MANAGING PAPERWORK
A Key to Productivity

MANAGING PAPERWORK

A Key to Productivity

FRANK M. KNOX

GOWER

Published in Great Britain by
Gower Publishing Company, Ltd.
1 Westmead
Farnborough
Hampshire, England

First published in the United States by Thomond Press,
an imprint of Elsevier North Holland, Inc., New York

Library of Congress Cataloging in Publication Data

Knox, Frank M
    Managing paperwork: a key to productivity.
    "An Elsevier professional publication."

    Includes index.
    1. Paperwork (Office practice)—Management. I. Title.
HF5547.15.K56   651.7   80-19685
ISBN 0 566 022621

Copy Editor   Ed Cone
Desk Editor   John Haber
Design   Edmée Froment
Art Editors   Kudlak, Ltd.
Production Manager   Joanne Jay
Compositor   Lexigraphics, Inc.
Printer   Haddon Craftsmen

Manufactured in the United States of America

CONTENTS

PREFACE

This is the age of information. The twentieth century will go down in history as the time when information became instantly available to all peoples in all parts of the world. In the home, the television gives us instantly what is happening next door and on the other side of the globe. In the business office the computer tells the executive within minutes of the variations in business operations in order that he can manage "by exception," or the price of gold on the world market in order that the treasurer can use the company's money to the best advantage.

In spite of all this mind boggling technological advance, the company is buried under a load of paperwork never before experienced. Business forms proliferate, the clerical payroll continues to mount, procedures get more complicated, the computer gives forth mountains of reports, and management, which is used to dealing with controllable factors, such as productivity and profit, wonders why someone doesn't do something to reduce this profit stealing, indirect paperwork expense.

Information is the end product of paperwork. Paperwork is the manufacturing process by which information is produced. No data come out of the computer without having been, somewhere, somehow, part of a paperwork operation. The computer is only a method, not a system or a procedure. It takes the data fed to it by paperwork procedures and, through incredibly fast electronic operations, turns it into management information—sometimes more than management can digest.

It is unfortunate that so much has been written about information and the electronic means by which it is produced and so little about the ground-level paperwork operations by which the computer's data base is built. As a result, paperwork has multiplied with frightening rapidity until it is robbing management of much of its potential profit.

Even though production processes in the factory have been subject for a century to work measurement and standards of production have been applied, productivity in the factory, at the time of this writing, has taken an alarming decline. It will, of course, be corrected but it will take time and will be a long and painful process.

On the other hand, productivity in the white-collar labor force, the paperwork area, is seldom studied and production standards, tailored to the white collar psychology, are generally nonexistent. This results in a field of cost reduction that is waiting to be tapped. Most offices have no counterpart to the industrial engineer in the factory. The office manager operates without the management tools he ought to have. The first line supervisor, the man in direct contact with the people who perform the paperwork, is given little or no training in the analysis of his paperwork or in its simplification for cost reduction. In other words, "no one is in charge here."

This need not be. If management can have an understandable definition of the paperwork problem, if someone will present management with a viable and effective program to solve the problem, and if management will then establish a policy and provide the means for its implementation, the white-collar productivity problem will be solved and profits will increase. This book shows how to accomplish that.

MANAGING PAPERWORK

A Key to Productivity

THE PAPERWORK
MANAGEMENT PROGRAM

Paperwork has become a drain on profit and must be controlled. The growing number of white-collar workers, approaching half the entire labor force of the country, plus the decline in productivity in business creates a situation in which top management must decide how to reverse the productivity trend. This can be done by attacking white-collar productivity through an integrated control program that encompasses the three areas of paperwork: manual paperwork procedures, forms, and clerical operations.

The effort must start with top management policy and be supported by a carefully thought out program that integrates a corporate paperwork management unit with all line units in accordance with spelled out authorities and responsibilities. The corporate unit must be furnished with proven techniques for operation that will not only control and reduce paperwork but will provide an information base for middle-management operation and reporting.

A. THE PAPERWORK PROBLEM

Business operates on paper. The whole body of business communication—systems, procedures, reports, clerical operations, and
information flow—depends on paperwork. No business operation can
be established, operated, changed, or even closed out without paperwork. No operating procedure can be devised, no meeting can be
held, no account can be paid or collected, no system can be
mechanized or computerized, in fact, hardly a conceivable business
operation can be carried on without some use of paper or business
forms.

Paperwork is the veritable foundation of business operation. As the
economy grows bigger and more complex the paperwork it requires
has grown with it; indeed, some think that the growth of paperwork has
far exceeded the corresponding growth of business.

The essential elements of business—money, people, machines, and
materials—are only static until they are put into motion by paperwork.
The requirements of expanding business have, throughout the years,
been accompanied by a corresponding expansion of the amount of
paper and the means of handling paperwork. The typewriter, the
key-activated business machine, the punched card tabulator, the
computer, and such later developments as optical character recognition, computer output microfilm, word processing, and computerized
composition and typesetting have come into being as the result of the
demands of business for faster and more accurate ways to perform
paperwork.

Decline in Productivity in Business

Productivity in private business has shown an alarming decline in
recent years. This dangerous trend can be modified, and quickly, by
addressing the issue of productivity in the white-collar labor force.

Productivity has traditionally been measured in the factory for
blue-collar workers and the machines with which they work. Factory
work has been measured for a century, and standards have been set for
productivity. The industrial engineer is an accepted part of factory

administration whose application of time and motion studies to factory work is an accepted fact of life. The same time and motion studies have not, however, been applied successfully to paperwork activities because paperwork does not lend itself to such detailed and accurate measurement. Where such predetermined standards have been used in the office they have met definite worker resistance and, by and large, they have not worked.

Productivity in the factory can and will be improved, but this requires capital expenditures, plant investment, equipment improvement, new or updated techniques, new labor training, and possibly additional research and development. All of these inputs take time and money, and their results will be measured in periods of at least many months, probably years. On the other hand, productivity improvement in the paperwork area can be accomplished in a relatively short time, months instead of years. All that is required is a genuine intent on the part of management and a viable coordinated program of paperwork management.

B. THE COST OF PAPERWORK

Paperwork is the largest single component of administrative overhead expense in the cost of doing business, and it robs business of much of its profit. What does paperwork labor do? Why is it there? How did it get so big? How can it be controlled? These questions are forcing themselves more and more on the attention of administrative management.

The white-collar worker cannot be singled out as a nonproductive element but must be considered within the context of the whole economic scene. What must be addressed is the way in which the work performed by the white-collar worker is done and the way in which paperwork productivity can be measured, analyzed, and improved to increase efficiency and to reduce administrative expense.

One clerk who earns £3500 a year plus fringe benefits of 25% may represent a drain on profits of £4375. This is equivalent to sales of the company's product of £62,500 if the company thinks in terms of only 7% profit on sales. Moreover, that sale of £62,500 must be repeated year after year just to balance the expense of that clerk for as long as he or she is on the payroll. If there are ten clerks, the company must sell some £625,000 of its product annually to compensate for their cost. Each year there are more, not fewer, clerks, and the drain on profit increases with each increase of administrative and paperwork labor.

Five hundred copies of a simple business form may cost £3.50–£4.50 to produce but as much as £350–£400 to use in paperwork practices. A clerk who earns £4550 (£3500 plus fringe benefits) costs £0.059 per minute, and a supervisor at £6500 (£5000 plus fringe benefits) costs £0.084 per minute. Only ten minutes of clerical time plus two minutes of supervisory time then cost £0.758. Thus 500 copies cost £379.00 and much of this is wasted because of inadequate paperwork control.

If a way is found to measure and apply standards to clerical work, if a way can be found to make first-line supervisors more creative managers, and if a way can be found to determine which forms are actually necessary and are designed for the most efficient paperwork—if all this can be done, the waste in administrative expense will be eliminated and profits protected.

C. INFORMATION AND PAPERWORK

Information is the end product of paperwork; paperwork is the manufacturing process by which information is created through the efforts of the clerical work force. It does not take a microscope or stopwatch to find that the paperwork clerical operations of the average company are woefully inefficient. The computer has eliminated many clerical operations but there are more clerical workers today than before the computer. The computer has eliminated many forms but there are more forms in use today than before the computer. The computer is a highly efficient electronic machine but it has not improved the efficiency of paperwork operations that create the data base on which it works.

Paperwork management must be a carefully planned, ongoing program encompassing all the factors of the problem, just as industrial engineering tackles the factory's problems.

D. PAPERWORK PRODUCTIVITY, A MANAGEMENT RESPONSIBILITY

White-collar productivity will never be improved unless management establishes a policy and provides a program to carry it out. The program must encompass the following factors.

The Five Ps of Administrative Management

An amalgam that knits together all administrative operations interrelates the following:

P-1. Policy. Management decision making and executive action; objectives; authorities and responsibilities; staff–line relationships and delegation for action.

P-2. Procedures. A step-by-step outline for action to put the policies into operation—what happens, where it happens, and when it happens.

P-3. Practice. The actual work of putting the policies and procedures into action—that is, the methods, techniques, and machines (including the computer).

P-4. People. The work force needed for the performance of the work—clerical and supervisory personnel.

P-5. Paper. The vehicle for information and communication flow—forms, reports, and records, which are the common denominator of all paperwork.

In the area of paperwork it is not unusual for management to get so involved in machine or computer *practices* (P-3) that it loses sight of the groundwork demands of the manual or non-EDP *procedures* (P-2). Management finds itself under a mountain of *paper* (P-5), which posits ever increasing demands for more *people* (P-4), who cost more money. It finds the office copying machine and the in-house print shop spewing out more and more forms in uncontrolled fashion, which requires more and more people to perform more and more operations until, hopefully, the situation forces management to do some soul searching in the area of paperwork *policy* (P-1), which, of course, it should have done in the first place.

The Anatomy of Paperwork Management

Paperwork management must be structured on the anatomy of the total paperwork problem as illustrated in Figure 1. Here we see just how the five Ps fit into the picture and furnish an approach to the measurement of white-collar productivity and paperwork improvement. The first and most important factor is, of course, the establishment and promulgation of a paperwork control policy. Without that policy no measure can be more than a temporary expedient.

But top management's part in the improvement of paperwork productivity does not stop with the establishment of a policy. Management must have a program and build that program into the organization of the company's structure. Such a program and its application is the subject matter of this book.

E. ORGANIZING THE PAPERWORK CONTROL PROGRAM

Top management should not be expected to be responsible for structuring the program. This is the job of the staff analysts, who unfortunately in too many cases are so involved with computer practices that they are either unaware of or not interested in the overall paperwork problem.

The Areas of Paperwork Management

The first task of staff analysts is to determine and closely define the areas in which the paperwork control program must operate. In practice the work of the program will naturally divide into systems and procedures control, forms control, and clerical work analysis and simplification. Other related areas are found in computer management, management reports control, and records management, but the first three are basic to the entire problem.

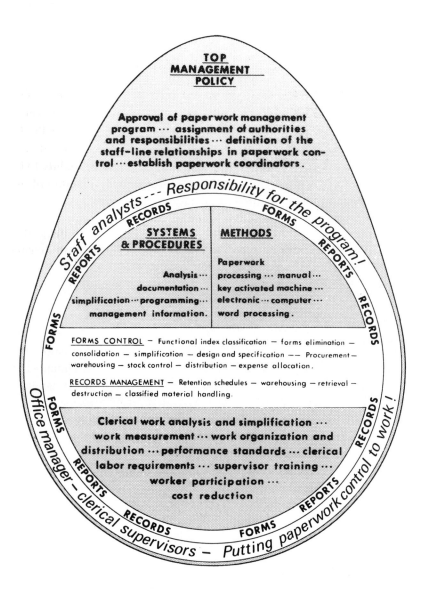

FIGURE 1. The anatomy of paperwork management.

In the average company the basic areas may be separate but closely integrated activities reporting to a common administrative point in upper management. Each activity serves to complement and support each of the others in addition to achieving its own assigned objectives.

Management Information Systems

This is, in reality, an extension of manual paperwork procedures and practices but it often assumes a special place in management because of decision-making requirements and its close association with the computer. As stated before, information is the end product of paperwork and it is common practice for the results of the procedure to be programmed into the computer as a data base for the production of the desired output information.

Whether MIS is located separately in the organization or integrated into the paperwork control program, there must be close liaison between the units.

Middle Management's Responsibility

Another factor is to be considered is the chain of command. The paperwork management responsibility should normally fall adminstratively under a vice president of administration or, if no such position exists, under the controller. The actual operation of the program will be delegated to middle management: A manager of general services, an office manager, an assistant to the administrative manager, an assistant controller (more apt an assistant to the controller), or a separate and distinct paperwork management unit may be created.

Wherever responsibility lies in the chain of command it should furnish a source of information for middle management, both staff and line, for reporting on all elements of business activity to their superiors. The specific areas of paperwork activity from which such reports are derived are described in detail in the ensuing sections (procedures auditing, Section II; forms control, Section III; and clerical work analysis, Section IV). Together these provide a base for management reporting in all areas of administrative activity.

F. AN ORGANIZATION OF STAFF–LINE RELATIONSHIPS

One of the prime causes of failure in this area of paperwork management is the absence of an organized relationship between the paperwork control and the line units of the organization.

In today's increasingly decentralized management, with a large degree of local autonomy, particularly in the case of profit center decentralization, it seems natural for management in larger companies to set up the corporate methods and procedures staff on a captive consultant basis and to let them depend on invitations to go into the line units to perform their services. In some cases this policy is successful, in others not. The unit is too often dependent on the ability or willingness of the decentralized line management to see the desirability or necessity of having help or on the ability of the methods and procedures group to sell themselves. When the line unit does request assistance it is too often in an eleventh-hour crisis.

In too many cases there is inadequate recognition of top management's prime responsibilty for the success of the program by establishing a carefully thought out program that does not have to depend on opportunism for success. What is required is an assignment of joint responsibility between the staff and line for a well-defined control over paperwork expense. This can be done without any danger of abrogating line authority.

An Assignment of Joint Responsibility

Unless management makes this assignment of responsibility, along with a statement of objectives, employees will not know quite where they stand in terms of paperwork management, and the opportunistic character of the operation will become dominant. In the experience of this author more paperwork programs have failed to achieve their objectives because of management's failure to establish the proper assignment of authority and responsibility between the line organization and the paperwork control unit than for any other reason. Either the control unit tries to exercise authority it doesn't have over forms and procedures used in the line units and the line units resent it, thinking that some of their authority is being eroded, or the line units refuse to fulfill their share of a joint responsibility because their obligation was not properly spelled out to them.

Appointment of Paperwork Coordinators

Each line unit should nominate someone it wishes to carry out the proposed paperwork control responsibility in that unit and submit the name to the central staff, which will then know whom to consult for information and approvals. In designating such persons by name the line units crystallize responsibility and put the staff—line relationship on a sound basis.

A large company with decentralized management may have divisions large enough to have their own divisional paperwork units. Each unit would control its own paperwork and have a functional relationship with the corporate paperwork control unit on all paperwork matters that cross divisional lines or have a corporate-wide application.

Since the line unit is already using forms and procedures, control may currently reside to some degree within the unit but probably on a fragmented basis under different persons with no real organizational authority.

Paperwork coordinators should be formally appointed by the manager of the line unit. The title given makes no difference as long as the function is performed. They are sometimes called forms coordinators, but the title should be broadened to cover paperwork management and the name ''paperwork coordinator'' is used in this book. The company ends up with a framework of paperwork coordinators in the line organization that ties in smoothly with the corporate control unit.

In the initial setting up of the program by management this arrangement should be spelled out and it should be made clear that it will not abrogate in any way the line authority by which the unit operates. Rather, the program entails the assignment of joint responsibility between the staff and line to increase white-collar productivity and achieve control over the ever increasing paperwork proliferation and clerical expense in the company.

The operation of the paperwork coordinators is a middle-management responsibility that provides an efficient channel for gathering and reporting results to corporate control or to upper management.

The Paperwork Coordinator's Manual[1]

The paperwork control unit should prepare a manual that spells out the objectives of the program and the duties and responsibilities of all concerned, whether staff or line. If such a manual is prepared and distributed to all units there should be no difficulty operating a successful paperwork control program.

---

[1]See Appendix I.

THE MANAGEMENT OF MANUAL PAPERWORK PROCEDURES

Forms cost money but the expense of using them can range from 20 to 100 times as much as the purchase price. Controlling the forms expense factor is the heart of the paperwork problem. This can be done only by controlling the manual paperwork procedures in which the forms are used. Auditing the procedure opens the door to the control over forms, paperwork methods, management reports, and clerical work measurement and simplification.

A simplified technique for charting and evaluating the procedure makes this possible and, in addition, permits a quick and easy documentation of the procedures for instruction to all levels of management, not only in paperwork but in job instruction and better supervisory management.

Methods for performing paperwork include everything from the pen or pencil to the computer but methods should never be studied, much less adopted, before the procedures to implement them have been analyzed, evaluated, and simplified. This is the first step toward an improvement in white-collar productivity.

A. PAPER-MONEY VERSUS PEOPLE-MONEY

Paperwork costs two kinds of money, *paper-money*, the cost of the *forms*, and *people-money*, the cost of the people who use the forms. The people-money can be anywhere from 20 to 100 times as much as the paper-money, and consequently they pose the real problem of managing paperwork.

Paperwork expands according to the means for its production. Twenty copies of a form can be produced on an office copier; a few hundred copies can be obtained from the in-house print shop; thousands of copies can be bought from a myriad of forms printers; and the computer printout is capable of producing hundreds of thousands of pages of information. All generate both kinds of paperwork cost: paper-money and people-money. How much? Hardly anyone knows for sure.

Furthermore, hardly anyone knows for sure how much of the paperwork is really necessary or contributes profitably to company operation or to management decision making. But management should know, and there is a way for it to find out, as well as to attain greater efficiency and lower paperwork expense as a by-product of finding out.

The way to do this is by auditing and analyzing the paperwork using a simplified procedures chart to measure both the necessity for the paperwork and its cost. The chart makes possible a detailed audit of the procedure and the paperwork that goes to make up that procedure.

B. THE NATURE OF THE PAPERWORK PROCEDURE

Every company is full of procedures. Nothing happens in administrative management except through a procedure. In the administration of a business, the procedure includes what happens, why it happens, and where it happens. The computer and other electronic machines have contributed greatly and profitably to speeding up the gathering and dissemination of information for decision making, but they have done little to control the proliferation of paperwork.

Manual procedures are not accomplished by pushing a button on electronic machines; they are accomplished by ordinary people using pens, pencils, typewriters, electromechanical machines, and other equipment short of the computer. They are subject to all the fancies and foibles of plain men and women working in ordinary offices and they create the people-money problem of the ever expanding clerical or white-collar work force.

Paperwork operations, particularly for lower-level officework, may be so disorganized, haphazard, and unplanned that they do not seem to be part of a procedure at all, but this is an illusion; the net effect of such operations is a procedure and, very possibly, an expensive and unnecessary one.

C. WHAT MANAGEMENT SHOULD EXPECT FROM PROCEDURES AUDITING

Too many procedures charts are drawn by and for procedures people alone and are relatively meaningless to others. This is of course wrong. Management should be able to get from procedures charts all the information to audit the procedure of which it is a picture, measure its cost, and make policy decisions on the necessity of the paperwork.

Experience in the use of the road map chart described further herein shows that all of the following management-related results can be attained from this simplified but effective technique of charting.

Evaluation of the Entire Procedure

Every paperwork operation being performed should be necessary or desirable. Paperwork elimination occurs mainly from the top down, seldom from the bottom up, and only when management has a chart or picture of the procedure that it can read, understand, and derive answers.

Only by these means can answers be given to such questions as, Is this paperwork operation necessary? What will happen if we eliminate it? Can two or more operations be combined? Can we take a calculated risk in eliminating paperwork controls? Are the operations being done in the correct place by the right people? Are authorities and responsibilities correctly placed?

All these and other questions vital to good management are revealed by the road map type of flow chart in a way that management can understand so that it can take action.

This provides for the all-important qualitative evaluation of paperwork necessary before any study of methods can be undertaken, whether they be manual, machine, electromechanical, or electronic, and before any office equipment is purchased.

Auditing the Form Design

By tracing the flow of each piece of paper through the chart you should be able to determine whether or not all the information necessary to the paperwork operation is included in the form design. Conversely you should find out whether or not there are data or information on the form that is not needed. You should be able to tell whether or not the same information appears on more than one form, how many times it appears, and whether or not repetition of the data is necessary or can be eliminated from the form or forms.

Related forms used in successive operations can be compared and, if the data are to be copied from one to the other, the design should facilitate such transference. If the form is a report to management at any level the data that are vital or interesting to management should be pinpointed and emphasized, thus relieving managers from reading unnecessary data or from having to hunt through the form for the only item of information they may need.

This provides an economy of operation in the processing of paperwork. Being sure that all necessary information is present on the form and that no unnecessary data are being processed guarantees that the first important step toward office economy and efficiency has been taken. This is a primary function of manual procedure auditing.

A Basis for Methods Study

When the qualitative analysis of the procedure is completed and management has approved the operations, responsibilities, and authorities, then and only then should the paperwork control unit start the study of methods. Existing work methods may be retained or new methods adopted. The control unit may change the construction or design of the form, but the paperwork operations will already have been audited and can easily be adapted to the new method.

Because the paperwork activities have been clearly stated and a workload study, with concurrent costs, is readily available, the study and evaluation of alternate methods becomes much easier. Management should receive meaningful statements of paperwork costs before managers are asked for decisions on new methods or machines.

The methods by which work is currently performed will have been observed during the construction of the chart but they are not entered on it. This is because management should not be confused during the auditing procedure by the introduction of information on processing methods. The methods should be studied only after the operations have been evaluated and determined to be necessary.

Too many paperwork studies start with attention to methods. Someone may say, "I think we should investigate such and such a method or machine," or management might say, "Let's get a computer." These are methods only (the computer is a highly sophisticated method) and are not the essentials of procedural operations. Methods should not be studied before procedures. But if the procedure has been properly audited the method problem takes care of itself.

It has become common for the manufacturers of forms and machines to promote symbols on their charts to represent the kind of form or machine they are selling. This may serve to promote the product but the practice violates the basis of objective paperwork auditing, which requires the qualitative analysis of the procedure and its operations for possible elimination or streamlining before any study is made of methods. The procedures chart must make this analysis possible.

Identification of Management Reports

The chart should show every report generated by the procedure, who makes it, and where it goes. It should show the operations involved in the creation of the report, where they are located, and the sequence in which they occur. This gives management the opportunity to study and evaluate the reports, learn what information they contain, and understand their relation to decision making and the management of the company. This identification is most important in good administrative management.

Combined with the functional index of forms (see Section III), which can insure that no forms have been missed, either in the construction of the chart or the review of reports, this study of reports can be of major importance to management.

A Basis for Clerical Work Measurement

The chart should identify every clerical operation in the procedure and show its relation to all other operations. It should provide either a broad basis for work measurement, merely by counting the documents handled, or a more detailed basis, by providing the starting point for reducing the work to measurable tasks (see Section III).

By counting the number of persons or the number of hours of work involved in each operation and applying salary factors, the economics of the operation can be determined. This factor is most important in evaluating new methods or machines by providing a basis of comparison between the costs of the old and the new methods.

A Framework for Documentation of the Procedure

By identifying every paperwork operation in the procedure, relating it to the department in which it occurs, and giving it a code or location number, the company can simplify the writing of procedures manuals. All that is necessary is to write the instructions or explanations necessary for each operation, relating them to the operation and the department by the location code on the chart. (This is treated in detail in Section IIG.)

A Basis for Job Descriptions

Identifying each clerical operation and showing its relationship to other elements of paperwork provides a basis for writing paperwork job descriptions and from that salary evaluations. If the procedures manual is adequately written to supplement the chart, the job descriptions are practically written except for the statement of responsibilities and authorities. From this point the listing of job qualifications becomes almost automatic.

Clerical Personnel Training and Work Instruction

The easy-to-read chart known as the "road map" chart, plus the procedures manual, become the supervisor's handbook. It describes the paperwork, its purpose, and its relations to other departments and sections. When new employees are trained, the chart can be used to explain the whole work situation and the framework in which each person operates. This gives more meaning to the work than if employees are merely told to do this and that without understanding the meaning of the operation they perform in relation to other operations of the firm.

A Means of Communication

Finally, it must be remembered that any paperwork chart is an effective means of communication only when it satisfies three major needs: first, communicating with upper management to determine whether all paperwork operations and clerical work are necessary or can be eliminated; second, communicating with suppliers of equipment in searching out and evaluating new methods after the qualitative analysis has been completed; and third, communicating with supervisors who have to make the procedure work after having been trained in the new methods.

If management cannot read and understand the chart, it may be taken for granted that it is the wrong kind of chart or it has been improperly constructed. A properly drawn and correctly constructed procedure chart can be one of the most effective tools in the whole range of administrative management.

The chart becomes the value analysis tool in the area of forms, paperwork, and clerical operations. Proper use of it should result in much money saved and efficiency improved.

D. DEFINITION OF TERMS

A great deal of confusion about paperwork is caused by a lack of understanding of the exact meaning of the terms used. Neophytes particularly may be faced with one of two situations: they read the elementary textbook on the subject or attend seminars and encounter discussions of the "what−when−where−why−how" factors that oversimplify the situation to the point of confusion or, on the other hand, they look in the other direction and see a proliferation of sophisticated terminology resulting from electronic data processing methods that may confuse them even more. There is no need for this confusion. The following definitions help clarify the matter, whether it be manual or electronic.

1. **The system.** A system is a coordinated series of procedures for the accomplishment of a designated management end. In normal business systems cover all the basic operational areas: financing, marketing, accounting, manufacturing, inventory control, procurement, receiving, payroll, personnel, timekeeping, and the like. Each of these systems is made up of a number of interlocking procedures. Figure 2 is a diagram of a typical industrial manufacturing system. The system is related to the strategy of business management.

2. **The procedure.** A procedure is a coordinated series of clerical or machine operations to perform a carefully defined part of a system. They provide the tactics for implementing the strategy of the system.

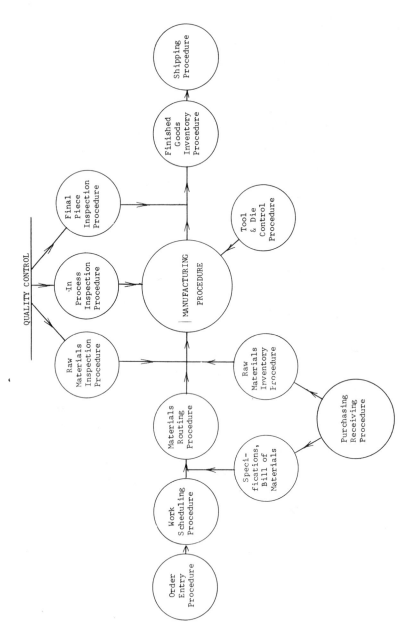

FIGURE 2. A typical manufacturing control system.

The 13 procedures in the manufacturing system shown in Figure 2 cover all the procedures common to basic manufacturing. In any specific case this number of procedures may vary depending on the type of business or the attitude of management or the systems manager, but it illustrates the composition of a typical system and the relation of the procedures to the system.

Figure 3 is a chart of the tool and die control procedure in the system chart, Figure 2. Each of the other procedures has its own flowchart to depict the operations and paper flow that make up the procedure. Output from one procedure becomes the input of the next related procedure.

3. The method. The procedure includes *what* happens, *where* it happens, and *when* it happens in sequence—not *how* it happens. That is the method, which may be manual (pen or pencil), key-activated machine (typewriter or accounting machine), electronic mechanical (typewriter tape output, word processing), or electronic (computer, optical character recognition).

For management analysis or auditing of the procedure the procedure chart should not include the methods. The first step is to audit the what–where–when factors; after they have been cleaned up and all operations determined to be essential, the methods—the "how" for accomplishing the essential work—should be studied.

If a machine or electronic method is adopted before the procedural requirements are determined, it may be found later that another method would have been better. Sellers of equipment should not be brought in before the auditing of existing or proposed procedures has been completed. Falling in love with a computer is not a substitute for "operation clean-up."

E. THE KEY TO CONTROL OF MANUAL PAPERWORK PROCEDURES

The key to control over procedures, particularly those areas of paperwork that are not computerized, is a technique for simplified paperwork flow charting that can be read and understood by all concerned. It is unfortunate that procedures charting has been made by some into an esoteric matter, which removes it from the ken of ordinary office managers, supervisors, and workers. Many procedures are not simple in themselves and some become quite complex, but the

22

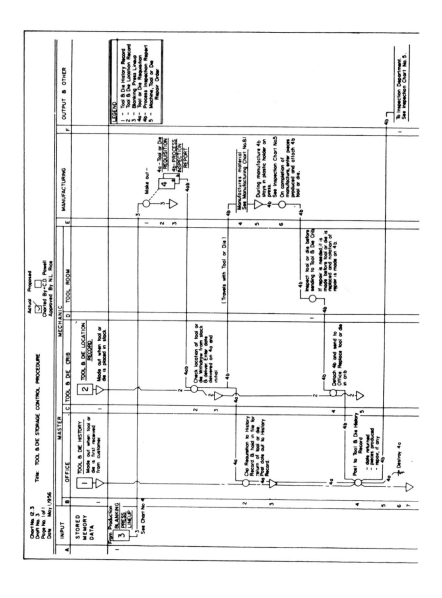

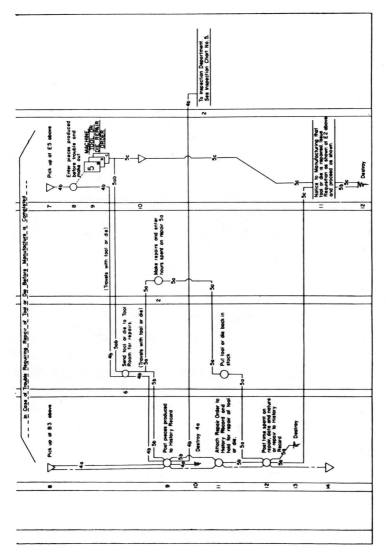

FIGURE 3. Procedure chart for tool and die control.

technique for charting the flow of paperwork in the procedure is neither complex nor difficult unless it is made so by the absence of proper know-how on the part of the analyst.

F. THE CHART REQUIREMENTS FOR PROCEDURES AUDITING

In order to meet management requirements for the preceding considerations the chart must do all of the following:

1. Show an outline of the total paperwork effort in that procedural area.
2. Show a continuous flow of work in its progression through the various operations in the procedure.
3. Show the paperwork input to the procedure and where it came from, plus the output and where it goes.
4. Show the paperwork responsibilities of each department or section involved in the procedure.
5. Show each paperwork operation involved in the procedure and tell briefly what is done in that operation.
6. Identify every form used in the procedure and each part of each form and show where that form came from, what is done to it, and where it goes, tracing the forms explicitly throughout the procedure.
7. Show the relationship between forms and the clerical operations involved in their use.
8. Give the supervisor a direct guide to his paperwork, responsibilities, and requirements.
9. Be readable and understandable to nontechnical people.
10. Lend itself to easy updating.

G. THE PROCEDURES MANUAL—DOCUMENTING THE PROCEDURE

It is not sufficient merely to draw a chart of the procedure; it should be documented in manual form. Writing a procedures manual is not easy and sometimes reading it after it is written is even more difficult. Figure 4 shows the manner in which the procedures charted in Figure 3 were documented.

The procedure chart is coded for each operation, and a paragraph or two suffices for each operation so that the step-by-step procedure is understandable to anyone having a copy of the chart. Gobbledygook is easily avoided by the simplicity of the technique. Accumulation of

Standard Procedure	Date	S. P. Number	Page 1
____ Mfg. Company		Chart 12. 3	of 5
		(draft 3)	

Subject:	Supercedes: SPI
Tool and Die Storage Control Procedure	Dated: Nov. 2, 1955

Issued to:

☐ All Locations   ☐ Purchasing   ☐ Stores

☐ General Office   ☒ Production Planning   ☐ Shipping

☐ Sales   ☒ Manufacturing   ☐ Personnel

☐ Accounting   ☒ Production Control   ☐ Public Relations

A1   Refer to Chart 4, Preparation and Scheduling of Production Orders. Production department prepares Blanking Press Line-up, schedules order for production and dispatches copy to Manufacturing department.

E1   Manufacturing receives copy of Blanking Press Line-up and determines tools and dies needed in the machine process. Makes out a Tool and Die Requisition for each tool and die needed in the manufacturing process. (Second copy serves as a Process Inspection Report.)

E-2-E3   Places Blanking Press Line-up in plastic holder on upper left side of press. Takes both copies of Tool and Die Requisition to tool and die crib to secure tools and dies that are required for manufacturing process.

C2-C3   Tool crib personnel reviews Tool and Die Requisition for completeness. Checks location of tool or die by referring to Tool and Die Location Record (maintained in a visible index). Withdraws item from stock to turn over to press operator. Enters date delivered, initials, and gets signature for the receipt of item on the first copy of Requisition. Operator leaves tool chit for each item taken from tool crib. First copy of Tool and Die Requisition is sent to the Master Mechanic's office for further processing.

B2   The Tool and Die History Record file is searched. When the record for the item appearing on the requisition is located, the requisition is clipped to the History Record and held in file until the return of the tool or die. Date item was charged out is posted to this perpetual History Record.

FIGURE 4. The procedure manual: documenting the tool and die control procedure.

seemingly endless detail, so prevalent in many narrative procedural writeups, is avoided since all interrelationships are shown on the chart.

All supervisors or departmental managers have their own area of operations identified and segregated and need read nothing other than what is essential to their work area. At the same time their work is clearly related to all other work in the procedure.

The manual should start out with a statement of the objectives of the procedure plus the responsibilities and authorities for each department or section. This is followed by simplified statements describing each operation, thus making it easy for employees to read and understand those elements of the procedure in which they are involved.

Procedures manuals are easy to keep up to date since changes need be marked only in the chart accompanying the manual. When the number of changes becomes considerable the chart can be quickly redrawn and only those pages of the manual that require changes can be reissued.

In this manner all the procedures in use can be charted and documented with a common language understandable to management, supervisors, and workers, who probably are neither technical-minded nor trained in systems and procedures analysis.

H. CONSTRUCTING THE MANUAL PROCEDURE CHART

In managing paperwork two basic techniques are critical to success: first, building a functional index of all forms in the company to provide access to and knowledge of the forms used in any particular procedure and, second, the construction of manual procedures charts to reveal what happens to those forms as they flow through the procedure.

In 1959 the American National Standards Institute, in response to requests by its members, appointed a committee to develop a standard format for manual procedures charting. That committee developed the format (ANSI Standard x, 2, 3, 4, 1959) used in Figure 3. In this book it is known as the "road map" type of chart. The road map chart is designed specifically to trace every piece of paper through all the clerical operations in the procedure just as the traveler's road map traces a route through the cities and towns on the journey. By tracing each form in this manner no form need be put in use with unnecessary information on it or lack data necessary to the processing of information. The route followed by each copy of a multicopy form is shown and unnecessary copies may be eliminated before they are printed, not after.

The Starting Point

A procedure is no more nor less than what happens to the paper that flows through it and is the basis for all clerical operations. Your procedure chart will be less than complete if it does not show every piece of paper, where it comes from, what happens to it, and where it goes.

The starting point in constructing the chart is, therefore, to lay your hands on each and every piece of paper in the procedure. How do you do that? If your company has a functional index of all forms this phase of the job will be greatly simplified since the subjects, operations, and functions by which the forms are classified in the index are identical to the subjects, operations, and functions in the procedure. (Section III gives complete instructions for building a functional index.)

Getting the Information on Work Flow

If you do not have a functional index of forms the alternative is to go to the supervisors of each department or section involved in the procedure and ask for a copy of each form used in their area that pertains to the procedure under study. On each form you will ask three questions:

1. Where did this form come from or how did you get it? Did you create the form in your own work area or did it come to you partly filled out from another work area and, if so, what area?
2. What do you do to or with this form in your area? Do you take information from it and put it on another form or do you add more information to it from data in your possession? Or do you use the data on the form for decision making?
3. When you are through with it where do you send it or how do you dispose of it? If you file it in your area how long do you keep it?

This action will give you the basic information for constructing the first draft of your procedures chart.

Drawing the First Draft

The answers to the preceding questions give you the information you need to construct your first draft of the chart. Remember that the chart is of the procedure only, not the methods by which the work is performed; therefore you should not seek detailed data on the methods. The study of methods comes after you have completed the chart, reviewed it with management, and determined whether or not operations can be eliminated. There is no need to study how the work should be performed before you determine whether it should be done at all. It is only natural that you will observe current methods as you gather data on the procedure and you may even want to make some notes, but don't let the way in which the work is done get in the way of management auditing of the procedure itself.

When you have the forms and the answers to your three questions you can draw the first rough draft of the chart. It will be unusual if it comes out right at this point. Some forms may not go where you were told they went. The people from whom you get your answers do not normally have the gift of instant recall and they are not to be condemned if they miss a piece of paper or two or give you some wrong information. But your first draft will instantly reveal gaps in the flow if your information is incomplete or incorrect, and then you will go back for a recheck. On the second time around you should get complete information and be ready to complete the chart.

Keep in mind that if you are charting a procedure that is part of a system as shown in Figure 2, you must dovetail the input and output of each successive procedure chart so they add up to the complete system. Forms do not come out of thin air; they must be the output from a previous procedure or be created in the work area under study. They have to go as input to a contiguous procedure, as output from the one under study, or be filed or destroyed in the procedure. The output is what comes into interface with the computer, which, as we have seen, is not a procedure, but only a method for which the procedure has to be programmed.

Tools and Supplies. Only a few simple tools are necessary for the construction of the road map procedure chart. A straight edge, perhaps a yardstick available from any five-and-ten-cent store, is useful for drawing long lines. For shorter lines a scaled triangle with template holes for drawing symbols is highly desirable. Such a triangle is discussed further and illustrated in Section IIJ under Symbols.

Paper for the chart can be purchased from most paper houses or your printer. The best is a sheet of ledger paper (for durability) measuring 22 × 34 in. in the number one sulphite grade. This standard size is large enough to accommodate most charts and the grade is necessary to take the amount of erasing that is almost inevitable.

The paper should be printed or penruled with faint blue lines running both ways of the paper. These lines afford guides to drawing the flow lines but are faint enough almost to drop out of sight when the chart is being read. This size paper can be folded into 8½ × 11 in. to fit in the normal letter file as shown in Figure 5.

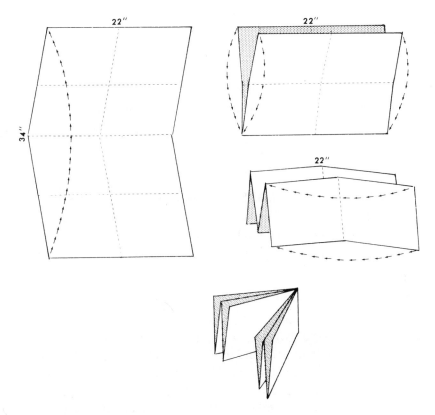

FIGURE 5. Folding the chart paper for filing.

I. DRAWING THE CHART

Study the chart in Figure 3 and see how the elements are arranged for following the flow of paper through the procedure. The following illustrations give step-by-step guides for the construction of the completed chart.

Identification

Each chart should carry a heading for identification. This should appear on the outside of the chart when it is folded into an 8½ × 11-in size (Figure 5) in order that it can be easily filed and the heading seen without being taken out of the file. Heading captions printed on the chart paper are impractical since if it is penruled it requires a separate printing for the words or type. Therefore the analyst will have to letter in the heading.

Figure 6 shows a suggested format for the heading. In any event the heading should contain the following information:

The name and number of the chart.

The date it was completed.

The sheet or page number and the total number of pages to the chart.

Whether the chart is preliminary or the finished draft.

The signature of the analyst who drew the chart.

Approvals if such be needed.

All heading or identification should appear in the left-hand half of the 22-in. edge of the chart. When the chart is folded to an 11-in. size this leaves all the heading visible on the face of the folded chart (see Figure 5).

Department and Section Column Headings

The chart is usually drawn on the sheet in a vertical position (i.e., with the 22-in. edge at the top), although in the case of some procedures that involve an unusual number of departments and require more columns than can be accommodated by the 22-in. width, the sheet can be turned with the 34-in. edge up and the chart drawn in that position. It is also possible to glue together two sheets in this position for a sheet 34 × 43 in. (with a 1-in. overlap). This permits the drawing of quite a large chart but it will be unwieldy and may repel people by its very size.

Columns. The blue vertical lines on the chart paper are 1½ in. apart on the vertical and 1 in. apart on the horizontal. The vertical lines offer positions for the departments and sections; those columns should be outlined with a darker blue pencil, dark enough to be distinguished from the faint printed lines but not so dark as to be confused with the black penciled lines that will later indicate work flow lines.

Each vertical blue line should have a secondary lighter line, very faint, printed ¼ in. inside the column from the left side (see Figure 6). This makes subsidiary space to enter the codes for the elements falling within that column.

Column Headings. The first and last columns on the chart should, in most cases, make provision for the input and output documents of the procedure. These columns can be fairly narrow since a minimum of data will be entered in them. The output column is often headed

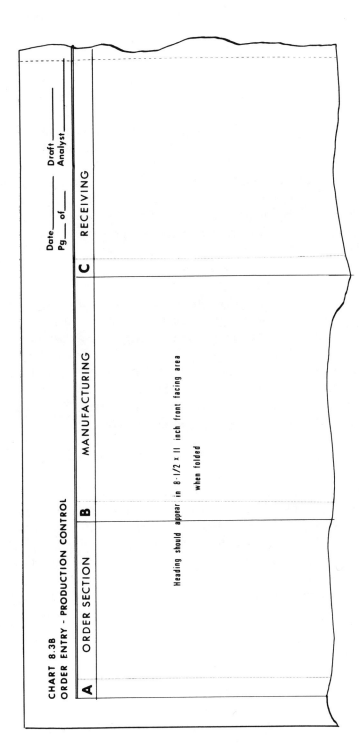

FIGURE 6. Identification and heading of the chart.

"Output and Other" for reference to some work unit or units that enter the procedure once only and do not justify full columns in themselves (see Figure 11). In some cases it is not necessary to use the actual words "input" and "output," although it is usually desirable to do so.

The sheet is divided into vertical columns, one for each work unit covered by the procedure. Columns should not be made the same width; rather, they should be varied according to the amount of data to be entered under each unit. In most procedures one or two of the operating units do most of the work. These should obviously have wider columns than others that do comparatively little in the procedure. It may not be possible at the outset to know just how much space to allot to each work unit, but this becomes apparent with the first rough draft of the chart. The second draft can then be rearranged to provide the correct amount of space for each unit.

Each column should be headed by the name of the work unit it represents. In many cases there will be subdivisions of work units, departments will be divided into sections, and so on. This arrangement, as well as the undivided column headings, are shown in Figure 7.

It is important to arrange the columns in a sequence as nearly as possible to the natural flow of work through the procedure. This prevents undue criss-crossing of flow lines on the chart. The general flow of documents is from upper left to lower right.

Symbols

The fewest possible symbols should be used on the chart in order to make it easily legible to those unaccustomed to procedures charting and the use of the charts. The following symbols are sufficient for most manual procedures charts: circle, rectangle, triangle, parallelogram, and light line (see Figure 8). These symbols have been built into a 12-in., 30−60-degree triangle especially for this type of charting as well as for forms designing. It is shown in Figure 9.[1] With this convenient tool it it a simple matter to draw charts without a drawing board and T square.

Operation Symbol. A circle with a ⅜-in. diameter is used to depict every clerical operation in the procedure. The circle should be drawn

---

[1]Such triangles may be obtained from Plastigraph Rules, 5530 State Road, Cleveland, Ohio 44134.

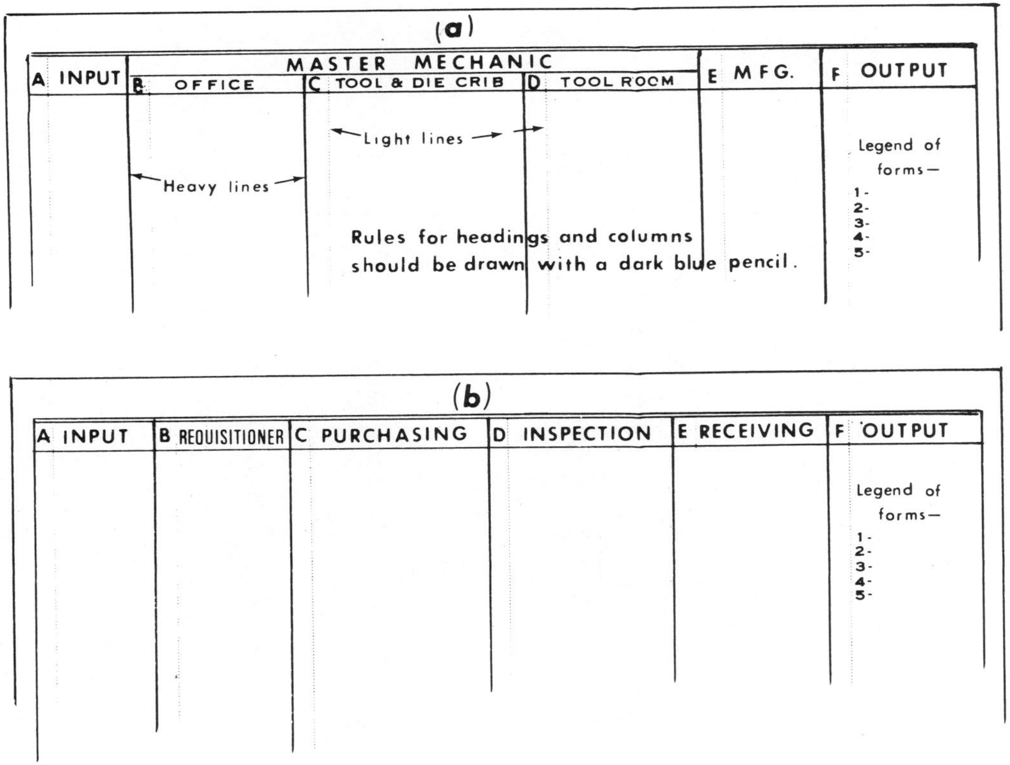

FIGURE 7. Structure and identification of columns and headings.

FIGURE 8. Symbols for procedures charting.

adjacent to the left side of the column in which the operation occurs, as near to the left margin as practicable in order to leave sufficient room at the right to enter the description of the operation.

Form or Document. A rectangle measuring ½ × ¾ in. is used for every form or document in the procedures chart. This rectangle should be drawn in the same relative position at the left-hand side of the column as the operation symbol (i.e., as close to the left-hand side as is

35

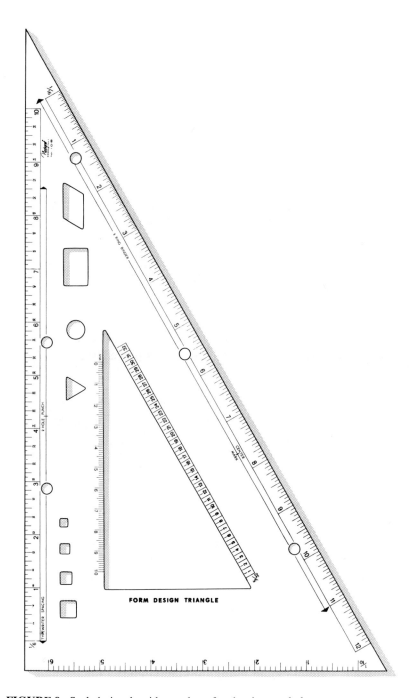

FIGURE 9. Scaled triangle with templates for charting symbols.

practicable in order to leave sufficient space at the right to enter the description of the form).

The rectangle is always drawn in a vertical position on the chart. Multiple-copy forms are indicated by a series of rectangles, one behind the other, fanned outward to the right and downward from the basic rectangle. As many rectangles are shown in the series as there are copies of the form.

File or Resting Place. An equilateral triangle, apex pointing downward, is used to represent a file or resting place of a form or document. This symbol can be used, if desired, to indicate a temporary resting place even if it is not a file in the strict sense of the word, if the delay of the form or document at that point is of sufficient importance to indicate on the chart.

If it is desired to differentiate between a temporary and a permanent file, the triangle may be left ''open'' for temporary use and blackened in to represent a closed or permanent file.

Physical Material. On rare occasions it will be desirable to show the handling of physical material in the paperwork procedures chart. When this occurs a parallelogram should be used.

Flow of the Form or Document. A straight line should be used to indicate the flow of paper within the procedure. This line is interrupted at intervals to contain the code for the paper represented. If desired, arrows can be added to these lines to show the direction of the paperwork flow.

Coding the Elements

The Chart Itself. If·the company intends to chart procedures on a planned basis, a numbering series should be established to cover all procedures. The code number of the individual chart should be placed in the heading of the chart as indicated in Figures 3 and 6.

The Work Columns. The narrow subcolumns as described in Columns and Column Headings should be headed with a capital letter, starting with A and proceeding with B, C, etc., until each work column on the chart has been so coded (Figures 7 and 11).

The Forms or Documents. Each form or document in the procedure should be coded with a number 1, 2, 3, etc. until every separate form or document carries its own code letter. This number is placed inside the rectangle symbol representing the document.

In the case of multiple-copy documents each copy should be further coded with a lowercase letter a, b, c, etc. until each copy of that form has been given a code letter. This makes the copies appear as 1a, 1b, 1c, etc. The code for the copy should be placed in the lower right-hand corner of the copy it represents (see Figure 10).

The Operations and Other Elements. Each operation, file, and any other element that appears in the procedure is coded in the narrow subcolumn at the left of the main column and exactly opposite the element it represents. This number combines with the capital letter at the top of the column to represent the element on the chart. They will be read later as A1, B2, C3, D4, etc. This permits easy and quick reference and location of any element on the chart (see Figures 6 and 11).

The Flow Lines. Each flow line on the chart should have placed in it at suitable intervals the form or document code which that line

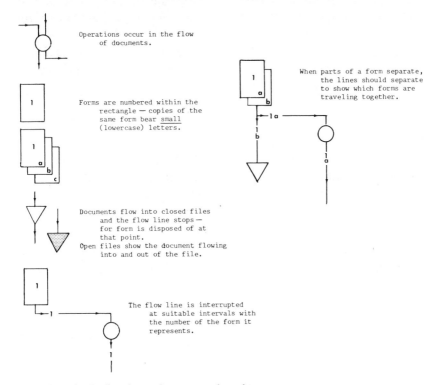

FIGURE 10. Coding the road map procedure chart.

represents. The line is broken to permit the insertion of the document code (see Figure 11).

Legend of the Forms and Documents. At the top of the right-hand column (Output and Other) and below the column heading there should be inserted a legend for the forms or documents entering into the procedure. This is for quick reference when reading the flow lines away from the original showing of the form or document. This legend consists of a listing of the forms and papers numbered the same as they are numbered in the symbols in the chart.

The reason for putting the legend in this particular place is that the top of this column is seldom used for charting and it establishes a standard position for the information.

Origination of Form or Document in the Chart

It is most important to show how each and every document gets into the procedure. *Show the Document Symbol* (the rectangle) *only once in the chart* for each form. Do not repeat the symbol each time that form enters into an operation. That practice (used on many charts) so loads the chart with document symbols that an entirely wrong impression is created in the mind of the reader as to the volume of paper in the procedure. It confuses the chart.

When the Document Comes from Another Procedure. The document symbol should be shown in the ''input'' column with a notation immediately above it as to its origin. If the procedure from which it came has already been charted, indicate its origin by the name or number or both of the procedures chart from which it came. In that chart it will be shown as an output document.

When It Originates Within the Procedure. The origination of the document is shown as a clerical operation with the circle symbol; a dotted line should come out of the circle at a downward slant to a rectangle representing the new document. If the chart is crowded the dotted line can be drawn almost horizontally, but under no circumstances should it slant upward since this would indicate a document coming into the operation instead of going out of it (see Figure 11).

39

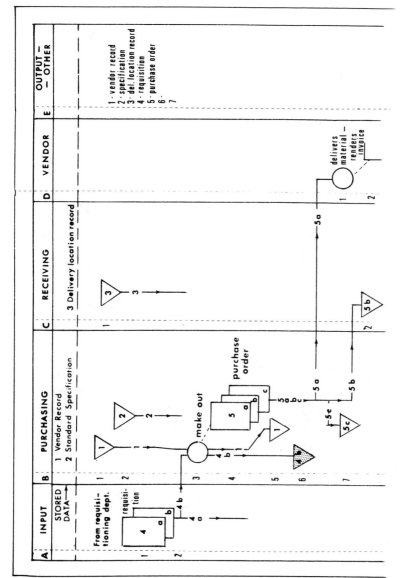

FIGURE 11. Charting the flow of paper through the procedure chart.

When It Already Exists as Stored Memory Data. The name of the form and its procedure code number (if available) should appear in the "stored data" space at the top of the form (Figure 11). In the column below enter the triangle file symbol and put the code number in the triangle. This is optional when the triangle is close to the top of the column. The flow line can then come from the file symbol down to the operation in which the form is first used. Always place the file symbol above the operation in which it is used and let the form come into the operation from above. Do not let the form appear to originate in that operation.

Flow of Paper Through the Procedure

The flow of paper through the procedure is shown by the straight line symbol. This line should be drawn from side to side and up and down (i.e., horizontally and vertically in so far as possible). Diagonal lines should be avoided as far as possible, although they may be used to save space on the chart. This always makes for a more orderly chart that is easier to read.

Identifying the Flow Lines. Each document in the procedure bears an identifying number that should also appear in the flow lines representing that form. The code number should be inserted in the line with enough frequency to prevent readers from having to search the chart to learn what form they are looking at as represented by the line. The form code should be inserted just above and below an operation unless these come close together, in which case judgment should be used (Figure 11).

When multiple-copy forms are shown, a single line should be used if all copies flow together and the code for the group should be inserted in the line. When the copies separate, additional lines should be used to represent the copies that are separated from the group. If only one copy is separated the code for that copy should be immediately inserted in the line for that copy. If two or three copies are separated but still stay together in a group by themselves a single line is used for the group and the code for several copies is immediately inserted in the line. In other words, do not use more lines than necessary to follow each individual copy of the form.

A different line should be used for every separate form. This may become clumsy when a number of different forms flow into the same clerical operation, but remember that the purpose of the chart is to show exactly what is happening. If a point on the chart represents a complicated situation, the chart must not be drawn in such a way as to make the situation appear to be simple.

The only time one line may be used to indicate more than one individual form is when the several forms are permanently clipped together for common flow or storage, such as the insurance daily report. If several forms are placed in a work folder and the folder itself flows through several operations, a single line can represent the folder and its contents, for example, a numerical file folder in a forms control procedure. The folder contains many different pieces of paper, only part of which enter into the current work, but it is desirable to maintain the complete record intact in the folder. In such a case it is necessary to indicate in the operation description just which of the several forms in the folder is being worked on.

When a form has been flowing as a separate piece of paper and at some point is put into such a folder, the lines for the form and for the folder may merge and become one. At that point the code for the form should be inserted in the line to identify it.

Positioning the Lines in and out of the Operation. The relative position of the flow lines as they enter into any given operation symbol will depend on where the lines come from on the chart. Whether they come from the right or the left or immediately above, they should be carried into the circle symbol in the same order to prevent, insofar as possible, the crossing over of lines.

The lines should come out of the circle in the same order in which they entered it. This may cause confusion if the forms travel in cross directions from the operation, but if the lines are permitted to change their relative positions between entering and leaving the circle readers are very apt to find themselves following the wrong lines. It is natural to assume that the same line will occupy the same position above and below the circle, and it should be so arranged.

Figure 12 shows several situations that may be encountered in this matter and the suggested manner in which they should be treated.

If several lines come out of a circle and must cross each other to continue through the rest of the chart, this is not justification for changing the position of the lines in relation to their position when entering the circle. It is better to have the lines jump each other, as shown in Figure 12, since experience has shown that the average chart

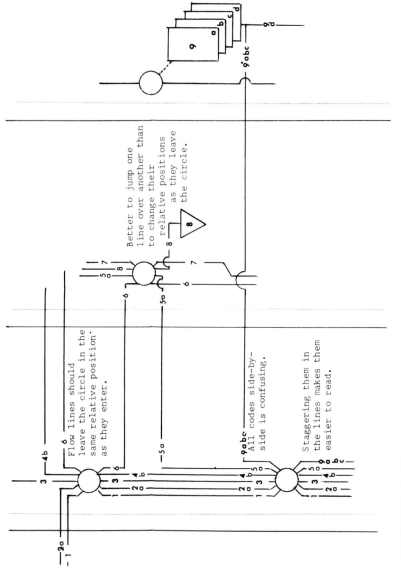

FIGURE 12. Positioning the lines in and out of the operation symbols.

reader follows the jumps more easily than the changed position of the lines.

Picking the Form out of a Preexisting Folder. When a form has been in a folder as preexisting stored data and enters actively into the procedure, the symbol for the file is placed above the operation in which the form is used. A line emerges from the triangle and, being identified with the form code, proceeds downward into the operation. If the form is to be returned to the folder, the line can be brought downward again into the triangle as a storage place.

If the line is dropped at that point and picked up again later in the procedure, the file symbol may be repeated and the line brought out of it again. In such cases it is necessary to indicate at the symbol of the file where it was dropped previously. The pick-up point must be identified (Figure 13).

J. CHARTING THE EXCEPTIONS AND VARIATIONS FROM THE RULE

No procedures chart is complete unless it shows the exceptions and variations as well as the basic flow of the procedure. It must show where the flow separates from the main channel or splits into two subsidiary channels and where it merges again into the main flow. It must show clearly the points of departure and give sufficient references to be able to pick up the flow at the proper point.

1. *Showing the beginning of an alternate flow.* When the main flow is interrupted to show the beginning of an alternate, two parallel lines should be drawn across as many columns as are involved in the break, the lines to be about ¼ in. apart. Between these two lines should be lettered the condition causing the alternate (Figure 13). It is advisable to turn downward the ends of the top parallel line to indicate that the material below the line is being bracketed.

2. *Showing the end of an alternate flow.* At the completion of the alternate another double parallel line should be drawn with the end of the bottom line turned up to indicate that the material above is being bracketed. Notation can be entered between these two lines as necessary to indicate the resumption of the flow (Figure 13).

3. *Instructions for picking up the flow.* Each break in the procedure should be coded in the left-hand code position in each column

44

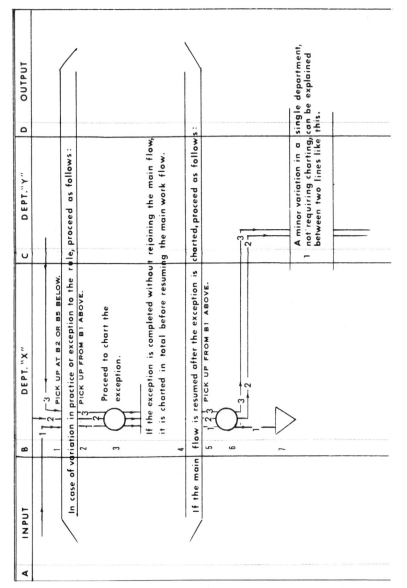

FIGURE 13. Charting exceptions and variations from the norm.

affected. A code should be entered to apply to the top and the bottom of the parallel lines in order that reference can be made to the break-off point (above the line) and to the pick-up point (below the line).

Above each break-off line should be indicated the pick-up point below where the reader should look for a continuation of the flow. This may be one point only or it may be several points, depending on how many alternatives are involved (Figure 13). Below each break-off line should be indicated the location from which the break occurred in order that the reader can establish the continuity (Figure 13).

4. *Minor exception.* In some cases the exception may be of a minor character, affecting only one department or work unit. In this instance the exception may not have to be charted but can be explained between two parallel lines in the column representing the affected department (Figure 13).

MANAGING FORMS

Some review of forms can be accomplished in the auditing of manual paperwork procedures, but the actual control over all the forms is the function of a separate forms control unit operating as part of the paperwork management program.

The key to forms control is in two control files, the numerical file and the functional index. The latter is indispensable to the total paperwork control program.

The index is made by classifying each and every form according to three factors basic to all paperwork operations: the subject, the operation or condition, and the function. A complete definition of all terms in forms control is necessary for this classification and a dictionary has been created for this purpose for use by analysts. With the standard terminology the functional index furnishes valuable information to all phases of paperwork management.

Procurement, warehousing, and distribution of forms is a necessary part of paperwork management. Much waste can be eliminated through an organized program of control contracting whereby the supplier not only stocks and distributes the forms but furnishes management with vital information on forms usages and costs by individual locations.

A. THE PLACE OF FORMS CONTROL IN PAPERWORK MANAGEMENT

If paperwork is done on forms it stands to reason that the paperwork cannot be managed or controlled unless the forms themselves are managed and controlled. If two or more forms in two or more locations are doing the same thing, perhaps in slightly different ways; if forms are created and produced locally that are really unnecessary; if standard procedures are being changed by the creation of local variations of standard forms; if standard forms are being produced locally instead of being requisitioned from the central stockroom; if these and other similar situations exist, probably unknown to management, the paperwork simply is not being controlled. Clearly, a way must be found to establish control.

The first requirement for this control is a forms control unit built into the organization with carefully assigned authorities and responsibilities plus properly defined relationships with the contiguous areas of systems and procedures and the purchasing department. Section IF describes the staff—line relationships that should have been established for the entire paperwork management program. The forms control unit works with the paperwork coordinators in the control of forms used in the line organization.

B. THE NATURE OF THE FORMS CONTROL PROBLEM

The real forms control problem is not with the purchase order or invoice, the insurance policy or the endorsement, the payroll register or paycheck, or any other forms that cover major business operations, or at least it should not be. Forms such as these should already be under careful administrative control. The problem exists because different divisions or departments create different forms for the same purpose; because forms of relatively infrequent use are produced in-house with no identifying numbers; because too many forms are produced with inefficient designs, causing waste in paperwork operations; and because too many forms are created under the assumption that they are temporary but are still in use two or three years later.

Most companies have many more forms than anyone in middle or upper management knows about, and these unknown forms are apt to be the most inefficient in use with the greatest waste in paperwork expense. Many are produced on someone's whim without consideration for procedures control or as local adjuncts to otherwise standard procedures. But all must be controlled if paperwork management is to be successful.

C. WHAT MANAGEMENT SHOULD EXPECT FROM FORMS CONTROL

A normally effective forms control program should assure management of the following:

1. All forms in the company are under some degree of effective control in relation to the paperwork management program.
2. All forms are properly identified with control numbers.
3. All forms are properly related to controlled systems and procedures or are available for study by the procedures analysts.
4. Different divisions or departments do not have different forms for identical paperwork operations.
5. All forms are designed for the most efficient clerical and paperwork operations and effort.[1]
6. Complete specifications are written for the proper procurement of forms whether in-house or purchased from the commercial market.
7. A data base of forms is available for a review of management reports at all levels of management.

D. THE KEY TO FORMS CONTROL

The key to forms control, once a control unit has been established, is the forms control files, of which there are two: a numerical file and a functional index. The building and maintenance of the control files is the most important factor leading to success or failure in the forms control program. Without properly constructed files the operation can be no other than an opportunistic attempt to "put out brushfires" or to work on only the most obvious cases of poor forms. Work will be done on the tip of the paperwork iceberg only and the four-fifths of the problem that lies beneath the surface will never be touched. Paperwork proliferation will continue unchecked.

---

[1]See Frank M. Knox, *The Knox Standard Guide to Design and Control of Business Forms,* McGraw-Hill, New York, 1965.

The Numerical File

The numerical file is an ordinary work file. It should contain a folder for each form with samples of the form together with all information currently related to that form insofar as design and specification is concerned. Work papers collect in this file and it becomes the reference source for the form. The file should contain, in addition to the form samples, a copy of the specifications for the form, a copy of the latest revision, and correspondence having to do with changes in the design. It also should contain information on who uses the form, the approximate usage for each user, and the date of revision plus any other information related to the form.

The Functional Index

A functional index, the most important tool in forms control, is a file in which one sample of every form in the organization is classified in such a way as to bring together in one easily accessible place all forms serving the same purpose or relating to the same subject and operation. It provides a key control over forms and paperwork by making available in one place the information necessary to analyze and correct situations of paperwork duplications and to uncover paperwork that management may decide to be unnecessary. The functional index does the following:

1. Reveals and brings together all forms doing the same thing.
2. Locates quickly and surely all forms relating to the same subject or paperwork operation.
3. Prevents the inception of new forms when one or more already exist for the purpose.
4. Identifies forms in relation to paperwork procedures for systems and procedures charting and analysis.
5. Assists in locating forms when the title or form number is unknown.
6. Identifies forms that report information to management at any level.
7. Makes possible a periodic review or audit of the forms situation.

The functional index is to paperwork management what the commodity classification of materials and products is to manufacturing. The industrial engineer wants to know what kinds and sizes of bolts, screws, nuts, and washers are available and in what applicable classifications. The purchasing agent or industrial engineer wants to know the different kinds of specialty steel available in the market and where they are. In like manner paperwork and forms control personnel must know how many forms there are, where they are, who uses them, and what they do. Otherwise it becomes difficult, if not impossible, to really manage the paperwork situation.

If the systems and procedures staff wants to analyze an existing paperwork procedure, the most direct route is through the forms being used in the procedure. Since subjects, operations or conditions, and functions—the factors by which the index classification is made—are common to all aspects of paperwork control, whether it be designing a form or programming a computer, a classification of forms by those factors provides a basic tool for the management of paperwork.

E. COLLECTING FORMS FOR THE CONTROL FILES

Obtaining all the forms is the first step and this is not always easy. As has been pointed out, many forms live out their entire lives within a single department and are never seen outside that department. Many of these create information that is transferred in one way or another to forms that do go outside that department. If management wants anything other than cursory or temporary control over forms, these intradepartmental forms must be collected and built into the control files.

No single place has samples of all these forms. Some forms are in purchasing department files, some in the stationery storeroom, some are produced in the in-house print shop or on the office duplicating machine, and some are buried in the department using them. The only way to get samples of all the forms is to make a complete collection from all departments. The impetus for the collection must come from some point in management high enough to command the attention of division or department heads. A letter should be circulated asking for several copies of every form used in that unit. ''Forms'' should be carefully defined. It is surprising the exceptions some people will make for themselves unless the meaning of the term is carefully spelled out. The following letter has been used successfully in collecting samples for the control files:

> To the heads of all units (Departments, Branches, Plants, etc.): The company has initiated a study directed toward the reduction and simplification of paperwork and the lowering of costs in clerical operations. This will include the standardization and simplification of

forms and records directed toward slowing the growth of clerical and administrative expense in the company.

In order to embrace an all-inclusive improvement it is necessary to make a collection of all forms as described below. Therefore, you will please assemble, pack, identify, and forward in accordance with the following instructions:

1. Five samples of every form which is wholly or in part used in the operations of your (unit).

   a. Include all office and plant forms including letterheads, envelopes, unit sets, continuous forms, salesbooks, labels, tags, checks, and other miscellaneous types of forms.

   b. Include all forms, whether printed, lithographed, or office duplicated; permanent or temporary; numbered or unnumbered.

   c. If the form is used in single sheets send five sheets; if it is made up in multipart sets send five complete sets; if the form is bound in books do *not* send complete books but send five sheets and indicate that it is bound and how many sheets or sets to the book.

   d. Checks and other negotiable forms must be carefully *cancelled* or rendered null and void before submitting.

   e. Indicate on *one copy only* the estimated usage of that form annually in your (unit). If the form is temporary tell its usage during its life.

   f. *Do not* submit information on how the form is used.

2. Each unit will make a separate package of its forms and identify on the outside of the package the submitting unit. Deliver the packages of forms to _____ .

3. All packages of forms should be received at the above receiving point not later than _____ . Signed.

When the forms come in from the using units they should be left intact in their original packages until they are removed for building the files. It is essential that every form be identifiable with its using location regardless of whether the form is used commonly by several or all departments or whether it is limited to one use point. It is important to find out just how many units use a given form.

F. CONSTRUCTING THE NUMERICAL FILE

In many companies such a file already exists; in fact it is hard to imagine any forms control program worthy of its name without an effective numerical file. The trouble with too many such files is that they include only those forms that have been worked on by the control unit or that have been purchased commercially. They may not include any of the unnumbered or temporary forms that create undue clerical expense.

The Numerical File Folder

Use straight-cut, legal-size folders for the numerical file if possible. The folder should show the form number (later the functional index code will be added), plus a record of all using locations and the annual usage of each. This record is important not only to the forms control unit but to the systems and procedures staff when they analyze the procedures.

Filing the Forms in the Numerical Folders

Only one location should be handled at a time to avoid confusing the record of using locations. If any study or survey of the forms is made prior to filing, the forms should be carefully replaced in their packages in order not to lose the record of using location and annual usage.

Of the several form samples collected, one should be set aside for the functional index. Before this is done care must be taken that all forms bear identifying numbers. It is almost certain that some, probably many, forms will not be numbered; these must be assigned temporary numbers before they are filed. It is best to use a five-digit number on these in order not to conflict with the assigned numbers. Start with 50,000, which will undoubtedly be above any previously assigned numbers. This temporary number should be stamped on all copies of the form plus the file folder.

The annual usage should be entered opposite the name of the unit under study. When the same form is encountered from other using units, that usage is also entered, and this accumulates not only the use points but the total annual usage.

It is inevitable that confusion will arise when different forms are found to bear the same number or different numbers are found on the same form or when prefixes and suffixes are mixed up. Correcting such situations is one of the purposes of the file.

G. CONSTRUCTING THE FUNCTIONAL INDEX

Three classification factors are common and applicable to all aspects of paperwork: a subject, an operation or condition, and a function. But these need to be defined. Different people call the same form by different names; different forms may be called by the same or similar names; many forms have no title at all or titles are assigned that are meaningless to all but the person who designed it. What is needed is a standard nomenclature for form titles that is understandable to all concerned. Such a nomenclature is found in the three factors listed above.

Classification Factors for the Index

The Subject of the Form. Every form relates to some specific subject in whatever activity in which the form is used: in commerce and industry, government, or the household or on the farm. Typical of this classification factor are such subjects as cash, assets, budget, commission, materials and supplies, depreciation, dues, inventory, claim, meal, lease, bank account, order, premises, product, quotation, vehicle, standard, tariff, rent, and many, many more for a total of more than 250. Subjects can be a veritable quagmire of confusion and misunderstanding unless some standard method of defining and recognizing them is used.

The Operation or Condition. An operation takes place or a condition exists in relation to each subject on each form. A personnel form may deal with a change in employment: the operation "change of" (active) or "status of" (passive). Therefore the second classification is either an operation or a condition.

Cash (subject) can be collected (operation) or spent or accounted for; estimates are computed or received and accepted or rejected; drawings are stored or issued; employees have seniority or other status and may be transferred or terminated. Work in process is inspected and accepted or rejected; insurance premiums are issued and paid; costs are distributed or allocated; workers are late or absent; materials and supplies are inspected while chemicals are analyzed and people are examined. Thus all subjects are modified by either an operation or a condition.

The Function. The function is the activating principle in the paperwork operation. The *issuance* (operation) of a *book* (subject) from the library is *requested* (function). Operations may be ordered or authorized, while conditions may be reported or recorded. The payment of cash is ordered or acknowledged. The employee is notified of his transfer or termination. The deduction of earnings is authorized or recorded. The amount of benefits can be estimated; the operation of a department is reported; time for an operation can be estimated and reported; work can be scheduled. Every paperwork operation involves and demands an activating principle, a function.

A successful functional index classifies all forms in terms of these three factors, which, as has been stated, apply to all forms and are common to all paperwork procedures and clerical operations.

Figure 14 shows the recapitulation sheet of a functional index in a medium-sized corporation covering the forms under the subject *employee*. Management had been shocked by the initial survey of forms and paperwork, which showed more than 3200 forms existing in the company, many more than anyone had anticipated. Managers were in complete agreement that there was no justification for as many as 172 forms dealing with employees, particularly since there were more than 80 additional forms under the classification *employment*, a total of more than 250 forms on personnel handling. Later consolidations and eliminations of unnecessary forms reduced this total to fewer than 140 forms.

Figure 15 shows a similar recap of forms under the subject *cash*. Again, there was agreement that it should not take 70 forms to deal with this one subject.

FUNCTIONAL INDEX SPREAD SHEET

FILE NO.	SUBJECT / OPERATION OR CONDITION	1	2	3	4	5	6	7	8	9	10	11	12	13	14	15	16	17	18	TOTAL
28.0	EMPLOYEE												1				1			2
.1	Absence Of				2									9	11	4				26
.2	Availability Of											3								3
.3	Death Of					2														2
.4	Examination Of													15	7					22
.5	Information About												1		1					2
.6	Instruction Of													1						1
.7	Interview Of										2									2
.8	Passage Of						6						2							8
.9	Qualifications Of												2							2
.10	Rating Of													3	14	16				33
.11	Reprimand Of											6								6
.12	Seniority Of							1												1
.13	Status Of												3	28	12					43
.14	Training Of												1							1
.15	Transfer Of														1					1
.16	Transportation Of												2							2
.17	Treatment Of												8	7						15 /172
29.0	EMPLOYMENT			3																3
.1	Acceptance/Rejection Of											7								7
.2	Change Of											8								8

FIGURE 14. Example of a functional index spread sheet on the subject "employee."

FUNCTIONAL INDEX SPREAD SHEET

Sheet 2 of 12

FILE NO.	SUBJECT / OPERATION OR CONDITION	1	2	3	4	5	6	7	8	9	10	11	12	13	14	15	16	17	18	TOTAL
15.0	Cash																	1		1
.1	Payment Of					4							2	3	11	1	7			28
.2	Receipt Of				13									1	3	1				18
.3	Reconciliation Of														1	3				4
.4	Replenishment Of																	1		1
.5	Status Of													12	4					16
.6	Transmittal Of												2							2
																				70

FIGURE 15. Example of functional index spread sheet on the subject "cash."

These figures illustrate how the forms become segregated in the index to cover paperwork and clerical activities in the company. Recording the status of employees is a paperwork function in every company, and the index automatically segregates every form doing that under the subject *employee*, 'the condition *status of*, and the function *to record*. In the case of Figure 14 it shows 28 different forms for that one purpose alone used in different departments and divisions of that company, many of them completely unknown to the personnel department.

Figure 15 shows no fewer than 28 different forms for the payment (operation) of cash (subject) covering the functions to acknowledge, to notify, to order, to record, to report, and to request. By charting and installing a standard paperwork procedure this number of forms was substantially reduced and the total of 70 forms on cash handling was reduced to a little over half that number. None of this would have happened if there had not been an initial survey of the company's forms and the subsequent construction of a functional index of all forms.

What Forms Should Be Built into the Index

Building a successful functional index is a long and arduous task. Management may well question whether it is worthwhile or whether the extent of the index might be diminished in order to speed up the work. Certainly, if a company has 10,000 forms (and many companies have more than that, although normally no one suspects it before a survey is made), it is permissible to question how many of them really must be included in the index. It depends on how the index is to be used.

Treatment of Small Usage Forms. Experience shows that half or more of the forms in any typical company are used in very small quantities, under 1000 or even 500 a year. Note the many daily, weekly, and monthly reports that are made out currently. If so many forms are used in such small quantities, are they really worth all the work of building them into the index? The answer depends on the use of the form and its relation to the processing of information. No one would think of questioning the importance of monthly budget reports, yet only 12 or 24 of them may be used annually by any one department. Even in 20 departments the usage would still be under 500 a year. Better put it in the index because it is a vitally important form with definite procedural and operational implications.

If the form may also be used by multiple locations in the company, it should be included no matter what the usage per year. If two forms doing the same thing in two or more locations can be combined into one, the result is a lower production cost for the form and probably a better design with greater efficiency in paperwork, perhaps even the elimination of the form as unnecessary.

If the form is used in small quantities and cannot possibly be used by any other department or location, then it may be permissible to exclude it temporarily from the classification but return it to the local paperwork coordinator for study and evaluation with corrective action at the local level, to be indexed at a later date. However, if the form relates to a paperwork procedure common to other departments or divisions or should be under corporate control, it should be included in the index, regardless of the usage quantities. This is particularly true if the information on the form relates to necessary information processing or management decision making at whatever level—first-line supervisor, middle management, or the executive committee.

Scheduling for Results. If the index is new to the organization and management has assigned staff personnel to compile it, it is probable that they will want some fairly rapid results or at least indications of productive action. This would seem to indicate the advisability of speeding up the completion of the index by laying aside temporarily some forms used in small quantities, or peculiar to local areas only, for later inclusion in the index. On the other hand, if management wants an in-depth audit of paperwork procedures, each and every one of those small usage forms creates paperwork expense and relates to some procedure or other, maybe one scheduled for study. In this case the availability of the small usage forms is important and the index provides the most feasible source for finding them quickly and surely. Witness the case of a large, multidivision, multiproduct company that decided to centralize all inventory accounting in one computerized procedure. While work was under way on the computer feasibility study, a functional index was completed of its more than 11,000 forms. The index revealed the existence of no fewer than 713 forms dealing with inventory, with 346 of them merely reporting the status of stocks on hand as of a given date. This was a shock to management as well as to the analysts making the study, who had no conception so many inventory forms were used in so many places. A quick decision was made to reduce the program to areas that could be handled and to find out in the meantime what those forms were doing and why they were there.

Those 713 forms fell into one of three categories: first, they were unnecessary and should not have been there in the first place; second, they represented local conditions that did not exist in other areas and either had to be excluded from the standard procedure or built into it as exceptions; or, third, they were unauthorized deviations from standard procedures that had to be analyzed and corrected. But if the original computer study had been completed and put into operation without the knowledge of the existence of these forms and the paperwork operations they represented, there would have been much backtracking with time and expense, delayed results, and probably some hard feelings or recriminations. Small usage forms are more often than not important to the paperwork procedures.

So deciding what and how many forms are to be included in the index is a matter of careful judgment. If the total number of forms in the company is under approximately 10,000, it is probably better to include all of them in the index at the outset rather than have to go over it again, possibly disrupting what had been accomplished before.

Preparing for Building the Index

The first step in building the index is to obtain the samples of forms to be classified, as described above.

Staffing for the Work. The index does not build itself. Index building is a long and arduous task. Management must assign personnel for its construction, and this is a full-time job for one or more people over a considerable period of time, depending on the skill and experience of the people and the number of forms to be classified. It is a time-consuming job and not something to be fitted in between other work assignments. If that is tried the index will probably never be completed or, at best, will be a halfway result.

A Common Terminology for Classification of Forms. As indicated above the greatest single problem in forms classification is the confusion of terminology in titles, even assuming the form has a title, which many don't have. Some titles are meaningless to anyone other than the designer of the form or the procedures person who authored it; some titles are technical and beyond the comprehension of the forms control staff; other forms are so badly designed that no one could know what they are used for. In many cases classifying a form may be a matter of guesswork with results that may be meaningless to users of the index.

It is almost a waste of time for management to invest time and money in building an index without some means of assuring that it will outlast personnel changes and be meaningful to others than the ones who made the classification.

There is only one practical solution to this confusion—the use of a standard terminology on forms as the index is built. This solution does the following: first, it guides the control unit in the original building of the index; second, it provides a means for future personnel to find forms when they are wanted; and third, it tells how or where new or combined forms should be integrated into the index as time goes by. Such standard terminology is provided in the dictionary of terminology in Appendix II. It has stood the test of application over many years in companies of all sizes—manufacturing, insurance, banking, and finance as well as government units.

The dictionary should be carefully studied and used as a basis for classification.

An Example of Classification. Figure 16 shows a form used in a manufacturing company entitled "Leaf Spring Test Report." This is an example of the "common garden variety" of forms used by the thousands in manufacturing, fairly well designed although it could be better. It is used in the final inspection as the last operation before the manufactured product is shipped to the customer or put into finished goods inventory. Let's classify it for the index:

LEAF SPRING TEST REPORT

| D.S.P.No. | CUST.No. | NAME | FRONT PROGRESSIVE
REAR PROGRESSIVE COMB.
AUXILIARY |

| FREE OPEN
MAIN SPG.
1ST UNIT | DROP
S.E.
L.E. | FREE OPEN
AUX. SPG.
2ND UNIT | INCREMENT TEST PROG.SPRING |

| DEFL | LOAD | AVERAGE RATE |

FREE LENGTH $[\quad][\quad]{\rightarrow}[\quad]$

| | 1 | | |
| | 2 | | |

MACH.
BED TO | PLATE   INCHES | 3
EYE   INCHES | 4

LOAD | HEIGHT @ | 5
OPEN @   LBS.   INCHES DROP | S.E. L.E. | 6

length at above load $[\quad][\quad H\quad]$

| | 7 | |
| | 8 | |

1" DEFL.BELOW
LOAD POSITION   LBS.   INCHES | 9
| 10

1" DEFL.ABOVE
LOAD POSITION   LBS   INCHES | 11

2"

RATE OF MAIN SPRING

2ND UNIT IN FULL CONTACT
@   LBS.LOAD

PL. NO.	MICROMETER THICKNESS	BRINELL HARDNESS
1		

CONTACT BRACKETS $[\quad]$ APART | 2 | |
| 3 | |

AUXILIARY SPRING CONTACT LOAD   LBS. | 4 | |

MACH.
BED TO | PLATE   INCHES | 5 | |
EYE   INCHES | 6 | |
| 7 | |

LOAD | HEIGHT @ | S.E. | 8 | |
OPEN @   LBS.   INCHES DROP | L.E. | 9 | |

LENGTH AT ABOVE LOAD $[\quad][\quad H\quad]$ | 10 | |
| 11 | |

1" DEFL.BELOW
LOAD POSITION   LBS.   INCHES | 12 | |
| 13 | |

1" DEFL.ABOVE
LOAD POSITION   LBS   INCHES | 14 | |
| 15 | |

2" | 16 | |

RATE OF COMB.SPRING | 17 | |

REMARKS | 18 | |
| 19 | |
| 20 | |

| TESTED BY | DATE |
| OK'D BY | DATE |

FIGURE 16. Example of a form to be classified: ''leaf spring report.''

1. *The subject.* According to the title on the form the subject is "leaf spring," but that surely is only one of the many products made by this company. If a separate classification were set up for each individual product, the index would be overwhelmed with subject titles. It would be unwieldy and would probably not work. Therefore the title is generalized into *product,* the definition of which is found in the dictionary. "Leaf spring" is, of course, not found in the dictionary. The definition of "product" is as follows:

Product (subject). The end result of a manufacturing or production process, usually offered for sale as an object of commerce; also, anything produced by generation or growth such as products of agriculture.

At some point the subject of a production process ceases to be work-in-process and becomes product. This usually is at the point of final inspection, after which work-in-process becomes saleable as a product.

The difference between "product" and "merchandise" lies in the nature of production. A product is produced by the organization that sells it, whereas merchandise is purchased for resale. A retail store sells merchandise, whereas a factory sells its product. The manufacturing concern may not only produce and sell its product but may also deal in resale merchandise (i.e., the product of another organization along with its own product).

See also "merchandise," "invoice," "statement," and "commodity" in the Dictionary of Terminology (Appendix II).

Thus, the definition not only defines the term but also distinguishes between that term and others that may overlap or be confused with it, telling the analyst which term to use in each case. Note that the definition delineates carefully work-in-process, production, and product. These are different stages in the manufacturing process and the distinction is important, each stage utilizing different forms. Also, *product* and *production* are two of the largest categories of forms in the average manufacturing company, and the distinction between them creates smaller groups of forms in the index folders, making it easier and quicker to look for duplication of paperwork. The analyst charting the procedure also treats the work-in-process and the handling of the final product as separate operations. By identifying the forms separately in the index, his or her work is made easier.

2. *The operation.* This appears quite simple. The title says "test," which is a standard term, but experience shows that considerable confusion arises between the operations *testing of, examination of, inspection of,* and *analysis of.* All four appear in classifying forms and they are used indiscriminately, making the job of classifying more difficult. To clear up this difficulty the dictionary provides a distinction between the four operations and assigns each a logical place in the terminology. According to these definitions, which are cross-referenced to each other, this form is classified under the operation *inspection of.* Admittedly the form might have been classified under *testing of,* but that could have confused other personnel versed in factory terminology because inspection is the commonly used term in manufacturing processes whether it be incoming materials and supplies, work-in-process, or final product, whereas testing is more often used in the laboratory.

3. *The function.* The title indicates a correct function, *to report.* The dictionary distinguishes between the functions *to report* and *to record,* being based on a to—from movement in the case of the report, which does not occur in the case of a record. Of course, many reports become records but the classification should be made on the basis of the first or primary usage of the form. In many cases report forms have the to—from movement specifically indicated on the form, whereas this one does not; however, at the bottom of the form the captions "tested by" and "ok'd by" indicate movement plus the fact that the general nature of the form indicates that it is not just filled in and filed at the point of origin without going anywhere else.

So we find this form classified under *product, inspection of,* and *to report.* There may be some disagreement as to this classification but it brings together in one folder all the forms used by the company that report the inspection of its product. This will reveal duplication and give the procedures analyst a quick source for all paper relating to that important procedure.

H. CLASSIFYING THE FORMS FOR THE INDEX

In making the classification, start with a pile of forms that have been collected for control purposes from the using locations, one sample of which has been laid aside for this classification. As stated before, all unnumbered forms must have a temporary identifying number and that number must appear on the form before it is built into the functional index.

For the actual work of sorting and classifying the forms an open file drawer (transfer file drawers may be used) should be placed within easy reach, easy to see and use. The file folders should be of the suspension type so that the forms can be easily and quickly dropped into the folders. Each hanging folder should have an index tab affixed into which slips can be inserted containing the titles being sorted.

The First or Initial Sort

The first or initial sort is by title only, not by operation or function. There are three reasons for this: first, to become accustomed to the forms presently in use, many or most of which have never been seen by the analyst before; second, to observe the use or misuse of captions and titles now on the forms; third, to become used to the dictionary of standard terminology. With the second round of classification it becomes clear that the first interpretation of many forms was not the correct one in the light of other similar forms encountered after the first one had been classified. In other words, the initial sort provides a preliminary working experience in the correct classification of forms and prevents a lot of backtracking to correct errors.

The initial classification should be limited to the better known subjects more or less common in industry and commerce and easily recognized by the analyst who may or may not be experienced in forms used in the more technical or specialized phases of the business. Those forms can be classified later. Typical of such commonly encountered subjects are accident, accounts payable and receivable, appropriation, bank check, cash, check, earnings, employee and employment, injury and illness, insurance, job, labor, lease, machinery and equipment, materials and supplies, merchandise, payroll, premises, premium, product and production, sales, shipment, tax, travel, vehicle, work and work-in-process, and other more commonly used subjects. There may be as many as 30 or 40 of these first-round subject classifications. No effort should be made to classify operations and functions in the first round, because that complicates the early stages and causes too much backtracking to correct wrong classifications.

The Second Sort

In the second round of classification each form previously classified is reviewed and many are changed to other folders, owing to the greater comprehension of terms and understanding of the forms gained from the first round. All forms are, at the same time, subclassified by the operation or condition and function, thus completing the index classification—complete, that is, except for those forms that are incomprehensible because of poor design and lack of identification. Such forms must be referred to the paperwork coordinator in the using location for explanation. This is a good exercise for showing coordinators design defects in their own forms.

In the second time around it may be found that some subject folders contain an unduly large number of forms. Such a case could well be in the subjects "product" or "machinery and equipment" in a large manufacturing company or "claim and loss" in an insurance company. The bulkiness of such large folders would hinder the efficient use of the index. Therefore, the forms should be broken down by some suitable subclassification.

In the example of machinery and equipment the subsort could be by types of equipment such as automotive, electrical, generating, maintenance, and the like. In the case of loss and claim the subsort might be by fire, personal property, fine arts, automobile, and so on. In each case the proper operation and function would be added.

By this stage all forms will have been classified and each folder will contain a sample of each and every form pertaining to one particular category of paperwork by subject, operation or condition, and function.

Coding the Index

The next step is to code the index folders. In the dictionary all subjects are numbered as are all operations and conditions and functions. Combinations of these numbers provide a Dewey decimal system for coding the index folders, and each index folder should be assigned its correct code. Thus, a folder containing forms having to do with reporting the status of employment are coded 91.214.15, "employment" being No. 91 in the subject list, "status of" being No. 214 in the operations list, and "to report" being No. 15 in the functions list.

A rubber stamp should be obtained reading FUNCTIONAL INDEX SAMPLE, DO NOT REMOVE FROM FOLDER NO. _____. This should be stamped on each form in the index with the folder code entered in the blank space left for that purpose. This serves to identify the form as belonging in the index and the specific folder in which it belongs. If this is not done the forms can, and probably will, be removed from the index and never returned, thus destroying the completeness of the index.

Cross-Referencing the Control Files

When all forms have been classified and coded they must be cross-referenced with the numerical forms file. This is a tedious job because the forms in the index folders are not in numerical sequence but are mixed as to form number. Since the numerical file is obviously in numerical sequence, it stands to reason that the easiest way to cross-reference is to get a sequential listing of the forms in the index by form number together with the applicable index code for each form.

One way to do this, probably the most feasible, is to go through the index with small slips of paper, entering the form number in one upper corner and the index code in the other upper corner, allotting one slip for each form in the index. These slips can then be sorted sequentially by form number, after which the index code can be entered from the slip onto the numerical file folder.

In the case of unnumbered forms a blank sheet of paper can be used to compile the list of temporary numbers as they are assigned. As each such form is numbered, stamp the number on the blank sheet in sequence. This not only serves to control the sequence of the numbers, but when the files are cross-referenced this blank sheet can be used to enter the index code opposite the temporary number, which makes it easy to cross-reference the unnumbered forms.

I. KEEPING THE INDEX UP-TO-DATE

After the index is built and put into operation many changes will take place. New forms will come into existence and old forms will be redesigned, eliminated, or combined with other forms. Each such case requires that the index be updated by removing the old forms and inserting the new forms in the proper classifications.

Experience shows that the best way for the index to get out of date is by not making the necessary changes to update it immediately. The press of current work, new personnel who don't know how to classify, even resistance to doing something that doesn't have to be done at that particular moment—all tend to accumulate a pile of forms that should have been put in the index but were not.

The use of the rubber stamp FUNCTIONAL INDEX SAMPLE, DO NOT REMOVE FROM FOLDER NO. _____ on every form in the index at the outset of building it is a strong deterrent to taking samples out and never putting them back. The stamp, by the way, should appear prominently on the front of the form even though it may cover some data on the form. If it is stamped on the back it may never be seen or probably no attention will be paid to it.

Every effort should be made to update the index periodically with new or redesigned forms. If someone wants to check on duplication of forms or find forms for charting a manual procedure and the forms are not in the index or the ones that are there are not the latest samples, paperwork control will suffer. With the passage of months and years there will be a constant change in paperwork and the forms will go out of date. The principle purpose of the dictionary, after the initial construction of the index, is specifically to make it easy to put new forms in their proper place and keep the index up-to-date.

J. FORMS CONTROL AT WORK

Figure 17 is a procedural flowchart of the operation of forms control in a typical company. This chart is made in accordance with the principles laid down in Section II, The Management of Manual Paperwork Procedures. It should be self-explanatory with but little study. Its use in the operation of the forms control unit is discussed below.

Auditing the Form Design

Section IIC is a discussion of auditing the form design, but the prime responsibility for form design lies with the forms control unit. Assuming that the system analyst has asked pertinent questions about the form as the manual procedure is designed, the forms control unit can go further with the following questions whether the form is under scrutiny in procedures analysis or in forms control independent of a current procedure study.

Questions on the Simplification of Forms

Necessity for the Form

What are the purposes of the form?

Are the purposes necessary?

Does the form completely accomplish its purposes?

Can some other form be used for this purpose?

Can this form be combined with some other form?

Should the form be divided into separate forms?

Is the form under a centralized control or is it a local uncontrolled form?

Is it a locally produced form to fill a gap in a standard procedure or are there local requirements not covered by the standard procedure?

Design and Content of the Form

Does the form bear a title and a control number?

Is the title descriptive of the form's purpose and use?

Are the most important data in the most visible and efficient locations?

For forms to be transmitted, have spaces been provided for the ''to'' and ''from'' information or instructions?

Is the sequence of data the same as on the next form to which the data must be transcribed?

Is the spacing sequence logical for the entry of data and the relationship of this form to others?

If the form relates to a data entry for a computer, is it designed to eliminate errors in and facilitate efficiency in key punching or key stroking?

Has sufficient space been left for the number of digits to be entered in the area allowed?

68

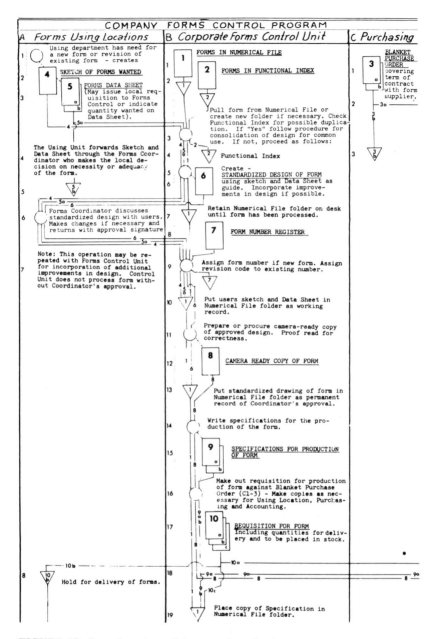

FIGURE 17. Procedure chart of the operation of a forms control unit.

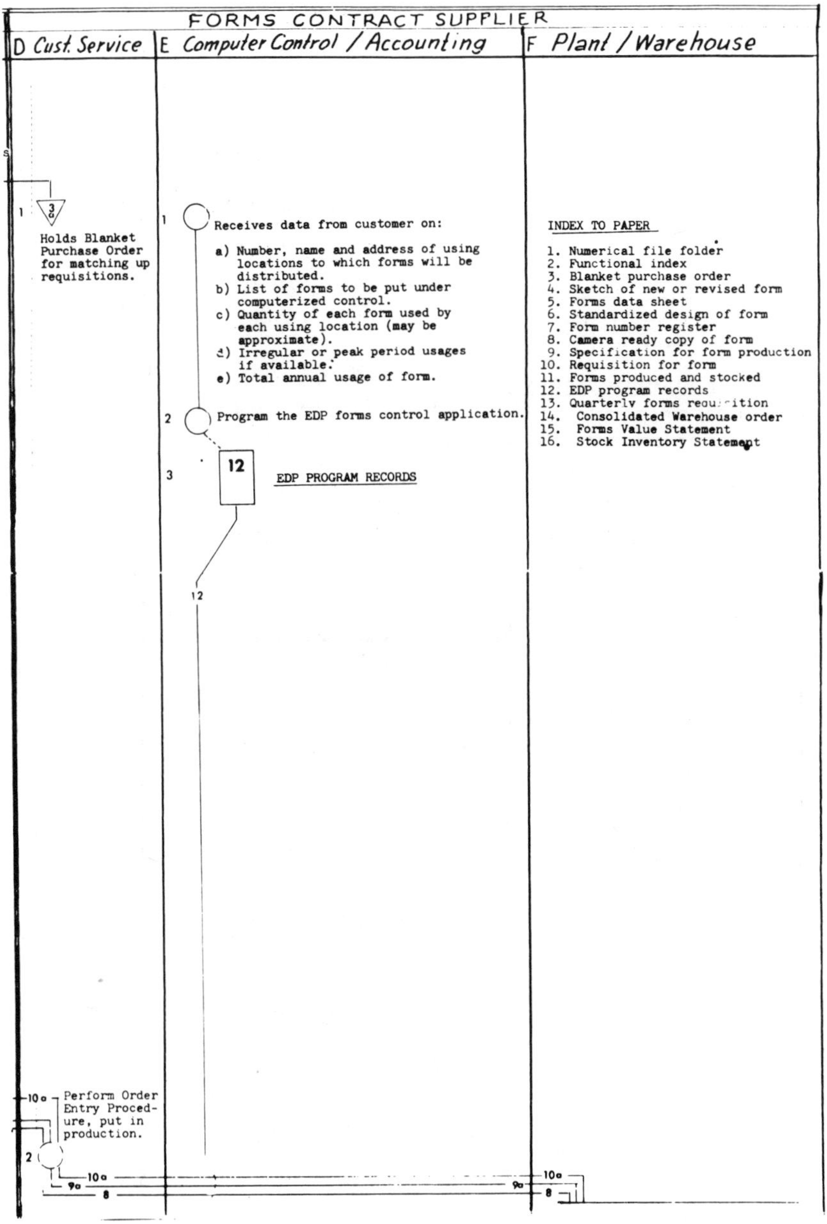

	FORMS CONTRACT SUPPLIER	
D *Cust Service*	E *Computer Control / Accounting*	F *Plant / Warehouse*

1 ▽ 3/c

Holds Blanket
Purchase Order
for matching up
requisitions.

1 ◯ Receives data from customer on:

a) Number, name and address of using
   locations to which forms will be
   distributed.
b) List of forms to be put under
   computerized control.
c) Quantity of each form used by
   each using location (may be
   approximate).
d) Irregular or peak period usages
   if available.
e) Total annual usage of form.

2 ◯ Program the EDP forms control application.

3 ☐ **12**   EDP PROGRAM RECORDS

12

INDEX TO PAPER

1. Numerical file folder
2. Functional index
3. Blanket purchase order
4. Sketch of new or revised form
5. Forms data sheet
6. Standardized design of form
7. Form number register
8. Camera ready copy of form
9. Specification for form production
10. Requisition for form
11. Forms produced and stocked
12. EDP program records
13. Quarterly forms requisition
14. Consolidated Warehouse order
15. Forms Value Statement
16. Stock Inventory Statement

10a ┐ Perform Order
    │ Entry Proced-
    │ ure, put in
    │ production.
2 ◯
    └ 10a
    └ 9a ── 8

10a
9a ─ 8

FIGURE 17 *(continued)*

70

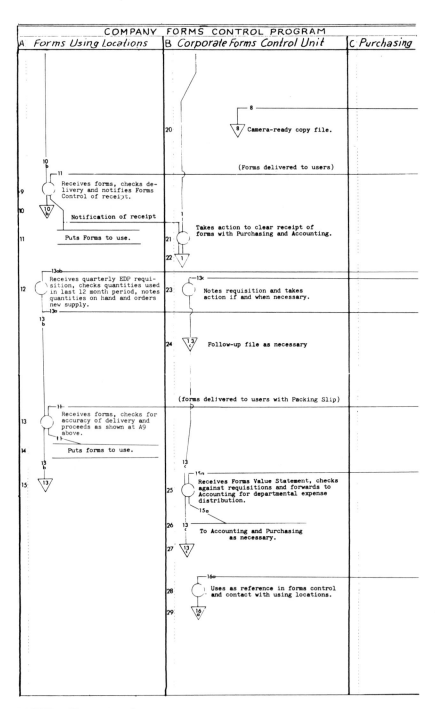

FIGURE 17 *(continued)*

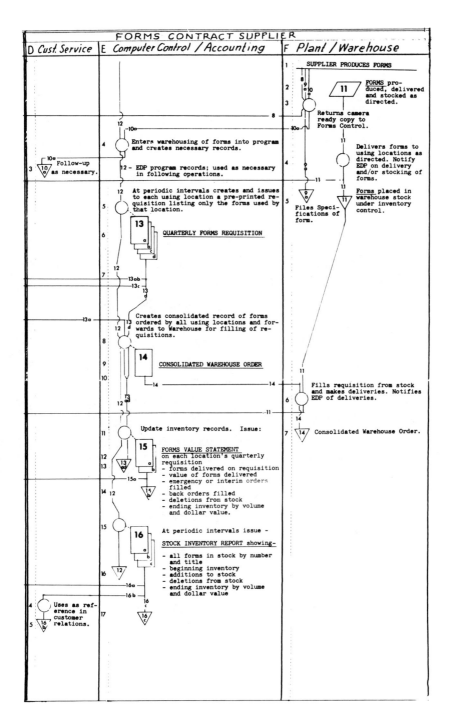

FIGURE 17 *(continued)*

Have spaces been left for necessary signatures and approvals?

Have the lines been properly weighted to facilitate reading the data horizontally or vertically on the form?

Is serial numbering necessary or desirable?

Are instructions for filing or sorting included in the proper place?

Are the necessary instructions for correct use of the form included in the proper place?

Have the lines been properly spaced for manual or machine entry of data?

Routing of Copies

Are all copies of the form necessary?

Have as many copies as are desirable or necessary for more efficient use of the form in subsequent operations been included?

Are routing instructions on the form in the correct places?

Has consideration been given to colored paper to indicate routing instead of printing separate instructions on each copy?

If the form is to be sent outside of the company has consideration been given to window envelope design?

Are departments that need clear copies for possible reproduction getting the proper copies on the right kind of paper?

If additional copies are needed in subsequent operations, will it be more economical to add copies to the form or reproduce them on duplicating machines?

K. PROCUREMENT, WAREHOUSING, AND DISTRIBUTION OF FORMS

Purchasing of office and plant forms is an administrative area with a considerable potential for cost cutting still untapped by many companies. Yet a company need only apply such modern business techniques as value analysis, economic lot ordering, and control contracting to realize the savings available in forms purchasing.

Volume of Forms Purchases Versus Expenditures

Forms are one of those ubiquitous, repetitive use items that may constitute as much as 80 percent of purchase orders issued but only 20 percent of the total dollars spent. Even with big-money forms, such as continuous and unit set, the average purchase is only a few hundred dollars at best, and for the general run of small usage forms the average purchase price or production cost is often well under a hundred dollars per form.

Ways of Obtaining or Purchasing Forms

Forms can be procured in one of four ways: from the office duplicating machine, the in-house print shop, commercial suppliers on spot order, and commercial suppliers under contract.

The Office Duplicating Machine. This is probably the most insidious way of producing forms. It is so convenient and "they don't really cost much of anything; the machine is there anyway." Office duplicating machines have, in some cases, really become printing presses. They reproduce the image by special processes and, if done carefully, produce visually acceptable results.

The main drawback to producing forms on office duplicating machines is that they are abused; the ease with which they are obtained leads to carelessness in the design of the form, producing poor clerical tools with resultant increased paperwork expense.

The In-House Print Shop. This is the source of a great many forms in the average company, hopefully under controlled conditions but too often under little or no administrative control. A small usage form produced in-house can produce exorbitant expense in clerical and paperwork operations. A form used in an annual quantity of only 500 can create as much as $600−$700 in paperwork expense with clerical work costing 13¢−14¢ per minute and supervisory work at 20¢−22¢ per minute. Half or more of all forms are used in such small quantities, and they account for a largely unrecognized share of total paperwork expense.

Commercial Suppliers on Spot Order. The large majority of commercially purchased forms are bought on spot order, a single order for a single form, with the total cost of issuing a purchase order on each such purchase. It is a quite expensive way to buy forms since the average order is a relatively small amount of money and the total cost of purchasing can easily match or exceed the cost of the form.

Commercial Suppliers Under Contract. Annual contracting for repetitive use materials is nothing new, not only in relation to office forms and stationery but in manufacturing materials as well. But seldom do such procurement contracts include management controls on the part of the supplier over stock maintenance, usage records, use point distribution, and costs when applied to business forms.

Printing is the only major business that operates largely on a job-shop instead of a production-line basis. Spot buying of forms forces a printer into the job-shop operation, in which each job is handled separately, often incurring the expense of rush orders, broken schedules, overtime, downtime on presses, and high operating costs. Contract buying is the key that opens the door to great economies in the procurement of ordinary forms if only buyers will take advantage of it, doing their part to make it possible.

Continuous computer forms are the ones most commonly bought under contract although in some larger companies other large usage forms, particularly if used in multiple locations, may also be bought under contract. Some purchasing departments have been known to use a blanket contract with a forms printer and the units of the company have freedom to buy or not to buy their forms under it. This is particularly true in companies composed of large units operating under a profit center decentralization with a high degree of local administrative authority. Such an arrangement usually offers savings to the units buying under the contract.

The Make-or-Buy Decision

The make-or-buy decision should be made by the purchasing department, not by the in-house print shop. Since the print shop undoubtedly prints a great many forms in small annual quantities, there should be a policy to determine what forms and what quantities of those forms should be printed in-house. Experience shows that in too many cases the manager of the print shop wants to enlarge his operation and points out that his press can print 9000 − 10,000 forms an hour, obviously an economical operation—economical, that is, when the true costs of operating the shop are not known, which is the case in far too many in-house print shops.

The make-or-buy decision, plus an objective analysis of the print shop operation and costs, is the key to this control.

L. WAREHOUSING AND DISTRIBUTION OF FORMS

The most expensive form is the form that is not where it is needed at the time it is needed. Delayed paperwork, lack of current information, makeshift records, frayed tempers—all add up to unnecessary costs and operational foul-ups.

Stocking or Warehousing?

There are three general methods of storing forms: in the company's stationery stockroom, in the using unit location, and at the printer's plant.

Most forms that are stocked at all are kept in the company's stationery stockroom with other general stationery items and maintenance supplies. Effective stockroom control is the exception rather than the rule. The absence of such control leads to unnecessary running out of stock or accumulation of excess stocks.

Inventory Control. Inventory control over forms is, again, the exception rather than the rule. Since cut or flat forms constitute 90 percent or more of all forms used and since most of them are used in small quantities, it is all too often considered not worthwhile to establish inventory control over them. Such control is often considered not worth the expense, but to run completely out of one such form might conceivably cause a work stoppage costing many times the value of the entire lot of forms.

Distribution of Forms. Distribution of forms to the using departments or locations is another part of the physical problem. Since most forms are kept in the stationery stockroom or in the using department, a parade of people goes to the stockroom to pick up a small supply of forms or fills up file drawers with forms used at that point. This is undoubtedly the most expensive of all methods of storing or distributing forms and may lead to large accumulations of forms throughout the company.

Four Areas for Consideration

There are four distinct areas for consideration in stocking and distributing forms based on the quantities used and the number of use points.

Small Annual Usage, Single Use Point. As has been stated, over 50 percent of all forms are used in comparatively small annual quantities. This comes as a surprise to the average administrative or systems managers, since their attention is usually centered on the large "big-money" forms. This attitude is reinforced by many forms salespeople who are not interested in an order for only 500—1000 forms because their commission will be minuscule. These forms are most often produced in-house and delivered entirely to the using department.

Small Usage, Multiple Use Point. This creates a distribution problem that normally does not have the usage data to control. In this case the form, even though used in small quantities, should be kept in the stationery stockroom and distributed from there. When one use point runs out of the form, it can be given a smaller quantity if necessary while the stockroom orders a reprint.

Large Usage, Single Use Point. Here we ask how large "large" is in terms of usage, the weight or bulkiness of the forms, the availability of storage space, the capacity of the central stockroom to handle the bulk, and the presence or absence of contract buying. In the case of very bulky or heavy forms, such as computer forms, shipping tags, envelopes, checks, and the like, adequate arrangements can be made by simple contract with drop shipments and stock status reports.

Large Usage, Multiple Use Points. This is where control contracting comes into its own with its facilities for bulk storage, requisitioning to multiple use points, delivery direct to the requisitioner, plus management reports on forms cost and shipping charges by use point by periodic requisition.

Without control contracting the parent company faces the problem of multiple use point requisitioning and distribution, which can create troublesome and wasteful situations resulting in forms running out of stock, work stoppages, rush orders at high cost, and, potentially, the taking over of the situation by using locations to avoid what they consider red tape. The solution to such a problem is a management decision for control contracting under an adequate paperwork management program.

M. CONTROL CONTRACT PROCUREMENT OF FORMS

What is control contracting in forms buying? It is the buying of forms (and possibly stationery supplies) from a supplier who takes over the responsibility for control of record keeping, requisitioning, and delivery plus reporting of stock activity and costs at designated intervals.

Obviously suppliers must be paid to administer the management controls for which they take responsibility, but for suppliers these become a major administrative action whereas for the purchaser they are a relatively minor activity and, too often, they are not carried out efficiently. Substantial savings in addition to convenience are an almost certain result of a well-managed control contract for forms buying.

Preplanning for Control Contracting

Essential factors in planning for this method of forms procurement include the following:

1. All forms must be identified by number.
2. All forms should be designed, insofar as possible, to fit standard printing processes and cut from standard paper sizes.
3. Complete specifications must be written for all forms under the contract.
4. A list of all forms initially covered by the contract must be furnished to the supplier together with the actual or estimated annual usage of each.
5. A list of all using locations must be provided together with complete names and addresses with, if possible, estimates of annual usages at each location for each form.
6. Irregular or peak usage periods should be indicated for each form when applicable.
7. A schedule for issuing periodic requisitions to use points must be prepared.

Handling Existing Stocks of Forms

Forms presently in the purchaser's stockroom must be inventoried, prepared, and removed to the vendor's warehouse as the nucleus of a warehousing and inventory control service. The vendor constructs the prototype control records on these forms.

N. HOW CONTROL CONTRACTING WORKS

The purchasing department issues a single purchase order covering the terms of the contract, presumably for a period of one or two years. It takes the better part of a year to establish the control contracting program and put it into full operation. It will probably be in the second year that the full benefits of the program are realized since the stocks of forms on hand must be worked off before they can be brought into the program.

Obviously vendors must have professionally managed warehouse facilities and the ability and willingness to handle all types of forms: flat, unit-set, and continuous. They must also have facilities for warehousing and controlling some forms such as envelopes or stock tab forms that they do not produce but that from the standpoint of the purchaser, must be brought into the program.

Last, but not least, the vendor must have computer capability and the ability to program control contracting into the computer.

The Periodic Requisition

At periodic intervals the supplier prepares by computer and issues to each using location a preprinted requisition (Figure 18), listing *only* the forms used by that location, showing the quantity of each used by that location in the preceding 12 months, with blank columns for taking stock count of forms on hand and indicating the number of forms wanted for the next period.

The supplier receives the requisitions from all using locations and prepares a consolidated list for checking stock and order picking. If consolidated wants are out of line with normal usages, the supplier checks with the customer's forms control unit to see if an error has been made in the requisitioning. The requisitions are then filled and the forms delivered directly to the using locations.

The Expense Distribution Statement

The vendor then prepares an expense distribution report (Figure 19) for customer accounting, showing the forms delivered to each location

PERIODIC FORMS REQUISITION
FORM 1009

TO General Manufacturing Company
420 So.Main St - District Office
Jefferson City, Nebraska

RETURN TO
Corp. Forms Control Unit
380 Third Ave.
New York, NY 10017

NOT LATER THAN

REQ. NO. 14 - 327 PAGE 1 or 6 DATE

PURCHASE ORDER NO | NEXT REQ DATE

FORM NO	TITLE	CODE	PRICE PER M	ORDER UNIT	12 MOS USAGE	QUANTITY ON HAND	QUANTITY WANTED	ACCOUNTING DISTRIBUTION
0008	A/c Rec. Ledger Sheet	00046	18.76	Sh 100	2,500	316	700	
0009	Accounting Analysis Sheet	00047	16.20	Sh 25	600	310	-	
0012	Deposit Slip - 3 Inch	00053	4.27	Pd 100	350	95	100	
0027	Perpetual Inventory Record	00072	22.76	Pd 50	750	300	-	
0031	Long Distance Telephone Slip	00078	5.03	Pd 50	200	100	-	
0038	E.E.O Activity Report	00086	9.78	Pd 50	150	25	50	
0047	Voucher Register	00098	10.50	Pd 25	200	37	75	
0057	Use Tax Report	00102	11.66	Pd 50	200	100	-	
0063	Employee Status Record Card	00117	9.99	Sh 25	900	225	100	
0068	Petty Cash Slip	00119	4.76	Pd 50	2,000	210	500	
0077	Attendance Record	00131	9.47	Pd 50	1,450	500	300	
0083	Cash Journal Sheet	00141	6.98	Sh 25	600	-	300	
0087	Separation Notice	00150	14.15	Pd 25	650	100	200	
0092	Employment Application	00162	21.50	Sh 50	200	50	-	
0098	Accident Report	00171	12.10	Pd 25	350	30	100	
0102	Expense Report - Weekly	00130	18.14	Pd 50	1,500	112	400	
0110	Check Request	00186	7.40	Pd 50	400	76	100	
0114	Misc. Payment Notice	00187	14.12	Pd 100	200	-	-	
0121	Salary Deduction Authorization	00190	9.12	Pd 50	400	115	-	
0129	Check Record	00193	16.40	Sh 25	100	40	-	
0130	Internal Memo, 11 Inch	00194	11.76	Pd 100	6,000	490	1000	
0131	Internal Memo, 5-1/2 Inch	00195	7.74	Pd 100	5,000	250	1000	
0132	Letterhead - Jefferson City	00196	18.77	Pkg 100	12,000	1100	2500	
0133	Envelope No.10 - Jef. City Return	00197	17.50	Box 500	15,000	550	4000	
0134	Envelope Kraft 9 x 12 Plain	00198	22.76	Box 100	800	145	150	
0147	Tool & Die Record Card 4 x 6	00221	17.76	Pkg 25	100	50	-	
0152	No.2 Die Press Production Record	00234	14.80	Pd 50	400	75	700	
0168	Labor Shift Schedule	00241	16.10	Pd 50	400	55	200	
0176	Quality Control J-16	00250	14.17	Pd 25	900	100	-	
0188	Gate Pass - Vehicle	00257	7.40	Pd 50	1,900	380	400	
0189	Gate Pass - Individual	00258	7.40	Pd 50	1,000	315	-	
0192	Visitor Register	00266	18.00	Sh 25	250	170	150	
0199	Request for Physical Exam.	00310	9.00	Pd 50	400	28	-	
0214	Hospital Report of Treatment	00321	14.12	Pd 25	100	50	-	
0215	Employee Health Record	00333	13.80	Pd 50	200	30	50	
0248	Factory Work Order	00376	143.00	Pkg 100	12,000	1250	4000	

FIGURE 18. The periodic forms requisition under control contracting.

FORMS EXPENSE DISTRIBUTION
FORM 1024

TO GENERAL MFG. CO	PERIODIC REQUISITION NO		DATE OF REQUISITION	
District Office	14 - 327			
420 So. Main St.	REFERANCE NO	P. O. NO.	ACCOUNT NO	
St. Louis Mo.	627 - 03			

FORM		QUANTITY			TOTAL THIS
NO	TITLE	ORDERED	SHIPPED	PRICE PER M	REQUISITION
SCHEDULED ORDERS					
0008	A/C Rec. Ledger Sheet	700	700	18.76	13.13
0012	Deposit Slip - 3 inch	100	100	4.27	.43
0038	EEO Activity Report	500	500	9.78	.49
0047	Voucher Register	75	75	10.50	.79
0063	Employee Status Record Card	100	100	9.99	1.00
0068	Petty Cash Slip	500	400	4.76	1.90
0083	Cash Journal Sheet	300	300	6.98	2.09
0087	Separation Notice	200	200	14.15	2.83
0098	Accident Report	100	100	12.10	1.21
0102	Expense Report - Weekly	400	400	18.14	7.26
0110	Check Request	100	100	7.40	.74
0130	Internal Memo - 11 inch	1000	1000	11.76	11.76
0131	Internal Memo - 5-1/2 inch	1000	1000	7.74	7.74
0132	Letterhead, Jefferson City	2500	2500	18.77	46.93
0133	Envelope No. 10.- Jeff. City	4000	4000	17.50	61.25
0134	Envelope Kraft, 9 x 12	150	150	22.76	3.41
0152	No. 2 Die Press Production Record	200	200	14.80	2.96
0168	Labor Shift Schedule	200	200	16.10	3.22
0188	Gate Pass - Vehicle	400	400	7.40	2.96
0199	Request for Physical Exam.	150	150	9.00	1.35
0125	Employee Health Record	50	50	13.80	.69
0248	Factory Work Order	4000	4000	143.00	572.00
	TOTAL SCHEDULED ORDERS				746.14
	INTERIM ORDERS				
0127	Daily Cash Report	500	500	11.45	5.76
0397	Rack Card	2500	2500	8.87	22.18
0478	Maintenance Work Sheet	20000	20000	6.40	128.00
0561	LCL Carloading Report	1000	1000	14.20	14.20
	TOTAL INTERIM ORDERS				170.14
	TOTAL ALL ORDERS				916.28
	TRANSPORTATION CHORGES				69.12
	TOTAL CHARGE FOR USE POINT, PERIOD				985.40

FIGURE 19. The forms expense distribution report under control contracting.

with prices, transportation charges, and any other items the customer may desire such as figures for local and state taxes. The customer then has only to make a transfer from a forms suspense account to the using location account to have all accounting completed.

The vendor updates the inventory records and issues low-stock notices to the customer for replenishment of stocks.

FORMS STOCK STATUS – FLAT FORMS
GM 795

CUSTOMER General Manufacturing Company

REFERANCE CODE 47 – 31 – 4333

FORM NUMBER	PRICE PER M	BEGINNING INVENTORY Quantity	Value	ADDITIONS	DELETIONS	YEAR ENDING / ENDING INVENTORY Quantity	Value	MAXIMUM STOCK	NOW IN PRODUCTION
0001	8.00	8,000	64.00	-	3,500	4,500	36.00	15,000	10,000
0003	12.14	6,400	77.70	4,000	5,000	5,400	65.56	8,000	-
0004	15.00	1,200	18.00	1,000	1,000	1,200	18.00	2,000	-
0008	18.76	27,500	515.90	30,000	38,450	19,050	357.38	43,000	20,000
0009	16.20	2,000	32.40	5,000	1,800	5,200	84.24	7,500	-
0010	15.70	4,200	65.94	-	2,000	2,200	34.54	4,000	-
0011	22.55	200	4.51	1,000	800	400	9.02	1,000	LSN
0012	4.27	1,000	4.27	7,500	4,550	3,950	16.86	7,500	-
0016	13.00	6,500	84.50	9,050	8,500	7,050	91.65	8,500	-
0027	22.76	8,400	191.18	25,000	29,050	4,350	99.00	30,000	25,000
0028	18.00	64,400	1,159.20	150,000	161,000	53,400	961.20	150,000	-
0029	19.77	2,200	32.49	10,000	6,400	5,800	85.67	10,000	-
0031	5.03	4,750	23.89	12,500	11,200	6,050	30.43	10,000	-
0038	9.78	1,000	9.78	1,000	1,750	250	2.45	2,500	LSN
0041	11.86	47,500	563.35	200,000	197,400	50,100	594.19	225,000	150,000
0042	33.00	250	8.25	-	800	450	19.85	1,000	-
0043	12.50	7,400	92.50	1,000	6,050	1,350	16.88	8,500	8,500
0044	20.00	4,000	80.00	-	-	4,000	80.00	4,000	-
0047	10.50	-	-	4,000	2,200	1,800	18.90	3,500	-
0048	8.40	22,500	189.00	75,000	77,950	19,500	164.22	75,000	75,000
0050	14.77	18,000	265.86	20,000	24,700	13,300	196.44	23,500	-
0051	29.50	200	5.90	1,000	780	420	12.39	1,000	-
0052	22.47	2,400	53.92	-	1,800	600	13.48	2,500	2,000
0054	11.20	34,500	386.40	50,000	52,000	32,500	364.00	60,000	-
0057	11.66	800	9.33	4,000	2,700	2,100	24.49	4,000	-
0058	11.66	1,200	13.99	4,000	3,300	1,900	22.15	4,000	-
0059	11.66	3,800	44.31	-	3,100	700	8.16	4,000	-
0060	47.60	9,500	452.20	20,000	27,500	2,000	95.20	22,000	4,000
0061	19.20	14,250	273.60	-	13,850	400	7.68	15,000	20,000
0063	9.90	2,400	23.98	6,000	5,500	2,900	28.97	6,000	15,000
0068	4.76	1,100	5.24	3,500	3,650	950	4.52	3,500	LSN
0072	21.00	8,500	178.50	-	2,000	6,500	136.50	10,000	-
0073	18.30	8,000	146.40	30,000	28,400	9,600	175.68	33,000	LSN
0077	9.47	2,850	26.99	10,000	9,600	3,250	30.78	10,000	LSN
0078	9.47	8,800	83.34	12,500	11,750	9,550	90.44	10,000	-
0080	12.53	11,250	140.96	22,000	19,800	13,450	168.53	22,000	-

LSN – Low stock notice has been issued

FIGURE 20. The warehouse stock status report on flat forms under control contracting. Another report covers other types of forms.

The Stock Status Report

The vendor prepares at stated intervals stock status reports for the customer (Figure 20), listing all forms in warehouse stock with beginning and ending inventories, additions and deletions to stock, forms in process of manufacture, and other inventory adjustments, all in terms of both physical volume and dollar cost. This report can be made separately for different types of forms if desired for the organization of gang runs, thus helping the printer into production-shop instead of job-shop practice. This should cut costs to the advantage of both the customer and the printer, who can include other customers forms in the gang runs. Slow-moving or obsolete forms will be identified.

O. FINANCING WAREHOUSE STOCKS OF FORMS

It is an interesting fact that purchasers who contemplate this type of contracting sometimes place strong importance on the cost of ware-housing such forms and demand that the printer finance the stocks and invoice them only as they are withdrawn from stock to fill requisitions. This attitude seems prevalent not only with stock tabulating forms and other large-volume items but also with smaller-volume forms going to multiple use points.

What is being paid for? No question about it, the financing of warehouse stocks requires money and money costs money no matter who is doing the financing. Some forms manufacturers have been known to say that they do not charge for stocking the customer's forms. To any thinking person this borders on the ridiculous; either the printer does not actually stock the form, counting on being able to print on demand in time to fill orders (with consequent higher production costs) or the printer does stock the form and must finance it, in which case someone has to pay the financing cost. Guess who.

More often than not any company that enters into forms contracting can "hire the money" more cheaply than can the printer and by doing their own financing they can take advantage of the printer's forms distribution statement to cut down their expense of handling many invoices contingent on charge-outs from the printer-financed stocks.

MANAGING AND SIMPLIFYING
CLERICAL WORK

With manual procedures audited (Section II) and with forms brought under control (Section III), the next step is to analyze and simplify clerical operations, establish standards for clerical performance, and thereby bring the total paperwork cost under control. This can be done only if the first-line supervisors are brought into the program and given new and more effective operating tools to make them better managers.

Management should expect positive results from the program. It should know what each paperwork operation costs, be able to forecast white-collar labor requirements, and cause a reduction in paperwork expense.

Clerical operations analysis can be accomplished through a simplified technique of clerical work measurement and analysis that can be operated by in-house personnel with a minimum of assistance. The key is a definition and measurement of clerical tasks that are the elements of the paperwork operation. It in turn is a segment of the procedure. In this way all elements of paperwork are integrated and brought under control.

By making the measurement and analysis techniques a normal tool of the paperwork supervisor, the controls are made permanent and administrative expense is reduced to a minimum, thereby increasing profit.

A. THE CLERICAL OPERATION

If the manual paperwork procedures—the strategy of paperwork management—have been charted and analyzed (Section II) and if the forms—the raw material of paperwork—have been brought under control (Section III), the next logical step is to analyze and simplify the clerical operations by which the paperwork is performed.

What Constitutes a Clerical Operation?

In paragraph D of Section II definitions are given for the "system," "procedure," and "method." The next successive element of paperwork is the paperwork operation, which entails people and can be done manually, mechanically, or electronically but which, however done, is a successive step in the procedure and costs money.

The clerical operation is work performed by office workers and is made up of tasks that comprise the elements of the operation. Approving an invoice for payment is an operation but it is made up of several tasks: removing the invoice from a file, matching it with a receiving report and/or a purchase order, checking the price for correctness, approving the amount, forwarding it for payment, returning the papers to the file, and possibly others.

The operation itself should have been audited in the manual paperwork procedure analysis but the individual tasks may be further analyzed and simplified, and that is the subject of this section.

B. THE FIRST-LINE SUPERVISOR AND CLERICAL WORK MEASUREMENT

If clerical work measurement is to be successful it must be more than a temporary effort. If most of the responsibility for control is delegated solely to a staff analyst, no matter how well qualified, there will almost certainly be results, but with almost equal certainty the results will be temporary when measured from a long-range viewpoint. It is economically impossible to keep a highly trained staff analyst permanently on the job of controlling clerical work in any local area; the analyst will move on to new pastures and afterward the permanence of clerical work economy will depend almost altogether on the degree to which the first-line supervisors have been built into the program and trained in the work measurement and analysis techniques. If this has not been done the results will surely be short-lived.

Even if the supervisor is responsible for paperwork management at that level, the results will be only partial if the work has not been carefully analyzed and measured as an initial step to give the supervisor more information about the work than he or she has ever had before. This can be done through a simplified clerical work measurement program that, again, is fitted to use by the supervisor and does not depend on a trained analyst for its long-range application.

This program for clerical work simplification and cost reduction should, therefore, be directed so that it can be continued by the supervisor to the greatest possible extent, with the staff analyst performing only the structural work and providing the basic installation and training of the supervisor in the techniques of the work.

The Supervisor's Interest in the Program

Such a program holds a vital interest for progressive supervisors. It offers them the opportunity to extend their field of knowledge about paperwork management and enhances their opportunity for advancement. Supervisors might ask, "Why should I as a supervisor be interested in being part of a general paperwork management program?" The answer is found in the following factors.

"Why Should We Have Such a Program at All?" First, my own interests are served by the following: new tools and techniques for better supervisory management practices; closer relationships with upper management; better communications, so that my ideas will be heard; greater opportunity through better performance; greater recognition of my accomplishments.

Second, the company's interests are served by a continuing program, not a one-shot deal; faster processing of paperwork; lower administrative and paperwork costs; more specific control over clerical work; preparing today for tomorrow's increased work load; a positive forecast of personnel requirements.

"What is the Program?" The program is one in which I will receive tools and techniques, plus training in using them, for work improvement, work simplification, work measurement, work scheduling, work layout and organization. The program is permanent, integrated at all levels of the company, and operated by us. It will make me a better supervisor.

"How Do We Start?" By recognizing the total administrative expense control picture plus my part in it. Then, specifically:

1. We gather data by flow charting to analyze the procedure and determine the *how* of paperwork within the department; analyze the overall paperwork requirements; measure the work; take a task inventory to find out exactly what each worker is doing and how much time is spent doing it; determine what machines are being used for what purposes and for how long; find out who does what, where, when, why, and how.

2. We analyze the data to find out how the work is divided among the workers; how the work is scheduled within the department; the time required for clerical operations; what can be done to improve the operations; how much time is required to process the data, in relation to current and future work loads; what the time lags are between operations and how they can be shortened.

3. We accomplish work improvements by eliminating all unnecessary work, simplifying all necessary work, scheduling work and eliminating waiting time, distributing work for greatest utilization of skills, determining the proper need for machines and equipment, and eliminating all unnecessary administrative expense.

With Continuing Participation I will be a better manager, with full opportunity for greater recognition for accomplishment, closer relationship with management, fuller utilization of my abilities, better possibility of advancement, *plus* greater pride and satisfaction in my own work and greater value to the company.

C. WHAT MANAGEMENT SHOULD EXPECT FROM CLERICAL WORK MEASUREMENT

Paperwork measurement can be so productive of information, if it is properly done, that the organization of the information for the greatest possible benefit becomes a vital matter. This requires that management know just what information is available or potentially available from the study. The following are the principal types of information that should be expected.

Better Management at the First-Line Supervisory Level

One major objective of clerical work measurement is to increase the level of management efficiency in the office, which is another way of saying decreasing office costs, all of which ultimately finds its focal point at the level of the first-line supervisor. The real measurement of lasting success in the field of paperwork expense control can be evaluated only in terms of increased supervisory efficiency and what that does to the productivity of the white-collar labor force.

The reduction of the labor force in the office, the reduction of any time lag in processing work, and the reduction of paperwork costs, all can be accomplished only through an increase in supervisory efficiency. If they are accomplished in any other way, the benefits will probably turn out to be temporary, the results of a periodic stimulation that cannot be kept up over a long period of time. Continued stimulation may well be a necessary part of any program, but the real changes should come about as the result of having created a new situation in supervisory management. That situation must become the new normal state of things without the necessity of too much continued stimulation.

Clerical Work Productivity

Productive Versus Nonproductive Time. The first basic data to be had from office work measurement is the effective utilization of worker time and effort. The technique for gathering data in the work measurement program must reveal worker utilization of available time in terms of productive output.

Personal Time Allowance.[1] The element of personal time to be allowed to the worker depends on the particular kind of work being done, the degree of fatigue inherent in the work, the seriousness of error in the performance of the work, plus other such factors as might require more than a normal allowance. Usually the personal allowance lies somewhere between about 10 percent and 20 percent of the total time available, ordinarily falling in the 14−17 percent range. Using 10 percent as a minimum and 20 percent as a maximum, the analyst can make a reasonable approximation, depending on the presence of the preceding factors in the tasks or operations being analyzed. Available time is total time less personal time allowance.

Experience shows that the utilization of available time by individual workers may vary widely within the same work unit, and there should

---

[1] All measurement results illustrated in this section are from an actual application of the task inventory method of measurement in an average industrial corporation with approximately 3200 employees, the study covering 14 stenographic and clerical workers in the accounting department.

be no great surprise if this turns out to be the case. Some workers may show work in excess of 100 percent of the available time; for instance, working supervisors may have a tendency to absorb overloads of work instead of distributing it as it should be. Supervisors or workers reporting more than 100 percent may be working overtime. Careful attention must be paid by management to the question of overtime in view of the legal restrictions on pay.

Figures 21 and 22 show a typical case of productive versus nonproductive time. Poor utilization of available time on the part of individual workers may be due to new workers who are not yet acquainted with the work, bad distribution of work by the supervisor, or simply poor performance. In any case the individual productive percentage gives the supervisor the most direct measurement of the efficiency of his or her own management of the unit. In some cases the low percent-

TIME REPORTED BY EMPLOYEES ON CLERICAL TASK INVENTORY

Dept. & Section, Stenographic and Clerical 84-3

Number of Employees, 14

Total Payroll Hours Monthly, 2,090

Available Time per Employee, 149.3 hours, or 8,958 minutes, monthly

EMPLOYEE	MONTHLY TIME AVAILABLE MINUTES	MONTHL TIME REPORTED MINUTES	TIME REPORTED PLUS PERSONAL ALLOWANCE, MIN.	% OF TIME AVAILABLE
No. 1	8,958	4,620	5,133	57.3
No. 2	8,958	7,068	7,853	87.7
No. 3	8,958	7,934	8,815	98.4
No. 4	8,958	8,386	9,318	104.0
No. 5	8,958	8,335	9,261	103.4
No. 6	8,958	7,433	8,259	92.2
No. 7	8,958	8,794	9,771	109.1
No. 8	8,958	6,995	7,772	86.8
No. 9	8,958	4,802	5,336	59.6
No. 10	8,958	5,742	6,380	71.2
No. 11	8,958	7,049	7,832	87.4
No. 12	8,958	7,402	8,224	91.8
No. 13	8,958	7,616	8,462	94.5
No. 14	8,958	6,608	7,342	82.0
TOTAL	125,412	98,784	109,758	87.5

FIGURE 21. Typical example of time reporting under the task inventory technique of clerical work measurement.

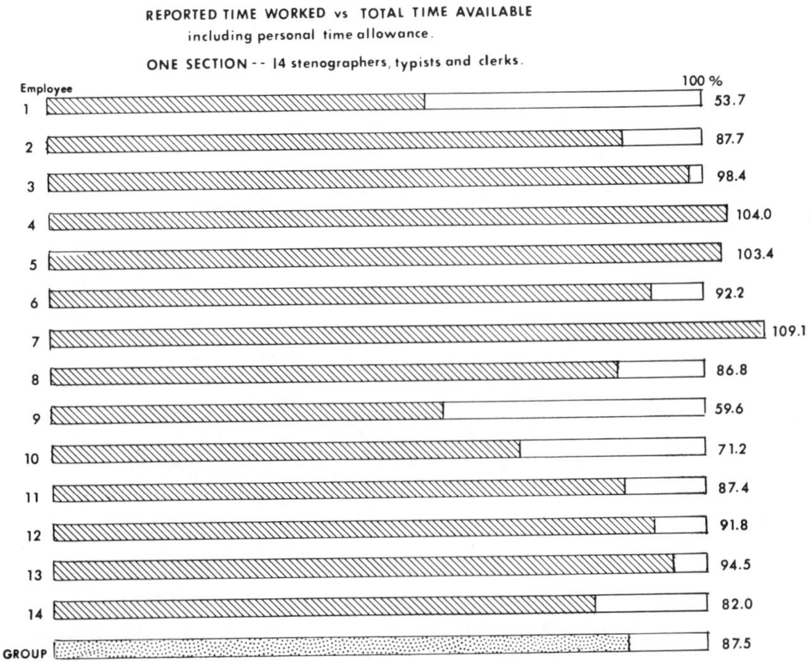

REPORTED TIME WORKED vs TOTAL TIME AVAILABLE
including personal time allowance.

ONE SECTION -- 14 stenographers, typists and clerks.

Employee | 100 %
1 | 53.7
2 | 87.7
3 | 98.4
4 | 104.0
5 | 103.4
6 | 92.2
7 | 109.1
8 | 86.8
9 | 59.6
10 | 71.2
11 | 87.4
12 | 91.8
13 | 94.5
14 | 82.0
GROUP | 87.5

FIGURE 22. The data in Figure 21 shown in chart form.

age may reflect a poor flow of work from another department; in that case the procedures analyst or the supervisors as a group should analyze the interdepartmental work flow and streamline the procedure. Such a case affords an excellent opportunity to get together and work as a team to create a degree of efficiency not possible by any single supervisor. The overall company management will benefit as well as the individual unit management.

Time Spent on Various Tasks or Types of Work

The work in any unit breaks down into that directly contributive to the output of the unit and that which, although it may be necessary, does not contribute directly to the output. These kinds of work would be known in factory measurement as direct and indirect labor. The principle is the same in the office, although these terms are not ordinarily used in the office.

It is important for the supervisor to know how much of the worker's time is spent on activities that contribute directly to the output of work and how much is not. The task inventory reveals this. It tells the supervisor how much of each individual worker's time is spent on each kind of work or on each task during the day or for the period of the survey. Figures 23 and 24 show a typical report.

The chart in Figure 24 shows graphically the distribution of work among the 14 stenographers, typists, and clerks covered in Figure 21. The 85.2 percent of the time devoted to the principal tasks of the group should normally be well under control by the supervisor, but the 23 different tasks that comprised the remaining 14.8 percent of the time were of the "cat and dog" variety that are hard to control in point of productivity. (This is not to be confused with a possible 15 percent personal time allowance.) In the task inventory each of these 23 tasks was defined and pinpointed and the supervisor was, for the first time, able to analyze them, find out why they were being done, and what needed to be done about it.

The purpose of this, again, is to give the supervisor more information about the work and worker performance in order to be able to make it more productive. As an example, in the clerical group represented in Figure 21 two workers turned in what looked like large amounts of conferring time (Figure 23). Conferring is a legitimate task, but in that department, analysis showed that those particular workers had to have considerable current data about their work and the only way to get it was to go somewhere and get it or ask someone about it. The amount of time so reported by the two workers looked inordinately high and the supervisor, being apprised of the fact by the statistics of the study, was able to investigate the situation. It was determined that by making certain information more readily available, this conferring time was eliminated and the workers' time was made more productive.

Sometimes things that look questionable in this regard turn out to be very much in order while other situations that, on the face of it, look sound turn out to be capable of improvement.

Data for Office Labor Forecasting

Nothing is more aggravating to a budget committee than to find out that the forecasts of office labor requirements have been made with little or no basis in fact with the result that the budget has to be revised during the year.

Work measurement gives factual information upon which labor

TIME REPORTED BY MAJOR TASKS PERFORMED

EMPLOYEE NO.	CALCULATE TASK 21	CONFER 40	DICTATION 48	TRANSCRIBE 93	POST 81	SORT 90	FILE 63	MESSENGER 74
No. 1	279	939			451			50
No. 2	1,849	1,600			628	17	187	213
No. 3		320			3,946	1,578	768	128
No. 4						2,474	2,562	1,962
No. 5	939	1,280	1,194	2,726	661	235	213	256
No. 6	100	2,666	640	2,433	568	64		128
No. 7	927	747	427	3,991	1,083		427	320
No. 8		1,792		323	1,116	763	320	320
No. 9		20	1,749	2,493	171			128
No. 10		85	1,066	4,347	21		113	85
No. 11		640	527	5,464				13
No. 12		171	1,579	4,654	768		30	35
No. 13		640	1,791	4,501	213	25	20	50
No. 14		449	1,067	3,998	106		63	
TOTAL	4,094	11,349	10,040	35,435	9,737	5,161	4,703	3,688
% of total reported	4.1	11.5	10.2	35.9	9.8	5.2	4.8	3.7

FIGURE 23. The time measurement in Figure 21 broken down by major tasks performed.

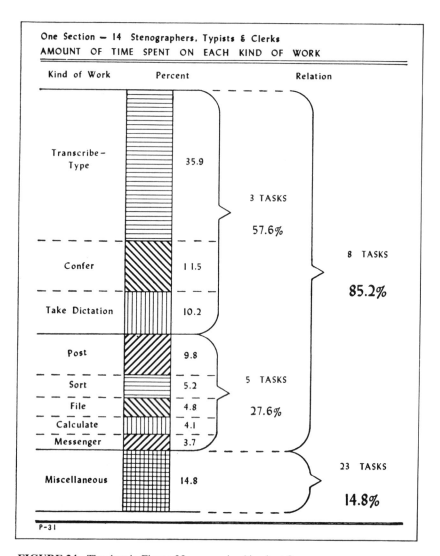

FIGURE 24. The data in Figure 23 summarized in chart form.

forecasts can be made with as much accuracy as is possible in line with general business forecasts. The degree of accuracy of the forecast depends on the accuracy of the basic data from work measurement and the skill with which the data are used.

In one case the use of the task inventory method in an accounts payable section showed that 39.7 hours of labor were required under present conditions to process each thousand invoices, not counting the work spent on them in the branch offices where they were approved for payment, nor in the tabulating section where the checks were prepared.

The current workload, about 13,000 invoices per month, was being handled by three employees with some overtime. A further increase in workload was expected. The workload study showed the labor requirements based on existing methods to be as displayed in the following table.

Monthly invoice volume	Required hours per month	Employees required
12,000	476	3.2
13,000	516	3.5
14,000	556	3.7
15,000	596	3.9
16,000	635	4.3
17,000	675	4.5
18,000	715	4.7
19,000	754	5.1
20,000	794	5.3

These figures did not include the supervisor, nor did they allow for vacation or sick leave time. The supervisor was expected to make necessary allowance for these factors in making up the budget.

The really important fact about these figures, however, was that they pointed out to the supervisor the real necessity of simplifying the work to avoid the increases in personnel. Some simplifying factors were uncovered during the task inventory and work analysis, some coming from the workers themselves who had been indoctrinated in the principles of work simplification during the course of the study. The supervisor could now measure the point at which one of two things had to happen: either more workers had to be assigned or productivity per worker had to increase. This gave the supervisor more information about the work and made sure he understood it, the first two steps in supervisory improvement.

All work measurement activities should and, if properly done, will result in data that point up the inevitability at a certain point of doing one of two things in the face of an increasing workload; hiring more workers or increasing productivity per worker to make the increase unnecessary. The case of a decreasing workload works in reverse; the reduction of force can be measured just as can the increase in personnel.

Productive Cost per Unit of Work

Work measurement tells how much it costs to do individual pieces of work. It provides not only an overall departmental total but gives a breakdown of the work and cost per individual part of the work. This measurement augments and greatly improves the costing out of complete clerical operations for use in the selection of new methods and machines.

An example is seen in the application of work measurement in the treasury department of a company with six employees doing stenographic and clerical work. It was found that, contrary to the general impression, only 45.6 percent of the total time was spent in transcribing or typing, while 13.5 percent of the time was spent in filing, 10.1 percent in taking dictation, and the remaining 30.8 percent was distributed among no fewer than 17 other kinds of work, including auditing, calculating, handling currency, conferring, correcting, entering data, removing material from files, arranging files, folding and inserting, handling income mail, messenger work, reading information, sorting, stapling and stitching, time stamping, writing, and general housekeeping.

In this situation about one-third of all the time was spent on a group of miscellaneous tasks, which indicated that the supervisor should give more attention to the organization of that area of the work, 30 percent of the total time in that case. Too many times this important miscellaneous area is neglected, probably because the supervisor was not sufficiently aware of its existence.

Machine Utilization in the Office

Companies have large amounts of money invested in office machines, and the current trend is toward more and more machines as a means of increasing output per worker. Records of present machine utilization are of vital importance in arriving at decisions on whether to buy additional equipment.

Clerical work measurement gives factual information as to the use made of all office machines. The approach through task inventory is particularly effective in this matter because it covers all work being performed, whether the large-scale repetitive type or small miscellaneous tasks. It relates each task to whatever machine is used in the performance of that task and measures productivity. In this way the idle time of machines can be determined and a sound decision reached on the necessity of buying another machine or spreading the work among existing equipment.

Forms and Reports Utilization

Each task is related to the form or forms used for it and, if desired, the total amount of time spent on any given form or report can be determined. Sometimes it is not practicable to do this because so many tasks relate to more than one form and the distribution of time between two or more forms is difficult to determine. However, any principal form, such as a purchase order, invoice, or receiving report, can be measured as to the time spent on it, including the time being spent on other less important forms related but subservient to it in the paperwork procedure. Actually, what we are doing is putting a price tag on a procedure of which the forms and reports are the major paperwork tools.

It is often important to know how much paperwork time goes into the creation of a given report in order to pinpoint its importance to the company's administrative management. The task inventory program should do this.

D. MEASURING CLERICAL WORK

The most satisfactory method of obtaining basic data for work measurement is to take a spot record by means of a task inventory over a limited period of time, but to take the time spent only on the work itself and to require no record whatever of nonproductive time spent by workers. This record may be kept over a period of two or more weeks, depending on the character of the organization and the cyclical nature of the work performed. It requires that both supervisors and workers be carefully indoctrinated as to the purpose and methods of the survey and, above all, that they understand that the work itself, not the workers, is being timed. This latter consideration is a psychological safeguard that has rightly become very necessary because of some efforts to impose predetermined standards on office workers with less than desirable results.

Where to Start

The unit for paperwork productivity study is the clerical task that is a definite segment of the clerical operation. Tasks include a multitude of such activities as calculating, dictating, typing, entering data, filing, posting, sorting, and using a messenger service. With all the tasks defined it is fairly simple to take an inventory of tasks performed by the paperwork personnel, much as the industrial engineer takes an inventory of the elemental motions that make up the factory operations. Each clerical worker keeps track during a predetermined period both of the number of minutes spent on each task and the output in terms of a previously determined unit of work.

Forms, machines, and files are also coded and related to each task. At the end of the measured period, time and output are averaged for each task by each worker and all the data are run through the computer. The resulting information lends itself to very detailed clerical work analysis for subsequent simplification and work improvement before standards of output are established.

The actual responsibility for doing this must be, to the greatest possible extent, that of the first-line supervisor. Structuring and administering the program should be by middle management, probably by a qualified systems analyst, but if the program is not to be a one-shot deal it must be made an ongoing part of the supervisor's management function. A major program objective, as has been previously stated, must be to make the supervisor a better manager of the work. Most supervisors will welcome this.

The Definition of Clerical Tasks

The success of the task inventory method of clerical work measurement depends to a very large degree on the manner in which the various tasks are defined and described to the workers in order that they may correctly report their time on any given task. Failure to do this has been a stumbling block to the average company since no widely available dictionary of clerical tasks has existed to fit the situation. Nevertheless, it is absolutely necessary that the task be defined beforehand in order that an intelligent analysis can be made and the same task can be measured in different parts of the company and the results compared on a common basis.

The measurement involves comparing "apples with apples" and not "apples with oranges." If one worker reports typing 50 purchase orders a day while another reports typing 75 receiving reports in the same time, the analyst will be completely lost unless the typing operations are defined with a further breakdown that permits a meaningful comparison of the work.

Figure 25 shows a workable definition of one task, typing or transcribing in the office. This breaks the task into four subdivisions: the kind of data typed, the arrangement into which it is typed, the kind of copy from which the typist works, and the number of copies made. This breakdown is fine enough to permit the comparison of relatively identical work done by typists who may work in different departments

Section 3. (Standard Task Title—Cont'd.)			Part I, Page 31	
Code		Description of Tasks	Count As Output	
Pre.	Suff.			
98		Transcribing—Typing		
		A. Kind of Data Coded (1st digit of suffix)	Sheets typed	
98	1 - - -	—Technical; Statistical—Symbols, Words and figures—Engineering, Medical Terminology, etc.		
98	2 - - -	—Non-technical; Common-usage words, some figures		
		B. Typing Arrangement (2nd digit of suffix)		
98	- 1 - -	—Lines—Single space		
98	- 2 - -	—Lines—Double space		
98	- 3 - -	—Fill-in blocks or spaces on forms under 100 key strokes		
98	- 4 - -	—Fill-in blocks or spaces on forms—100 to 500 key strokes		
98	- 5 - -	—Fill-in blocks or spaces on forms of over 500 key strokes		
98	- 6 - -	—Columnar, using 3 tabulation stops or less		
98	- 7 - -	—Columnar, using 4 to 7 tab stops		
98	- 8 - -	—Columnar, using over 7 tab stops		
98	- 9 - -	—Irregular fill-in		
98	- 0 - -	—Unclassified		
		C. Kind of Copy Transcribed (3rd digit of suffix)	Sheets typed	
98	- - 1 -	—Longhand copy		
98	- - 2 -	—Longhand and typed copy, combined		
98	- - 3 -	—Typed copy		
98	- - 4 -	—Typed copy requiring re-arrangement		
98	- - 5 -	—Dictating-machine records		
98	- - 6 -	—Stenotype tape		
98	- - 7 -	—Stenographic notes		
98	- - 0 -	—Unclassified		
		D. Copies Made (4th digit of Suffix)		
98	- - - 1	—Original		
98	- - - 2	—Original and 1 carbon; includes assembling sets and removing carbons		
98	- - - 3	—Original and 2 carbons; includes assembling sets and removing carbons		
98	- - - 4	—Original and 3 carbons; includes assembling sets and removing carbons		
98	- - - 5	—Original and 4 carbons; includes assembling sets and removing carbons		
98	- - - 6	—Original and 5 carbons; includes assembling sets and removing carbons		
98	- - - 7	—Original and over 5 carbons; includes assembling sets and removing carbons		
98	- - - 8	—Snap-out set—4 copies or less—includes removing carbons		
98	- - - 9	—Snap-out set over 4 copies—includes removing carbons		
98	- - - 0	—Varying number of copies		

Example:

Typist is typing nontechnical words, single-spaced, from dictating machine record, in original and two copies including assembly in sets and removing carbon.

Codes:

Typing   98
nontechnical   2---
single-spaced -1--
dict machine --5-
two copies   ---3

98.2.1.5.3

FIGURE 25. A standard task title definition coded for transcribing or typing.

or even be geographically separated. The definition is stated in a way that both the supervisor and the typists understand and can use.

Figure 25 is taken from the dictionary of clerical task titles developed over a period of years in the application of the task inventory technique in many companies and organizations. It is given in full in Appendix III of this book. Each task is coded for easy identification and study for work measurement results.

With the tasks properly identified and defined and with the supervisors properly indoctrinated in the taking of a task-time inventory, the next important requirement is making it easy for workers to report their time correctly. The natural tendency on the part of most workers is to wait until after the whole operation has been completed and then to mark down the time spent on each task. After a few days they are apt to grow careless and wait until a break period, coffee break, or even lunch or the end of the day and then try to recall and reconstruct the day's work for the record keeping.

Needless to say this destroys much of the value of the record. Some method must be found for making it so easy for workers to report the time correctly that they do not succumb to the tendency to let it wait until later. This can best be done by giving workers a temporary form with the two-minute intervals of the work day in vertical columns wide enough for them to indicate the task, checking the beginning and ending time for each task.

E. PUTTING THE TASK INVENTORY TO WORK

Before starting a clerical work measurement program it must be assumed that management has made the decision to measure the cost of office operations and paperwork and a suitable assignment of staff personnel has been made. The analyst assigned to the program will have studied this text carefully to understand the basics of task inventory work measurement. Management should then issue a directive to all concerned—the staff analyst, the supervisors, and the workers—outlining the program and their duties and responsibilities. The line management of the departments concerned will be briefed by means of the directive.

Responsibilities in the Program

The Paperwork Manager. The paperwork manager, who will probably be a staff analyst, must assume responsibility for the overall management of the program, working with the supervisors in establishing understanding and acceptance of the program. He or she must provide the basic analytical ability to handle the statistics and be able to synthesize answers. The paperwork manager arranges whatever degree of training the supervisors of the program require, either in the details of the program itself or in the overall exercise of the management of their work. (Obviously the personnel department should bear the prime responsibility for general supervisory training.)

The First-Line Supervisor. The first-line supervisor must accept and discharge a responsibility for working in close cooperation with the paperwork manager in conducting the program. He or she will take an active part in working with his or her own clerical staff to make them understand the program. Supervisors should be given a manual of instructions to assist them in this phase of the work. This is a most important phase of preparatory work in the program since worker attitude can easily make or break the program. The supervisor will cooperate with the analyst in analyzing the work after the task inventory has been taken and should receive adequate credit for all simplification results.

The Clerical Workers. The workers must be so indoctrinated that they understand fully the objectives of the program and then accept and discharge their own responsibility for cooperating in the task inventory. Every possible incentive should be made to have the workers themselves offer suggestions for work simplification. If there is a suggestion award system in operation in the company, that system and the work simplification should be closely integrated.

Determining the Scope of the Program

Experience shows that the best results are obtained by limiting a single application to not more than 8 – 12 supervisors with a total of not more than about 100 workers collectively.

After the analyst has thoroughly studied and understands the program, he or she selects, with management, the exact areas to be covered in this phase of the program and the number of supervisors and workers to be covered. Following this a meeting of the supervisors should be called and the program introduced and thoroughly explained to them.

This can be a critical point in the program. Although the general capacities and performances of each supervisor should already be known through performance evaluation done by the personnel department, it is at this meeting that the enthusiasm or reluctance of the supervisors to become party to this kind of program becomes apparent. It is also at this point that the ability of the analyst to conduct this kind of program also becomes apparent. Analysts must be able both to instruct and to lead; without these qualities they probably will not do a good job with the program.

F. TAKING THE TASK INVENTORY

The following pages give full and detailed instructions for the actual taking of the task inventory using a four-page inventory form as illustrated in Figures 26–28. Figure 27 shows a typical inventory of the tasks performed by one worker over a two-week period. The tasks were identified beforehand by the supervisor through the dictionary of standard task titles (Appendix III) and the ones performed by the particular worker listed. The inventory of forms, machines, and files was made on Figure 26 and codes assigned to each.

The worker then reported the number of minutes spent on each task and the volume of output for each of the ten days. At the end of the period the record was reviewed by the analyst and the supervisor and an average time and output per day was established. The items were then coded and analyzed.

Coding the Data

The first requirement of a successful analysis of the information is that it be properly defined at the outset and then coded in such a way that it can be organized. The adequate and correct definition of tasks is stressed again for a definite purpose; the whole final result of work measurement depends so much on proper definition of tasks and operations that much time and effort will probably turn out to have been wasted unless this definition is properly made.

A very effective and quick way to organize the information for purposes of analysis is by use of data processing equipment. If the company does not have such equipment it should contact a service bureau at the outset of its study in order to produce the information in such shape that it can be key stroked efficiently and with an absolute minimum of mistakes. It is then a simple matter to obtain the organized records for analysis. Coding is done in the extreme right-hand column of the Figure 27, daily and weekly work detail.

Factors that must be coded include work unit, forms used in the work, the equipment and files used, reference manuals if any, worker, the task, time, and amount of output (Figure 27). All these factors are necessary for the complete utilization of the work measurement effort. Figure 27 is used for this listing.

Every form used in the work of the unit must be identified and coded for analysis. This generally precludes the use of the form number itself as a code since there may well be alphabetical prefixes and suffixes that may be difficult for the use of data processing equipment. If the company has an effective forms control program, such as is envisaged in Section III of this book, the identification of the forms should be a relatively simple matter. All forms will already have been filed with the identification of the using unit, and it merely remains to pull a sample of each form used in that work unit and let the supervisor indicate which ones are used in connection with each task.

Reference must be made here again to the small usage and apparently unimportant forms so often left out of a so-called forms control program. Every one of these small usage forms enters somehow or other into a clerical task, and the measurement of that task necessitates relating that form to the task no matter how small the usage or how unimportant the form appears. Unless these forms are collected and built into a control program at the outset, they will have to be added piecemeal as the work measurement program goes along. This is more work in the long run than collecting and organizing them properly in control files in the first place. It must be remembered also that these apparently unimportant forms may represent variations from the normal procedures and can cause much trouble in such important procedures studies as an automation feasibility program if they are not known beforehand. All this points to the increased necessity of a complete forms control program.

Each form used in the tasks of the unit being measured should be assigned a code number that can be used easily in EDP equipment. A cross-reference sheet must be made out to show the actual form number and the arbitrary work measurement code for that form in order that they can be related to each other later.

An inventory should be taken of each and every piece of equipment used in the unit, and a code number assigned to each. It would seem reasonable that an inventory could be taken from the property records

102

Let's • • • SIMPLIFY YOUR JOB • • • MAKE YOUR

We want you to help us improve, everybody's position, to eliminate waste and do the work better. You can help

NAME OF EMPLOYEE	JOB TITLE

DIVISION OR DEPARTMENT	PLANT OR OFFICE

WHAT FORMS OR REPORTS DO YOU USE IN YOUR WORK?

	FORM NUMBER	TITLE OR NAME *(If no title or name attach a blank copy to this form)*
1		
2		
3		
4		
5		
6		
7		
8		
9		
10		

WHAT OFFICE MACHINES DO YOU USE IN YOUR WORK? *(See list of office machines for description*

NO.	KIND OF MACHINE	NAME OF MANUFACTURER
1		
2		
.3		
4		

WHAT FILES DO YOU USE IN YOUR WORK? *(See list of files for description and name.)*

NO.	KIND OR TYPE OF FILE	WHAT MATERIAL IS KEPT IN THE FILE
1		
2		
3		
4		

HOW CAN YOUR JOB BE MADE EASIER?

JOB ANALYSIS RECORD
FMK-87   PAGE NO. 1

FIGURE 26. The job analysis record. (Note: this is page 1 of the four-page form used for the task inventory. See also Figures 27 and 28.)

WORK EASIER • • • IMPROVE THE METHODS

by filling in this form carefully after studying the in-
structions. Ask your supervisor if you don't understand it.

OR CLASSIFICATION		HOW LONG ON PRESENT JOB	
		HOW LONG WITH COMPANY	
SECTION		NAME OF SUPERVISOR	

	WHAT REFERENCE BOOKS OR LISTS DO YOU USE IN YOUR WORK?	
	NO. OR CODE	NAME OR TITLE OF BOOK OR LIST
	11	
	12	
	13	
	14	
	15	
	16	
	17	
	18	
	19	
	20	

and name.)   DO NOT WRITE IN THIS SPACE

	MODEL	SIZE	DO OTHERS USE THE MACH.	DO NOT WRITE IN THIS SPACE
			☐ YES ☐ NO	
			☐ YES ☐ NO	
			☐ YES ☐ NO	
			☐ YES ☐ NO	

		NO. TIMES USED DAILY	NO. FEET FROM DESK	DO NOT WRITE IN THIS SPACE

FIGURE 26 *(continued)*

DAILY AND WEEKLY WORK DETAILS		The total daily time should be less than 8 hours. Do not report personal time.							
LIST BELOW EACH DIFFERENT KIND OF WORK YOU DO. YOUR SUPERVISOR WILL HELP YOU SELECT THE PROPER TASK TITLE TO USE	REFER TO PAGE 1 AND SHOW WHAT EQUIPMENT OR PAPER IS USED	MONDAY		TUESDAY		WEDNESDAY		TH	
		PCS.	TIME	PCS.	TIME	PCS.	TIME	PCS.	
1 Remove From File 64-1013	FILE NO. 4 / FORM NO. 1	122	74	76	42	50	15		
2 Post 81-2312	FORM NO. 3	80	40	160	87	130	75		
*3 Numbering 76-2	MACHINE NO. 2 / FORM NO. 8			60	10				
4 Transcribe Type 98-2111	FILE NO. 1 / FORM NO. 10	40	17	80	45	75	55	67	
5 File 63-1313	FILE NO. 1 / FORM NO. 8	50	24	30	15	50	27		
6 Housekeeping 101		5		5		5			
7 Conferring 40		10		10		10			
8 Sort 90-353	FORM NO. 21	40	5	60	5	95	17	38	
9 Coding 1-1	FORM NO. 8			60	30	30	15		
*10 Auditing 9	FORM NO. 8			60	45				
11 Auditing 9	FORM NO. 23			60	65			44	
*12 Post 81-2222	FORM NO. 13			60	65				
13 Fold + Insert 67-2	FORM NO. 8			30	5	15	3		
14 Address 2-517	FILE NO. 1 / FORM NO. 9			30	25	60	37		
15 Messenger 74	FORM NO.						8		
16 Fold 66-3	FORM NO. 16								
17 Calculate Checks 21-1183	MACHINE NO. 3 / FORM NO. 19								
18 Insert 68-3	FORM NO. 22								
19 Mailing Incoming 72	FORM NO.	60	10						

FIGURE 27. A two-week task inventory by one worker (with pages 2 and 3 of the four-page form used for the task inventory; see also Figures 26 and 28).

of the company, but actual practice shows in many cases that such records are not as complete as management thinks. If that is the case the work measurement program will have the added advantage of bringing the records up to date.

Coding the work unit and the workers poses no particular problem, since an arbitrary number will do for each element in that area. It may be a good idea to use a code for the company itself, since the occasion

Enter "add jobs" on page 4. Enter time in minutes only — SHEET 1 OF 2

	FRIDAY		MONDAY		TUESDAY		WEDNESDAY		THURSDAY		FRIDAY		AVERAGE			CODES	FORM
	TIME	PCS.	TIME	PCS.	TIME	PCS.	TIME	PCS.	TIME	PCS.	TIME	PCS.	TIME	PCS.	TIME			

DO NOT WRITE IN THIS SPACE

														164-1013				
				90	59							169	95	71-421	50053			
				90	118			30	80			240	200	81-2312				
														3	53751			
										30	5	76-2						
												54-001	53005					
92	88	78	110	104	111	122			105	165		67	69	99-2111				
												41-111	11044					
			60	15	250	70					50	15	245	83	63-1313			
5	5		5		5		5		5		-	5	81161	50053				
														101				
			10		10		10		10		-	8	40					
19		60	14	50	6			550	54	89	12	90 -	353	53058				
			60	30						75	38	1-1	53005					
55	42	60	38					87	63	9	53005							
			40			142		180	-	360	9	53005						
57		60	72					82	94	81-2222	53910							
			30	14	65	24		70	23	67-2	53258							
			30	15	25	30		72	54	2-517	53262							
								-	1	41-111								
			250	10				250	10	74	53260							
380	12			500	10	1760	44	21- 1183	11046									
				500	43	70	14	1140	114	13- 212	11046							
								60	10	68-3								
										72								

USE ADDITIONAL SHEET IF NEEDED — PAGE 3

FIGURE 27 *(continued)*

may arise in the future for an intercompany comparison of task times, possibly through some trade association or other medium. Certainly, in the absence of any real or adequate information in the area of office work measurement, such comparisons could be of real value to the companies involved and can undoubtedly be made without revealing any company secrets.

The next item to be coded is the task itself. This relates back to the

WORK DETAILS — INFREQUENT TASKS — *Enter here the different kinds of work during the past two weeks. Give a gene*	
LIST BELOW EACH DIFFERENT KIND OR WORK YOU DO WHICH WAS NOT SHOWN ON PAGES 2 AND 3	REFER TO PAGE 1 AND SHOW WHAT EQUIPMENT OR PAPER IS USED

LIST BELOW EACH DIFFERENT KIND OR WORK YOU DO WHICH WAS NOT SHOWN ON PAGES 2 AND 3	FILE NO.	MACH. NO.
1	FORM NO.	
2	FILE NO.	MACH. NO.
	FORM NO.	
3	FILE NO.	MACH. NO.
	FORM NO.	
4	FILE NO.	MACH. NO.
	FORM NO.	
5	FILE NO.	MACH. NO.
	FORM NO.	
6	FILE NO.	MACH. NO.
	FORM NO.	
7	FILE NO.	MACH. NO.
	FORM NO.	
8	FILE NO.	MACH. NO.
	FORM NO.	
9	FILE NO.	MACH. NO.
	FORM NO.	
10	FILE NO.	MACH. NO.
	FORM NO.	
11	FILE NO.	MACH. NO.
	FORM NO.	
12	FILE NO.	MACH. NO.
	FORM NO.	
13	FILE NO.	MACH. NO.
	FORM NO.	
14	FILE NO.	MACH. NO.
	FORM NO.	

FMK - 87

FIGURE 28. The task inventory of infrequent tasks. (Note: this is page 4 of the four-page form used for the task inventory. See also Figures 26 and 27.)

done infrequently which you did not do
ral estimate of pieces and time.

HOW OFTEN IS IT NECESSARY TO DO EACH KIND OF WORK	ESTIMATED		DO NOT WRITE IN THIS SPACE			
			AVERAGE		F R E Q	
	PCS.	TIME	PCS.	TIME		C O D E S
☐ MONTHLY ☐ ANNUAL ☐ SEMI ANNUALLY ☐ ONCE IN A WHILE						T M F
☐ MONTHLY ☐ ANNUAL ☐ SEMI ANNUALLY ☐ ONCE IN A WHILE						T M F
☐ MONTHLY ☐ ANNUAL ☐ SEMI ANNUALLY ☐ ONCE IN A WHILE						T M F
☐ MONTHLY ☐ ANNUAL ☐ SEMI ANNUALLY ☐ ONCE IN A WHILE						T M F
☐ MONTHLY ☐ ANNUAL ☐ SEMI ANNUALLY ☐ ONCE IN A WHILE						T M F
☐ MONTHLY ☐ ANNUAL ☐ SEMI ANNUALLY ☐ ONCE IN A WHILE						T M F
☐ MONTHLY ☐ ANNUAL ☐ SEMI ANNUALLY ☐ ONCE IN A WHILE						T M F
☐ MONTHLY ☐ ANNUAL ☐ SEMI ANNUALLY ☐ ONCE IN A WHILE						T M F
☐ MONTHLY ☐ ANNUAL ☐ SEMI ANNUALLY ☐ ONCE IN A WHILE						T M F
☐ MONTHLY ☐ ANNUAL ☐ SEMI ANNUALLY ☐ ONCE IN A WHILE						T M F
☐ MONTHLY ☐ ANNUAL ☐ SEMI ANNUALLY ☐ ONCE IN A WHILE						T M F
☐ MONTHLY ☐ ANNUAL ☐ SEMI ANNUALLY ☐ ONCE IN A WHILE						T M F
☐ MONTHLY ☐ ANNUAL ☐ SEMI ANNUALLY ☐ ONCE IN A WHILE						T M F
☐ MONTHLY ☐ ANNUAL ☐ SEMI ANNUALLY ☐ ONCE IN A WHILE						T M F

FIGURE 28 *(continued)*

initial definition of the tasks. The codes should identify not only the basic task but enough variations within that task to make possible a really meaningful comparison of task times. These will be taken from the dictionary of task titles.

Coding the time and output is a simple matter, requiring only the numerical values of the number of minutes reported as being devoted to the particular task and the number of units of output. The latter requires that a unit for output count be assigned to each task in the dictionary of task definitions. In the case of typing, the unit of output count is sheets typed. This measure of output would probably not satisfy the situation in a time-and-motion approach since it is too general for the very specific measurement made under that approach, but under the task inventory approach it is usually satisfactory. Again, care must be taken to keep the situation at the level of the normal understanding and ability of the supervisors and workers, not making it unduly technical or too detailed for them. A count by lines typed would be more accurate than mere pages, and key strokes would be the most accurate of all, but counts of that kind involve statistical details of accounting for results that go beyond the needs of the average company. Output units for coding are included in the dictionary.

With a complete coding established for all the elements necessary to the work measurement program, and with the task inventory taken, the next step is to do the actual coding and production of the necessary records of results. The coding is an important stage inasmuch as it affords the first real opportunity of bringing the supervisor into the program on an analytical basis. The analyst should sit down with the supervisor to evaluate the record of the task inventory before the actual coding is done. This gives the supervisor a first overall look at the situation, together with a responsibility for evaluating the individual time-and-output records turned in by workers. If at that time the supervisor feels that any one of the records of time and output does not look reasonable, he or she can check back with the worker and discuss it. This does not mean the supervisor should try to talk the worker out of something that the worker honestly feels represents the actual situation, but it does mean the supervisor should use judgment as to the correctness of the record, and if the worker agrees, a correction can be made. What is wanted is the best possible record in line with the facts, not a carelessly prepared record that is not in accordance with the facts.

Management can use this situation for its first direct contribution to increasing the management skill of the supervisor by having the procedures person, or whoever is directing the program, work carefully with the supervisor in this evaluation. It is a first step toward giving the supervisor more information about the job and being sure that information is understood. It also means that management should have given thought to the additional step of supervisory improvement (i.e., increasing the supervisor's skill in using the information).

Once the data on time and output are agreed upon as being reasonably in line with the facts, they can be coded and entered into data processing equipment with the other measurement data and run for analytical records.

G. AFTER TAKING THE TASK INVENTORY

The all-important analysis of the data is the next step.

Analysis of the Data

At the end of the two-week study period each task should be carefully scrutinized and for repetitive tasks the pieces and time should be compared. On a daily task the pieces and time should be reported ten times or once each for ten days. If the task is performed weekly it is reported only twice.

There may be tasks that the worker does intermittently or only occasionally or that may not even occur during the two-week reporting period. Each of these tasks should be reported with an estimate of pieces and time. Very infrequent tasks are entered on page 4 of the job analysis record, as shown in Figure 28.

Each supervisor reviews the job analysis record in a uniform manner in order that an accurate comparison can be made of all tasks in all of the departments under study.

Steps to Be Taken

1. Codes should now have been assigned to all tasks. This is done by referring to the dictionary of task titles.
2. Assign codes to all machines and files by information gained from supervisors on the relation of the office machines and equipment to the tasks, using the dictionary for coding.
3. Assign codes to all forms used in connection with each task. The manual procedure chart helps in identifying the forms as they relate to the clerical operation.

4. Assign codes to each job analysis record (Figure 26), to identify the department or section where the tasks are performed, the employee, and the employee's job classification.
5. Establish normal daily output (pieces) and time for each task reported on the job analysis record. Normally this is an average obtained (1) by dividing the total pieces and total time by 10 if the employee performed regular duties during the full inventory period, or, (2) if the employee was absent during part of the period, by using the number of days present as a divisor or by applying other special treatment as required. Any abnormal work volume also requires special treatment.
6. Assign an alphabetical code that represents the frequency with which each task is performed, as follows:

D—performed daily

W—performed weekly

O—performed occasionally (approximately 2½ times monthly)

M—performed monthly

Q—performed quarterly

S—performed semiannually

A—performed annually

Tabulating the Data

At this point we have uncovered all tasks and established an average of pieces and time, by employee and by day, week, or month. We have also assigned codes to all the different factors involved. We are now ready to summarize our findings to compare like operations and develop workload studies of clerical work as it is now being done.

To do this we transfer all of the coded data on the job analysis record to data processing equipment. The data will then be sequenced in different arrangements and tabulated to report the following:

1. Total time, productive and nonproductive, by department, section, and job.
2. Total output and time for each task title, broken down by department, section, and job.
3. Total output of work and time expended on each individual form by department, section, various job classifications, and individual tasks.
4. Total output and time for each machine classification.

Other analyses can be made from the records to develop data for use in studying special situations.

Why Have We Done This?

The program has now developed to the point where we have accumulated a mass of facts about clerical work as it is being done. All this information is vital to the final phase of the clerical work analysis program.

Having measured each operation, the procedures staff can then evaluate the entire procedure, or that portion that falls in each work section, or the total forms usage. Such figures are valuable in evaluating alternate methods and procedures.

H. THE TASK INVENTORY IN RELATION TO PROCEDURES ANALYSIS

Having taken a task inventory and organized the data with data processing equipment, and having given the supervisors all the data they need for better management, the procedures staff can now measure every clerical operation in the procedures in the area studied.

Look at the segment of a procedures chart shown in Figure 29. Notice that each clerical operation is identified in two ways; first, by the work area in which it is performed and second, by the forms or paper that enters into it. By using the task inventory technique and by merely tab listing all tasks by work unit by form, each task that enters into any given operation on the procedures chart can be identified. These can then be listed as shown in Figure 30 and the task time converted into operation time. By the addition of salary figures to the records, each operation can be measured in payroll dollars as well as in minutes or hours.

In the next phase of the program, teams of supervisors and analysts analyze each procedure by arranging the essential operations and tasks in the sequences necessary to perform each one as indicated on the procedures charts. This step of the program will result in an operations analysis sheet (Figure 30) for each department's activities related to each procedure. Following the development of operations analysis sheets, each operation should be analyzed using sound principles of work simplification. Performance standards are determined in the form of "allotted time" specified for a given output on each task.

Ultimately possibilities will be explored on different forms, rede-

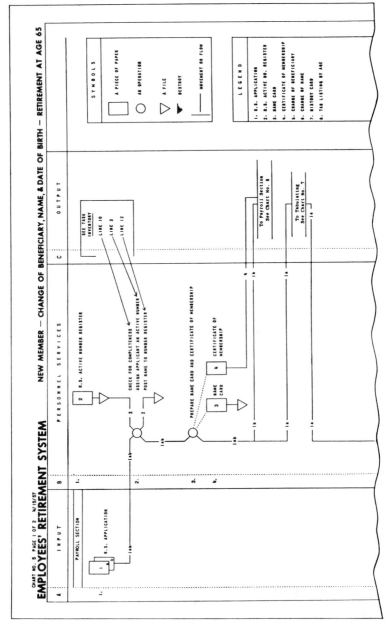

FIGURE 29. Application of the task inventory time to operations on the procedures chart.

OPERATION ANALYSIS SHEET

TM 58-A

| CHART NO. 5 | PROCEDURE TITLE Employees Retirement System | | | | DATE | | PAGE 1 OF 1 |
| DEPT. Personnel Services | SECTION Retirement | | | | ANALYST J.mc | | |

								TIME PER REPORTED DATA		
L I N E NO. OPER NO	NORMAL OUTPUT FACTOR D/W/M	STANDARD TASK CODE	TASK	FORMS CODE	MACHINE CODE	FILE CODE	TASK TIME A	OCCUR PER NORMAL OUTPUT B	TIME PER NORMAL OUTPUT C (AxB)	TIME PER MONTHLY OUTPUT D (C x FACT.)
1 B-2	60	9	Check R.S. Enrollment	53005	—	1.	.7	60	42	180.6
2	4.3 W	81-2222	Post name to R.S. No. Register	53710	—	—	1.15	60	69	296.7
3	R.S. En-rollment	76-2	Assign Active No. to R.S. Enrollment	53005	—	—	.16	60	10	43.0
									121	520.3

FIGURE 30. The operations analysis sheet.

signed forms, new machine operations, and any other changes in methods that will result in a reduction of paperwork or clerical costs.

I. DEVELOPING THE OPERATION ANALYSIS SHEET

The working tools of this phase of the program are the operation analysis sheet (Figure 30), the procedure flow chart, and the tabulated work load data summaries. This phase of the work deals with the method by which the data, which have been compiled by task title in the first phase of the program, are related to each operation shown on the procedure flow chart with the result that the "how" of each work detail will be fully stated in the proper sequence.

The analysts on the study teams are responsible for the preparation of the operation analysis sheets, assisted by the supervisor of the section or department concerned. The operation analysis sheet brings together the tasks and related time data that comprise the operations in a given procedure as it is now performed.

The following steps are involved, using the procedure flow chart, the job analysis record, and the tabulated work load data as source information:

1. *Chart number—procedure title:* taken from flow chart.

2. *Department—section— analyst:* Enter appropriate names.

3. *Operation number:* This is the location within the column on the procedure chart at which the operation is shown. The operation number is the code at the immediate left of the circle showing the operation.

4. (a) *Normal output:* This is a figure that represents the number of measurable units processed through the various tasks on a "normal" day, week, month, etc. A measurable unit is the single unit of output for *all* of the tasks and operations of the department or section under study. (In Figure 29 the unit is the enrollment of a member in the employees' retirement system.)

 Because different "counts" were used to measure output when taking the task inventory, the measurable unit is the common yardstick that can be applied to component tasks of a procedure.

 (b) *Factor:* This is the decimal equivalent of the frequency code letter shown in the Freq column of the job analysis record (Figure 27) as follows:

D = 21.3, W = 4.3, O = 2.5, M = 1.0, Q = 0.33, S = 0.17,
A = 0.083.

(c) *D/M/W:* This is the frequency code letter.

5. *Standard task code, task, forms code, machine code, file code:* These are all taken directly from the job analysis record and are entered in the actual sequence of performance known by the supervisor.

6. *Task time:* This is obtained by dividing the total monthly time by the total monthly pieces shown on the tabulating listing. If an identical task is performed by more than one employee in the same section, the figures for pieces and time for each employee are to be combined before computing the task time. The result is the time required to perform each task under present procedures and conditions.

7. *Occurrences per normal output:* This is the number of times a task is performed in relation to the normal output.

8. *Time per normal output:* This is the result of multiplying the task time by the number of occurrences per normal output.

9. *Time per monthly output:* This is the result of multiplying time per normal output by the factor. The sum total of the task times shown in this column represents the time required to perform an operation under present procedures and conditions.

Use of the Operation Analysis Sheet

With the completion of the sheets for all operations associated with a procedure, as indicated by the procedures flow chart, we have completed the data development phase of the supervisors' work analysis program. The objective is the reduction of clerical costs by means of simplifying and streamlining office routines.

Control of costs has been started by establishing uniform procedures, as defined by the flow chart plus the operations sheets, and an awareness has been created on the part of all clerical workers of the importance of consistent and uniform practices.

This phase of the program has also created a common language—a new medium of communicating the details of procedures. More than that, in the course of developing the flow charts and the operations sheets, every task and operation has been scrutinized and some have probably been eliminated. These eliminations were made without any formal action merely because they did not fit into any essential operation or procedure. They failed to pass the productivity test of being essential to an essential procedure.

Now comes the last phase of the work analysis. This most important team activity requires participating supervisors to apply sound principles of work simplification to the operations under their control. By employing the uniform techniques and following the same steps in analyzing operations, the findings of the individual supervisors can be consolidated and reviewed by all supervisors while working as a methods improvement team. Recommendations can be developed, new procedures instituted, forms combined, eliminated, or revised, new machines procured, and training programs undertaken.

In addition, this phase of the program will develop revised time and output data under the new conditions established as a result of work simplification.

J. DEVELOPING THE PERFORMANCE ALLOWANCE SHEET

This form (see Figure 31) shows who does each activity and how much time is spent on it. The task inventory, of course, does this as an end result and is a complete, quite accurate statement of every single task done by every worker. The possibilities for work simplification on each of these tasks will have been revealed by the detailed work of reporting and analyzing these tasks by the worker, the supervisor, and the procedures analyst. Having seen the possibilities, management should be able to project a new operating-performance time allowance that, in effect, becomes a standard of performance.

The big advantage of this type of standard is that it has been developed by the worker and the supervisor in conjunction with the analyst, and not superimposed by some predetermined standard developed by someone else from somewhere else.

K. SIMPLIFYING CLERICAL WORK

Figure 31 is a chart that can be used for work simplification as a direct adjunct to the clerical work measurement program. It relates directly to the tasks listed on the operations allowance sheet and provides a direct follow-up for supervisors in the analysis of the work of their units.

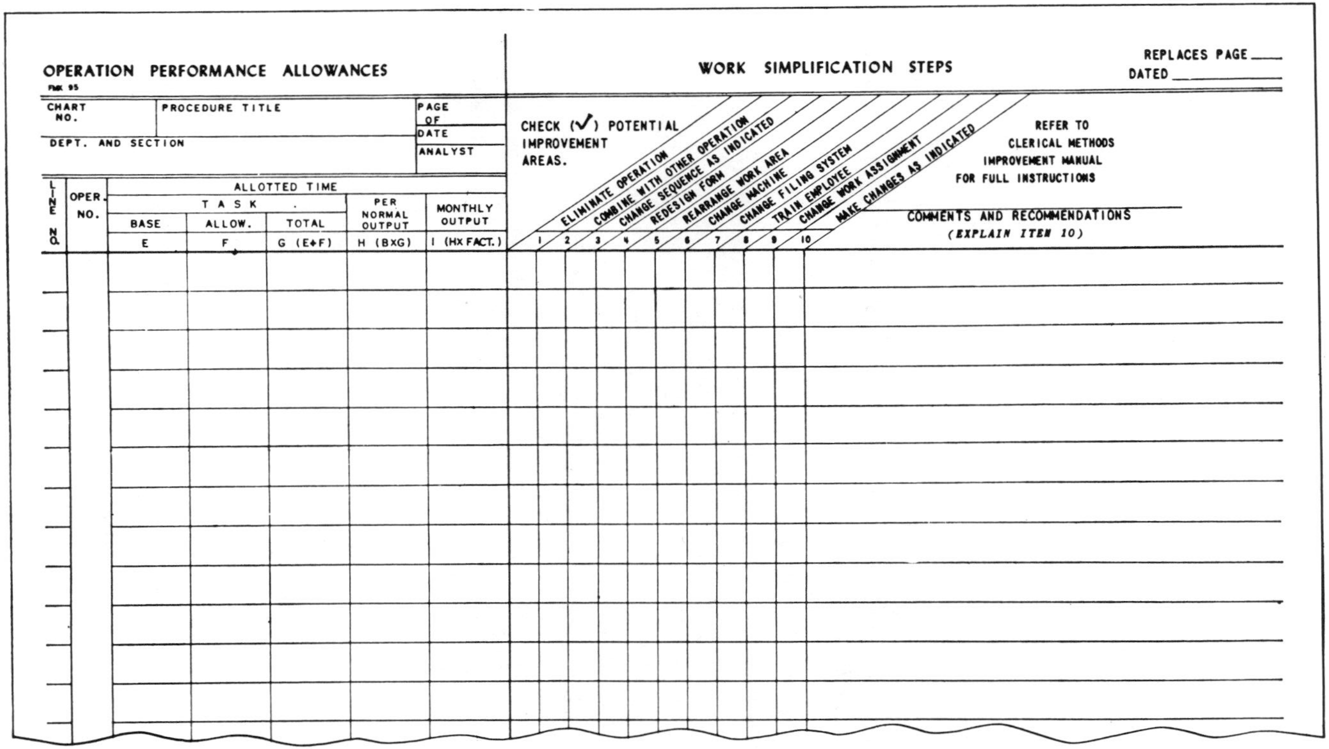

OPERATION PERFORMANCE ALLOWANCES

WORK SIMPLIFICATION STEPS

REPLACES PAGE ___
DATED ___

CHART NO.

PROCEDURE TITLE

DEPT. AND SECTION

PAGE ___ OF ___
DATE
ANALYST

CHECK (✓) POTENTIAL IMPROVEMENT AREAS.

REFER TO CLERICAL METHODS IMPROVEMENT MANUAL FOR FULL INSTRUCTIONS

ELIMINATE OPERATION(OTHER AS INDICATED)
COMBINE OR REARRANGE WORK AREA
CHANGE LINE OR SECTION LAYOUT
CHANGE TOOLS OR EQUIPMENT
CHANGE FILING SYSTEM
CHANGE WORK SEQUENCE
CHANGE THE EMPLOYEE
CHANGE METHOD OF THE WORK
CHANGE IN WORK AREA AS INDICATED
CHANGE FORM AS INDICATED

COMMENTS AND RECOMMENDATIONS
(EXPLAIN ITEM 10)

LINE NO.

OPER. NO.

ALLOTTED TIME

TASK

BASE ALLOW. E

TOTAL F

G (E+F)

PER NORMAL OUTPUT H (BXG)

MONTHLY OUTPUT I (HXFACT.)

1 2 3 4 5 6 7 8 9 10

FIGURE 31. The performance allowance sheet.

The ten work simplification steps are listed with a checkmark column for each in order that the supervisor can give full consideration to each step in connection with each task. With the completion of the left-hand portion of the performance allowance sheet the supervisor is in a position to analyze each operation in terms of backlogs and unfinished work, excessive time required to prepare for a given task, simple jobs taking too much time, and nonproductive time that appears to be excessive.

Section L gives a partial list of the many questions that may be asked and answered by the supervisor or the project team related to the factors in order to achieve simplification.

L. QUESTIONS TO BE ASKED FOR WORK SIMPLIFICATION AND COST REDUCTION

Elimination or Combination of Operations

The elimination of unnecessary operations should have been done in the charting and auditing of the manual procedures as set forth in Section II. However, the task inventory will probably have uncovered additional views of the work from a different standpoint, and the team can use these questions to form further conclusions as to whether or not an operation can be eliminated or combined with another operation.

1. Is the operation performed to satisfy the actual requirements of the procedure or merely at the demand of certain individuals or departments?
2. Can the end result be changed to eliminate the purpose of the operation?
3. Is the result accomplished by the operation necessary?
4. Is the operation necessary because of the improper performance of previous operations?
5. Was the operation established to correct a condition which has since been eliminated?
6. If the operation is performed to improve appearance only, is the added cost justified?
7. Is the operation performed as a result of habit?
8. Was the operation established to decrease the cost of a previous or subsequent operation?
9. If the operation was established to improve accuracy, is the cost greater than any foreseeable loss or difficulty?

10. Can elimination of a report result in elimination of the operation?

Can this operation or task be combined with another if:

1. Employees are given proper training?
2. More versatile machines are used?
3. Office arrangements are changed?
4. Operation is transferred to another department?
5. Filing system is changed?
6. Accuracy of preceding operations is improved?
7. Report is eliminated?
8. Record or form is redesigned?
9. Flow of work is evened out?
10. Exceptions to established routines are minimized?

Work Organization in the Office

Office Layout and Work Place Arrangement
1. Is the available space being used to best advantage?
2. Would the work flow more easily and quickly if the office equipment and desks were rearranged?
3. Are the recipients of forms provided with the proper place to keep them? Could guides or form holders be used to better position the work?
4. Are desk tops and drawers organized in an orderly manner so that time spent in seeking and finding material is reduced to a minimum?
5. Could supplemental information and reference materials be made more accessible to the worker? Could they be put on rotating tables or another facility to be made available to more than one worker?
6. Is a desk necessary or could work be done as well on a flat table top?
7. Would a specially designed table facilitate use of office machines?

Flow of Work and Form Handling
1. Is the work flow in your area consistent with the most efficient and economical operation?
2. Can the amount of time the work is delayed while awaiting forms be reduced?

3. Is the messenger service adequate?
4. Can pneumatic tubes or other forms-carrying systems be used to advantage?
5. Can the incoming forms be delivered directly to the first work station without intermediate handling or storage? Is it necessary to leave the desks or location of work for information in order to use the form?
6. Can backtracking of work be eliminated?
7. Would it be more economical to move machines to the work than the work to the machines?

Scheduling of Work
1. Can bottlenecks be eliminated by better scheduling?
2. Can low and peak periods of work be leveled out by better scheduling in the areas from which work is received?
3. Is much time consumed in moving forms to the next operation?
4. Will batching save time in movement between stations?

Use of Office Machines

The consideration of office machines will have been taken care of to a certain degree in the analysis of the procedures charts. However, the completion of procedures charting of the work in a particular area may be some time off; if that is the case, it behooves supervisors to look into the use of machines in their area prior to the completion of procedures charting. The following questions serve as reminders for that purpose.

Necessity for the Machine
1. Has the volume of work performed been costed out with relation to the machines now in use or that may be desirable?
2. Can special machines or equipment be utilized that do more than one operation at a time?
3. Are machines being operated at maximum capacity?
4. Is the present type of machine correct for the operation being performed?
5. Is each typewriter suitable for the use to which it is put?
6. Could a duplicating process or automatic typewriter be used more economically in place of a manual typewriter?
7. Could a recording machine be used to save a stenographer's time?

8. Will electrically driven equipment save time over manually operated equipment?
9. Can additional fixtures be added to present machines to simplify work or increase output?
10. Is the design of the existing fixture correct?
11. Are other fixtures available that can be adapted to the job at hand?
12. Can gathering or sorting aids be used to advantage?

Maintenance of Machines
1. Are machines properly maintained by qualified maintenance personnel?
2. Is periodic inspection maintained on equipment?
3. Have all precautions been taken to prolong the useful life of the machines?
4. Are any of the machines in need of repair at the present time?

Files and Filing

Systems and Equipment
1. Do you have access to specialized knowledge of filing and filing systems?
2. Is it economical to have a central filing system and, if so, what of your material should be so filed?
3. Is the present system of filing so arranged that work can be done with a maximum of efficiency?
4. Could files be labeled or indexed to make the work easier and eliminate errors?
5. Is the records retention system such that you have suitable access to dormant records when needed?

Organization of Material for Filing
1. Are forms designed to facilitate filing and file search?
2. Is material organized and compiled in the manner most suitable for filing?
3. Do you have adequate information at hand to facilitate moving papers into dormant filing or dead storage areas at the proper time?
4. Is the file now being used the best suited to the operation?
5. Are the files close enough to the work to provide for efficiency?

6. Are files taken up with unnecessary reports or records that should be killed or moved to other areas?
7. How long has it been since your files have been "cleaned out"?

Forms

It is not to be expected that the line supervisor will have professional knowledge of forms design, and it is to be hoped that the company does have a forms control unit that possesses such knowledge and capability. However, even if there is a forms control unit, it will behoove the supervisor of the operating departments or units to be aware of the very large possibilities for waste or efficiency in the design of forms as it affects his or her work.

Reports and Their Necessity

The answers to these questions may have to be found in other areas or in management policy.

1. Is the purpose of the report essential to the performance of the major work function?
2. Is the report used as intended?
3. Does the report convey information essential to another operation?
4. Does the report merely give assurance that necessary work has been performed?
5. Is this an "in case of" report—in case someone wants to check back sometime?
6. Could the information be obtained elsewhere?
7. Is the cost of the report justified by results?
8. Is more than one individual or department reporting similar data?
9. Are all copies necessary?
10. Have conditions changed since the report was started?

Checking and Controls

It is of prime importance to the control of clerical costs that essential operations be correctly performed in the first instance and that "make over" work be kept at a minimum. This is particularly important in computer input forms. Errors are inevitable and corrections must be made. However, if errors can be prevented by establishing properly located control points in the operations sequence of a procedure and if errors can be detected and corrected at once, a substantial elimination of "make over" work can be accomplished.

Error and the Necessity for Checking

1. Could procedures be clarified to prevent errors? Is the degree of checking now employed necessary?
2. Has checking become merely a habit through repetition?
3. Is the proper employee doing the checking? Are workers checking their own work?
4. How many rejections result from work in this area and what do they indicate? Do workers need more training?
5. To what extent do the preceding or following operations affect the work in terms of checking for accuracy?
6. Could spot checking take the place of total unit or detailed checking?
7. Are the standards of quality higher than the end use justifies? Can checking requirements be improved?
8. Is incorrect work being properly handled in terms of correction and do the workers receive proper instruction to prevent repetition?
9. Would the use of modular numbering be justified for accountability of all copies of the form.

General Conditions Checklist

These questions may not be the responsibility of the supervisor but certainly someone should be aware of them. It will behoove the supervisor to know about them and be in a position to know whether something may be done to improve the paperwork or clerical operations. Some of the conditions are physical, some psychological, but all are or may be important.

1. Do conditions foster concentration on work at hand?
2. Is lighting uniform and sufficient?
3. Are workers' eyes protected from glare and reflection?
4. Is proper temperature provided for maximum comfort at all times?
5. Has proper safety equipment been provided?
6. Would installation of air-conditioning equipment be justified?
7. Is ventilation good?
8. Are drafts eliminated?

9. Are drinking fountains conveniently located? Is the water cool, and
    is there an adequate supply?
10. Is the floor smooth but not slippery?
11. Have all loose wires or extension cords been removed?
12. Are employees who use machines that soil the hands provided with
    proper cleansers?

CLERICAL EFFICIENCY REPORT P-87-A				FOR MONTH OF *May 1962*	
DEPARTMENT *Accounts Payable*				NO OF EMPLOYEES *12 clerical workers*	
POSITION	BASIS OF MEASUREMENT	UNIT TIME	MONTHLY VOLUME	STANDARD HOURS	PAYROLL HOURS
Accounting Clerk *6 workers*	*Voucher*	.1167	7461	871.7	
	Fixed hours			55.0	
			SUB TOTAL	926.7	1127
Voucher clerk *2 workers*	*Voucher*	0266	7461	198.5	
	checks	0188	212	4.0	
	Fixed hours			4.1	
			SUB TOTAL	206.6	251
File clerk *2 workers*	*Voucher*	.0078	7461	59.2	
	Correspondence	.0972	912	88.6	
	Fixed hours			32.2	
			SUB TOTAL	180.0	246
Expediter *2 workers*	*Purchase Order*	.3572	361	128.9	
	Fixed hours			9.4	
			SUB TOTAL	138.3	183
			TOTAL HOURS (REGULAR)		1807
			PLUS OVERTIME		14
		TOTAL STANDARD HOURS VS AVAILABLE HOURS		1451.6	1821
		% EFFICIENCY 79 %			
REMARKS *9½ workers should handle the work load*					

FIGURE 32. Clerical efficiency report: application of time allowances.

13. Does the office present a neat, orderly appearance at all times?
14. Are new employees properly introduced to their surroundings, and are sufficient instructions given to them?
15. Are suitable facilities provided for personal belongings?

M. APPLICATION OF THE PERFORMANCE TIME ALLOWANCES

With the completion of the performance time allowance sheets (Figure 31) and the simplification of the clerical work, reference may be made to the manual procedures charts, and clerical operations or groups of operations within the total procedure can be identified for the application of the performance time allowances or clerical work standards. The findings and recommendations that have been adopted as a result of the work performed in the methods improvement and work simplification phases of the program will, of course, affect both the tasks and the time and output data that have been listed on the operation analysis sheet.

We are now ready to establish the revised list of operations (and their component tasks) within the procedures studied and to determine new time and output data. If the only change that has been instituted is the elimination of some tasks, then time and output data can be taken from the original operation analysis sheet. In the majority of cases, however, it may be desirable to take another task inventory at some time in the future to determine productivity under the revised conditions.

The new task time should be entered in column E, Base, on the form Operation Performance Allowances. To this time we must add an allowance for personal time (see page 87), which should be entered in column F, Allow. These two amounts should be then added and the sum entered in column G, Total. The occurrence per normal output, which was previously determined and entered in column B on the operation analysis sheet, should be multiplied by the total allowed time and the product entered in column H. If the method improvement and work simplification phases altered this figure, a new normal output should be established. This amount should in turn be multiplied by the factor to convert the time to a monthly basis, and the result entered in column I.

When these steps are completed for each task within an operation, the figures in column I should be totaled. The answer will be the amount of time required each month to process the normal output of measurable units through one operation of a procedure under the revised conditions established through methods improvement and work simplification. This amount can then be used as a standard against which productivity may be measured.

Figure 32 shows such an application in the accounts payable section of an accounting department, consisting of 12 clerical workers. Four positions are involved using four forms or documents. The principal document, the voucher, is shown to be used in three of the four positions, and this provides a means of accumulating hours and cost by a single document if desired.

For the whole operation the payroll hours now used are 1821, whereas the measurement analysis showed that only 1451.6 hours should be needed, a percentage of efficiency of 79 percent. It is hardly to be expected that the operation would reach 100 percent efficiency, but management would be justified in wanting an improvement of at least 10 percent and, more probably, 15 percent in the work.

Such an improvement in clerical work on a wide basis would be of great value in increasing white-collar productivity and should show a discernible result in the profit column.

CONCLUSION

Paperwork and white-collar productivity can be controlled. The results are positive and add to profits. With the white-collar labor force equaling or exceeding the hourly rated or blue-collar force, it is absolutely necessary that management take steps to control this vital segment of indirect operating expense. Merely issuing an order that the white-collar labor force be reduced by 10 percent is almost sure to be counterproductive. The wrong people will be let go, the most efficient areas will be penalized, and the supervisor may decide to overstaff in order to be protected when the ax falls the next time. An orderly, intelligent program of management put into effect in the office, parallel to the industrial engineering in the factory, is the way to do it.

But the program requires a companywide management policy and a carefully thought out program of implementation. That program must be built into the table of organization with carefully defined statements of objectives. It must be coordinated with the assignments of authorities and responsibilities in order that staff-line relationships are not disturbed. It must accomplish its objectives through cooperation between the various units of the company—departments, plants, and divisions—with an effective central staff to guide and coordinate efforts and results.

The program must consist of proven techniques covering the several basic elements of paperwork, the systems, and the procedures that make up these systems; the forms and documents that are the raw material of paperwork; and the clerical operations that are the productive efforts of the white-collar work force. Selection of methods for performing the work will be a logical and effective outgrowth of the auditing and simplification of the procedures, forms, and clerical operations. No procedure or paperwork operation will be tailored to a preconceived selection of method—manual, mechanical, or electronic—without having been first audited and evaluated for necessity and simplified to eliminate unnecessary operations.

Continued and permanent management of paperwork and productivity in the office must, of necessity, be centered in the first-line supervisor who is in immediate contact with the clerical labor force. The supervisor must be given more information about the work and tools with which to implement that information. This is the objective of clerical work measurement and simplification in which the supervisor will have been trained after the procedures have been audited and streamlined. Unless the supervisors are built solidly into the program, no lasting results are possible.

Forms will be controlled and designed for the greatest possible paperwork efficiency. Unnecessary forms will be eliminated; duplicate forms for the same tasks will be consolidated into standard designs; unnecessary new forms will be prevented. A data base for the study of procedures and clerical work analysis will be created through a functional index of all forms in the company in which the forms are segregated by function, operation, and subject matter—factors common to all aspects of paperwork. Procurement, warehousing, and distribution of forms will be implemented through control contracting.

The expression "Thar's gold in them thar hills" was never more true than in today's office with too much paper, too many clerks, too much emphasis on advanced technology without having carefully considered the need before installing the machine, and too little management attention to the indirect expense that robs the company of a goodly part of its profit.

To repeat: Paperwork and white-collar productivity can be controlled. The results are positive and can add to profits.

THE PAPERWORK COORDINATOR'S MANUAL

This appendix contains a suggested copy for the important paperwork coordinator's manual, a fundamental tool in establishing a correct and workable staff-line relationship in the paperwork management program. It has been used in substantially this form by many companies in which forms and paperwork management programs have been installed, although it may be changed to meet conditions or situations existing in any given company.

A. TO THE PAPERWORK COORDINATOR

The work of our divisions or departments is accomplished, or reported, or controlled through paper and the flow of paper. Hence forms and reports are essentially interdepartmental in character.

This is most easily appreciated upon considering that a division or department or work unit is only a part of our entire organization and that the work of our whole company is accomplished only through the combined and integrated efforts of all divisions, departments, and work sections.

It follows that the forms, which are the raw material of this paperwork, are equally interdepartmental in character. They often start in one department or division and travel into another.

Hence, if paperwork control is to be effective it must be done on an interdivisional, interdepartmental level and must be established companywide as a staff function.

B. THE PAPERWORK CONTROL PROGRAM

In our company the work of forms and paperwork control is carried on in the paperwork control unit reporting to _____. Management has delegated to this control unit the prime responsibility for controlling and coordinating the company's forms and paperwork and for providing a service in all paperwork control functions according to company standards for efficiency and economy. This service is rendered by the control unit in close cooperation with departmental paperwork coordinators to all divisions, departments, plants, and work units of the company.

C. THE PAPERWORK COORDINATOR

Throughout the line organization of the company there must be an equal responsibility for controlling and coordinating the forms and paperwork used in each division, department, plant, and work unit of the organization.

In order to make the relationship between the paperwork control unit and the line organization a two-way proposition and provide a good foundation for the success of our control of paperwork expense, we believe it advisable for the head of each division, department, or work unit to assign one person the responsibility for controlling forms and paperwork in that area. This person will be known as the "paperwork coordinator."

Importance of Coordinators in the Company Paperwork Control

The importance of good paperwork coordinators cannot be overemphasized. They are the channels through which the objectives of the control program are achieved. Possessing an intimate knowledge of the proper requirements in their particular area, or being in a position to obtain such knowledge quickly and efficiently, and also having an understanding of company objectives in paperwork control, the coordinators are in a position to know the answers to the many questions bearing upon a given problem and to correctly determine its disposition.

Furthermore, the suggestions and proposals arising within the area and submitted by the coordinators to the control unit are invaluable to the program and often lead to accomplishments that would otherwise be impossible to obtain. In short, the success of the control program can depend on the proper selection of paperwork coordinators and the cooperation and understanding they evidence in relation to it.

Advantages of Paperwork Coordinators in the Program

The primary advantage is to be able to carry on a comprehensive and successful paperwork expense reduction program without the necessity of employing a large number of staff analysts to coordinate the work throughout the organization.

All contact between the control unit and the division, department, or work unit will be with and through the paperwork coordinator. Before any forms used by that unit are changed or reprinted, or before any paperwork procedures are revised by the corporate control unit, the approval of the coordinator will be obtained.

This is the best and most effective way of ensuring that the prerogatives of the line organization are not abrogated or abused in the forms or procedures affecting the paperwork of the unit.

If discrepancies or obvious inefficiencies in paperwork flow are uncovered in the paperwork procedures analysis, the staff analyst will depend on the coordinator to determine why such situations exist and what can be done to correct them.

In many cases inefficiencies in paperwork flow result from a lack of coordination between divisions or departments. In such cases it is the function of the staff analyst to work with the coordinators of the several units to synchronize the paperwork flow.

It is only by this cooperative effort by the staff and the line units in interdepartmental or divisional relationships that the results in efficiency and economy of paperwork management will be achieved.

Another important advantage is that the paperwork coordinators will become, over a period of time, experts on the paperwork in use in their respective units. Assisting greatly in the successful disposition of all forms and paperwork problems arising in or affecting their particular locations, they develop an intimate knowledge of their forms, how and where they are used, and why they are necessary. As a result they become quite adept at discovering procedural improvements that increase efficiency and facilitate the handling of their paperwork problems, particularly when specific procedures are under review throughout the organization.

D. RESPONSIBILITIES OF THE PAPERWORK COORDINATORS

Paperwork coordinators have a dual responsibility in our company's paperwork control program. Their first responsibility is to the division, department, or work unit with which they are affiliated to ensure that forms and paperwork they use are correct and clerically efficient. Their second responsibility is to the companywide paperwork control program to ensure that the objectives of that program are achieved, insofar as it is possible to achieve them, within the unit in which the coordinator is located.

These two primary responsibilities are not incompatible. They do, however, often give rise to the necessity for studied judgment in arriving at the disposition of paperwork problems. This, of course, only emphasizes the importance of the coordinators in our paperwork control program.

E. DUTIES OF THE PAPERWORK COORDINATORS

The duties of the paperwork coordinators in the company's paperwork control program are listed below.

The Case of Manual Paperwork Procedures

The corporate staff has trained procedures analysts but they must depend on the paperwork coordinators for information on the procedural flow of paper in the coordinators' unit. When a procedure is to be analyzed and the analyst wants to chart it, he or she depends on the paperwork coordinator for guidance and assistance in obtaining the basic information necessary to charting the procedure: the forms used, where they come from, what happens to them within the using unit, and where they go or how they are disposed of within the unit.

The duties of the coordinator include cooperation in the following functions:

1. Identifying the procedures in any given paperwork area, whether manual, machine, or electronic, for auditing and simplification.
2. Charting the procedures in a manner understandable to management—supervisory, administrative, and executive—in order that all clerical operations and paperwork flow may be analyzed and audited for necessity and efficiency.
3. Studying the methods used in paperwork operations and evaluating

them in the light of possible better methods. This includes machines and equipment of all kinds.

4. Eliminating all unnecessary paperwork and improving that which is necessary to the profitable operation of the business.
5. Measuring the cost of individual paperwork operations for labor budgeting and establishing standard time allowances.
6. Assisting line supervisors in better management of their operations.

The Case of Forms Control

A relatively small staff group working in the corporate office handles the detail of reviewing the company's forms situation, as revealed by the functional index that shows interdepartmental or interdivisional duplications in forms usage, and prepares efficient and economical designs to meet specific forms situations. These designs and other pertinent data are cleared with the line organization through the paperwork coordinators whose duty is to approve or disapprove the changes. The result is that a cooperative organization smooths the way for handling and clearing forms problems quickly without imposing too heavily on any one unit.

Another great advantage of the coordinators is the avoidance of any confusion or disturbance in the divisions or departments in which the forms are used. The coordinators are affiliated with their particular segment of the organization, are known and accepted by the personnel of the unit, can "speak the language" of that unit, and know where to get answers. Hence the normal routine work of the program can be conducted with a minimum of disturbance in the divisions and departments or plants.

This cooperation between the corporate paperwork control unit and the paperwork coordinators will produce the following benefits:

1. Elimination of unnecessary existing forms and preventing the inception of unnecessary new forms.
2. Consolidation into standard designs of all forms serving the same identical operation or asking for the same information.
3. Applications of standards in design or redesign of forms to ensure the greatest possible economy in production or procurement.
4. Reduction in the cost of storing and distributing forms to using locations and ensuring against running out of a form when it is needed.

5. Elimination of overstocks of current forms, thus lowering inventory costs or avoiding the necessity of disposing of excess obsolete stocks.

The Case of Clerical Work Analysis and Simplification

The corporate staff formulates and supervises a special program to be applied through the paperwork supervisors in each unit. The paperwork coordinators will be fully advised of this program before its application in their unit and will play an appropriate part in its use.

DICTIONARY OF STANDARD FORMS TERMINOLOGY FOR CLASSIFICATION OF FORMS IN THE FUNCTIONAL INDEX

INTRODUCTION

The control of office and plant forms is dependent to a considerable degree on an understanding and usage of terms and words common to all concerned. Since there has never been any standardization of terminology in forms, systems, and procedures work as it relates to office work and practices, there has grown up a maze of confusion in the words used.

It becomes necessary, therefore, to establish common definitions of terms in order to organize the thinking of the individuals engaged in the work and to be sure that everyone concerned is thinking of the same thing when a word or term is used.

It is not necessary to reorganize the thinking of everyone who uses forms, for this would take in almost everyone in the organization, but it is very necessary that those charged with the responsibility of controlling paperwork should have organized thinking, particularly in the building and use of the functional index.

Since a primary purpose of the functional index is to bring together every form doing the same thing, and since different forms doing the same thing are often called by different names, it is essential that some terms be used that cut through this confusion and relate to the essential meaning of the forms.

This dictionary represents more than 15 years of study and experience in arriving at such a set of standard terms for the classification of forms in a functional index. All definitions in the dictionary have been coordinated insofar as possible with existing definitions and with accepted practices in industry and commerce.

The dictionary is based on a logical breakdown of all that goes on in paperwork into the basic divisions of subject matter, operations or conditions, and functions.

Since these terms themselves need definition in order to clarify the basic assumption, they are defined as follows:

Subject—That concerning which anything is said or done; thing or person treated of; matter; theme; topic. In forms control the subject becomes the matter or thing in relation to which an action takes place or to which a condition refers.

Operation—In general, act, process, or effect of operating. A doing or performing action; work. In forms control, the operation represents the action which takes place in relation to the subject.

Condition—A mode or state of being. In forms control the condition refers to the state in which the subject may be at any given time.

Function—The natural or characteristic purpose of a thing; that purpose which the thing or person is supposed to accomplish or fulfill. (Webster defines function in terms of an ''action'' whereas other standard dictionaries use the term ''purpose,'' which fits better into this classification and is therefore used.)

In working with forms, procedures, records, and other phases of paperwork, it will be found that everything which takes place may be related to these categories of subject, operation or condition, and function. Examples are seen as follows:

Bank check—The purpose of a bank check is to order the payment of cash or its equivalent. Hence we have a *subject* ''cash,'' an *operation* ''payment of,'' and a *function* ''to order.'' Put together they constitute a logical statement of the purpose of the check.

Inventory report—The purpose of an inventory report form is to report the status of materials, supplies, etc. Hence we have a *subject* ''materials, etc.,'' a *condition* ''status of,'' and a *function* ''to report.'' Again they are put together as a logical statement in reference to the form.

One of the problems which arose in establishing standard terminology in this field was the fact that many terms have several different definitions and many forms are called by different names. In such cases where a legitimate difference of opinion may exist as to which term or definition to use, the one which appears most logical has been adopted as standard. This is not to deny the validity of others, but from a purely practical viewpoint only one definition can be used in a given case if confusion is to be avoided. As long as the definition is usable and everyone concerned uses it confusion will be avoided and the control can be made effective.

This is particularly important in the use of the functional index over a period of time with changes in the personnel using it. What may have appeared most logical to the first person may not seem so to subsequent personnel, in which case the absence of a standard, if arbitrary, definition would endanger the work and probably lessen its effectiveness.

Although the dictionary represents the results of many years experience and the building of many functional indexes, it is possible that new subjects, operations, or conditions may be encountered in any given index. These may be added as necessary or desirable.

The functions used have been reduced to 18 since many others are, or seem to be, synonyms. Over a period of years it has not been found necessary to use more than 18 listed.

The subject, operation or condition, and function of any given form can be put together in a logical, sensible phrase to describe the purpose of the form. Examples are as follows:

"Personal Record"—*To record the status of an employee.*

"Receiving Report"—*To report the receipt of materials and supplies.*

"Appropriation Request"—*To request the expenditure of cash.*

In each case the subject is expressed by a noun; the operation or condition is a noun phrase referring either to a verb or an adjective; the function is expressed by an infinitive.

Unless the classification can be so expressed, it should be questioned since the entire purpose of the classification of forms into the functional index is to simplify and make clear a confusing situation.

Study your dictionary of standard forms terminology. It will clarify many situations and help keep your paperwork control effective.

LIST OF SUBJECTS

1. Accident	41. Carrier
2. Account	42. Cash
3. Account Payroll	43. Cash Item
4. Accounts General	44. Certificate
5. Accounts Payable	45. Check
6. Accounts Receivable	46. Claim
7. Action	47. Class
8. Address	48. Code
9. Admission (legal)	49. Collateral
10. Advertising	50. Communication
11. Agent	51. Committee
12. Analysis	52. Community
13. Applicant	53. Company
14. Appointment	54. Complaints/Trouble
15. Appropriation	55. Contact
16. Assets	56. Container
17. Assigned Risk	57. Contract
18. Audit	58. Contribution
19. Award	59. Control
20.	60. Correspondence
21.	61. Costs
22.	62. Course
23.	63. Credit
24. Bad Debt	64. Credit Card
25. Bail Bond	65. Curriculum
26. Bank	66. Customer
27. Bank Account	67. Customer Service
28. Bank Check	68.
29. Beneficiary	69.
30. Benefit Plan	70.
31. Benefits	71.
32. Binder	72. Damages
33. Bond	73. Demurrage
34. Book	74. Department
35. Budget	75. Dependent
36.	76. Deposit
37.	77. Depreciation
38.	78. Dictation
39. Call - Sales	79. Die
40. Candidate	80. Diploma

81.	Distributor	124.	Hazard
82.	Dividend	125.	Hearing
83.	Document	126.	Housing
84.	Draft	127.	
85.	Drawing	128.	
86.		129.	Idea
87.		130.	Incident
88.		131.	Income
89.		132.	Indemnity
90.		133.	Injury/Illness
91.	Earnings	134.	Inquiry
92.	Education	135.	Instructor
93.	Electrotype	136.	Insurance
94.	Employee	137.	Insured
95.	Employee Benefits	138.	Interest
96.	Employment	139.	Invention
97.	Entertainment	140.	Inventory
98.	Error	141.	Invoice
99.	Estate	142.	
100.	Estimate	143.	
101.	Event	144.	Job
102.	Experience	145.	
103.		146.	
104.		147.	Key
105.		148.	
106.		149.	
107.	Facility	150.	Labor
108.	File	151.	Land and Buildings
109.	Food	152.	Law
110.	Foreign Exchange	153.	Lead
111.	Forms	154.	Lease
112.	Formula	155.	Ledger
113.	Freight	156.	Legal Documents
114.		157.	Letter of Credit
115.		158.	Liability
116.		159.	License
117.	Garnishment	160.	Lien
118.	Guage	161.	Loan
119.	Gift	162.	Loss
120.	Grievance	163.	
121.		164.	
122.		165.	
123.		166.	

167.	Machinery and Equipment	210.	Personal Property
168.	Mail	211.	Plant
169.	Mailing List	212.	Plate
170.	Manuscript	213.	Policy
171.	Market	214.	Postage
172.	Materials and Supplies	215.	Power of Attorney
173.	Meal	216.	Premises
174.	Media	217.	Premium
175.	Medical Examination	218.	Price
176.	Medicine	219.	Prints
177.	Meeting	220.	Problem
178.	Member	221.	Procedure
179.	Membership	222.	Product
180.	Merchandise	223.	Production
181.	Messenger Service	224.	Profit and Loss
182.	Model	225.	Program
183.	Mold	226.	Project
184.	Mortgage	227.	Property
185.		228.	Prospects
186.		229.	Proxy
187.	Name	230.	Publication
188.	News	231.	Purchase
189.	Note	232.	
190.	Notice	233.	
191.	Number	234.	
192.		235.	
193.		236.	Quotation
194.	Order	237.	
195.	Organization	238.	
196.	Overhead	239.	
197.		240.	
198.		241.	Railroad Car
199.	Package	242.	Rate
200.	Parent	243.	Real Estate
201.	Part	244.	Recipe
202.	Passport	245.	Records
203.	Patent	246.	Regulation
204.	Patient	247.	Reinsurance
205.	Pattern	248.	Rent
206.	Payroll	249.	Report
207.	Pension	250.	Reservation
208.	Period	251.	Reserve
209.	Person	252.	Resolution

253.	Returnable Container	296.	Title
254.	Revenue	297.	Tool
255.	Rights	298.	Trade Mark
256.	Risk	299.	Training
257.	Room	300.	Transportation
258.	Royalties	301.	Travel
259.	Rubbish	302.	Trouble
260.	Rules and Regulations	303.	Trust
261.		304.	Tuition
262.		305.	
263		306.	
264.		307.	
265.	Safe Deposit Box	308.	
266.	Salary	309.	Utilities
267.	Sales	310.	
268.	Salvage	311.	
269.	Sample	312.	Vacation
270.	School	313.	Vehicle
271.	Scrap	314.	Vendor
272.	Securities	315.	Visa
273.	Selective Service	316.	Visitor
274.	Service	317.	Vote
275.	Shipment	318.	
276.	Signature	319.	
277.	Social Security	320.	Wages
278.	Specifications	321.	Waiter's Check
279.	Specimen	322.	Weather
280.	Standard	323.	Work
281.	Standard Practice	324.	Work-in-Process
282.	Stock	325.	Work Measurement
283.	Student		
284.	Suggestion		
285.	Suit		
286.	Summons		
287.	Supplier		
288.			
289.			
290.			
291.	Tariff		
292.	Tax		
293.	Teacher		
294.	Ticket		
295.	Time		

LIST OF OPERATIONS AND CONDITIONS

1.	Absence of	41.	Completion of
2.	Acceptance—Rejection of	42.	Computation of
3.	Access to	43.	Contents of
4.	Addition to	44.	Control of
5.	Adherence to	45.	Correctness of
6.	Adjustment or Correction of	46.	Cost of
7.	Admission of	47.	Coverage of
8.	Aging of	48.	Credit of
9.	Allocation of	49.	Credit to
10.	Analysis of	50.	
11.	Application for	51.	
12.	Appointment of	52.	
13.	Appraisal of	53.	
14.	Appropriation of	54.	Damage to
15.	Approval of	55.	Death of
16.	Assignment of	56.	Debit—Credit to
17.	Attendance of	57.	Debit to
18.	Audit of	58.	Deduction of
19.	Availability of	59.	Deferment of
20.		60.	Delay of
21.		61.	Delinquency of
22.		62.	Delivery of
23.		63.	Demonstration of
24.	Back Order of	64.	Departure of
25.	Birth of	65.	Deposit of
26.	Budget of	66.	Depreciation of
27.		67.	Description of
28.		68.	Design of
29.		69.	Destination of
30.		70.	Destruction of
31.	Calibration of	71.	Development of
32.	Cancellation of	72.	Disbursement of
33.	Certification of	73.	Discount of
34.	Change of	74.	Disposition of
35.	Charge-off of	75.	Distribution of
36.	Citizenship of	76.	
37.	Classification of	77.	
38.	Clearance of	78.	
39.	Closing of	79.	
40.	Collection of	80.	Efficiency of

81.	Eligibility for	124.	Lease of
82.	Employment of	125.	Limitation of
83.	Enrollment of	126.	Listing of
84.	Evaluation of	127.	Loading of
85.	Examination of	128.	Loan of
86.	Exemption of	129.	Location of
87.	Expiration of	130.	Loss of
88.	Exportation of	131.	Lost and Found
89.	Extension of	132.	
90.		133.	
91.		134.	
92.		135.	
93.		136.	Manufacture of
94.	Filing of	137.	Marriage of
95.	Filling of	138.	Maturity of
96.		139.	Minutes of
97.		140.	Mortgage of
98.	Garnishment of	141.	Movement of
99.		142.	
100.		143.	
101.	Handling of	144.	
102.	Hiring of	145.	
103.	Housing of	146.	Obsolescence of
104.		147.	Opening of
105.		148.	Operation of
106.		149.	Organization of
107.	Identification of	150.	Orientation of
108.	Incorrectness of	151.	Overage of
109.	Indoctrination of	152.	Overage–Shortage of
110.	Information About	153.	Ownership of
111.	Inspection of	154.	
112.	Installation of	155.	
113.	Instruction of	156.	
114.	Insurance of	157.	
115.	Interview of	158.	Packaging of
116.	Investigation of	159.	Participation in
117.	Issuance of	160.	Passage of
118.		161.	Payment of
119.		162.	Performance of
120.		163.	Placement of
121.		164.	Prevention of
122.		165.	Price of
123.		166.	Procurement of

167.	Properties of	210.	Safety of
168.	Protection of	211.	Sale of
169.		212.	Seniority of
170.		213.	Settlement of
171.		214.	Set-up of
172.		215.	Shipping of
173.	Qualification of	216.	Shortage of
174.		217.	Shrinkage of
175.		218.	Shut-down of
176.	Rate of	219.	Size of
177.	Rating of	220.	Specifications of
178.	Recall of	221.	Status of
179.	Receipt of	222.	Stocking of
180.	Referral to	223.	Storage of
181.	Reconciliation of	224.	Substitute of
182.	Recovery of	225.	Suspension of
183.	Refund of	226.	Switching of
184.	Refusal of	227.	
185.	Registration of	228.	
186.	Reinstatement of	229.	
187.	Rejection of	230.	Termination of
188.	Release of	231.	Testing of
189.	Remittance of	232.	Training of
190.	Rental of	233.	Transfer of
191.	Repair−Maintenance of	234.	Transmittal of
192.	Replenishment of	235.	Transportation of
193.	Repossession of	236.	Treatment of
194.	Reprimand of	237.	
195.	Reproduction of	238.	
196.	Requirements of	239.	
197.	Reservation of	240.	
198.	Responsibility for	241.	Use of
199.	Retention of	242.	
200.	Retirement of	243.	
201.	Return of	244.	Vacancy of
202.	Review of	245.	Value of
203.	Rework of	246.	Variance of
204.	Rooming of	247.	Violation of
205.	Routing of	248.	
206.		249.	
207.		250.	Weight of
208.		251.	Withdrawal of
209.		252.	Withholding of

EIGHTEEN ESSENTIAL FUNCTIONS

1. **To Acknowledge:** To recognize a fact or condition; to admit the existence, authority, truth, or genuineness of; to give validity to through recognition; to make known the receipt of.

2. **To Agree:** To offer and accept in writing; to concur in; to come to terms or common understanding; usually applying to actions or events to take place in the future as opposed to ''to certify,'' which applies to past actions.

3. **To Apply:** To make application for something that may or may not be granted; to ask consideration—usually a request made without formal authority to demand action, to be decided under conditions beyond the control of the applicant as opposed to ''to request,'' where action may definitely be expected as a result.

4. **To Authorize:** To permit, allow, or make possible an action; to clothe with authority; to grant license or liberty; usually where subsequent action is optional, as opposed to ''to order,'' where subsequent action is mandatory.

5. **To Cancel:** To cause or bring about the annullment, revocation, or recall of things; to abolish or repeal things or former actions.

6. **To Certify:** To attest, verify, endorse, or guarantee authoritatively, usually applying to existing or past conditions as opposed to ''to agree,'' which applies to future conditions.

7. **To Claim:** To ask for or seek to obtain something in the possession of another; to demand something due or supposed to be due, usually when there is actual or potential question as to the right of possession or justification for the claim.

8. **To Estimate:** To fix or calculate approximately; to form an opinion of something in the absence or unavailability of all actual facts; usually pertaining to values, qualities, or time; usually subjects or matters treated in the singular as opposed to ''to schedule,'' which usually treats of repetitious or recurring events.

9. **To Follow up:** To pursue an initial effort; to keep attention fixed upon or to recall attention to.

10. **To Identify:** To establish the identity of; to recognize or establish something or someone to be the same.

11. **To Instruct:** To impart knowledge to; to teach, or furnish with direction; to educate, train, or indoctrinate; usually without authority to enforce subsequent action, as opposed to "to order," which carries authority.

12. **To Notify:** To give notice of or make known facts that were not known before, usually where another person will be bound to some degree by the information as opposed to "to report," where no binding action is carried.

13. **To Order:** To rule or regulate by competent authority; to commission the purchase or sale of things or the performance of services or work; usually where subsequent action is mandatory, as opposed to "to authorize," where subsequent action is optional, or to "to instruct," where no binding action is involved.

14. **To Record:** To copy or reduce to writing as evidence; to perpetuate a knowledge of events or facts, usually where the making of a record of some permanency is the primary function of the document, as opposed to forms in which the record is secondary to another primary function.

15. **To Report:** To give an account of events, happenings, performance, things, or conditions; to communicate knowledge of, to make known, tell, or enlighten; to gather data or information from records to present a current picture of conditions; to gather primary data or information from which records are to be compiled; usually where the other person is not particularly bound to specific action by the information, as opposed to "to notify," where it is known that action will be affected or circumscribed by the information.

16. **To Request:** To ask for something; to requisition the procurement of delivery of things, materials, or personnel required for operation, usually by those in a position to expect action as a result as opposed to "to apply," where the request carries no assurance of action.

17. **To Route:** To send forward or transmit by a certain route or to a specified place or person.

18. **To Schedule:** To place in a formal written or printed list; to set forth the times of projected operations; to outline regularly occurring events or to write a plan of future events placing them in the time element; to place chronologically, as opposed to "to estimate," which involves elements other than time and is only an approximation in the absence or unavailability of all actual facts.

LIST OF FUNCTIONS AND SYNONYMS

Abolish, To—see, To Cancel
Accept, To—see,
   To Acknowledge
Account, To—see, To Report
Acknowledge, To
Agree, To—see, To Certify
Allow, To—see To Authorize
Annul, To—see, To Cancel
Apply, To—see To Request
Appraise, To—see, To Estimate
Ask, To—see, To Request
Attest, To—see, To Certify
Authorize, To
Calculate, To—see, To Estimate
Cancel, To
Certify, To
Claim, To
Commission, To—see,
   To Authorize
Compute, To—see, To Estimate
Confirm, To—see, To Certify
Consent, To—see, To Agree
Contract, To—see, To Agree
Demand, To—see, To Claim
Endorse, To—see, To Certify
Establish, To—see, To Identify
Estimate, To
Follow up, To
Grant, To—see, To Acknowledge

Guarantee, To—see, To Certify
Identify, To
Inform, To—see, To Notify
Inquire, To—see, To Request
Instruct, To
Inventory, To—see, To Report
Invoice, To—see, To Notify
Notify, To
Order, To—see, To Authorize,
   To Instruct
Permit, To—see, To Authorize
Promise, To—see, To Agree
Recall, To—see, To Cancel
Receipt, To—see, To Acknowledge
Record, To
Regulate, To—see, To Order
Repeal, To—see, To Cancel
Report, To
Request, To
Requisition, To—see, To Request
Route, To
Rule, To—see, To Order
Schedule, To
Tell, To—see, To Report
Testify, To—see, To Certify
Transmit, To—see, To Route
Validate, To—see, To Acknowledge
Verify, To—see, To Certify
Warn, To—see, To Notify

THE DICTIONARY OF
STANDARD FORMS TERMINOLOGY

Absence of (condition)—The state of being absent or withdrawn from. In personnel work absence applies to an employee and may be authorized or unauthorized, the latter usually being treated as an offense. See also "Leave of Absence."

Abolish, to (function)—To do away with wholly; to annul; to make void. Use the function "To Cancel."

Accept, to (function)—To receive or admit and agree to; to assent to. Use the function "To Acknowledge."

Acceptance—Rejection of (operation)—The act or process of accepting or rejecting. May apply to physical things such as acceptance or rejection of materials, work-in-process, or product following inspection or to personal matters such as acceptance or rejection of an offer of any kind.

Access, to (operation)—A right of entry or passage to some place or something.

Accident (subject)—An event that takes place without one's foresight or expectation; undesigned, sudden, and unexpected event, particularly of an unfortunate or afflictive character. As used in forms control, the subject "Accident" refers to the event or incident itself and not to the result or product of the event or incident. Accidents may involve persons or inanimate objects or things, such as machinery, equipment, etc. No distinction is made in the application of the subject "Accident" insofar as that which is involved in the accident is concerned.

In forms control, a distinction is made in the result of the accident. The result "Injury—Illness" can be sustained only by persons, and is treated as a subject. The result "Damage" can be sustained only by inanimate objects, and is treated as a resultant condition, "Damage to" modifying the specific subject.

In treating with the general subject of insurance it must be remembered that an accident gives rise to a train of related factors as follows:

The Accident—or its result, death.

The Claim—request for benefits as a result of the accident.

The Loss—payment of the benefits.

The Experience—a recapitulation of the above factors.

The Rate—premium amount resulting from the experience.

Account to (function)—To render or state the terms of; an account or relation of particulars; to answer in judgment or explanation. Use the term "To Report."

Account (subject)—In forms control the subject "Account" refers to a record, usually kept in a ledger under an appropriate heading or title, of business transactions with persons or other business organizations, involving cash or its equivalent; or of other types of transactions dealing with the same identical elements of the business, or similar enough to be classed together. See also Accounts Payable, Accounts Receivable, Accounts General.

In banking the term "Account" is used also to indicate the relation between the bank and its customers, particularly depositors. Forms relating to the fact of a bank−customer relationship or to information about the depositors, either individually or corporation, may be classified under the subject "Account." See also "Bank Account."

Accounting (department)—In forms control, "Accounting" refers to that phase of operations, and that portion of a business organization, having to do with the recording of financial or business transactions involving cash or its equivalent, and all other closely related operations or subjects.

Account Payroll (subject)—An account devoted solely to payroll.

Accounts, General (subject)—Accounts in general, not classified as a specific class (i.e., "Receivable," "Payable," etc.). See also "Account."

Accounts Payable (subject)—The individual account of a creditor from whom merchandise has been purchased or by whom services have been rendered on open account. Also, in a collective sense, the creditors' accounts as a group. See also "Account."

Accounts Receivable (subject)—The individual account of a customer to whom merchandise has been sold or to whom services have been rendered on open account. Also, in a collective sense, the customers' accounts as a group. See also "Account."

Acknowledge, to (function)—To recognize a fact or a condition; to admit of the existence, authority, truth, or genuineness of; to give validity to through recognition; to make known the receipt of.

Acknowledgment (form)—A form the function of which is to acknowledge. A formal declaration of recognition in a particular character or relationship, or recognition of the existence, authority, truth, or genuineness of something. In forms control, acknowledgments are classified under the function "To Acknowledge" and the specific subjects and operations under that function.

Acknowledgment of Order (form)—To acknowledge the receipt of an order (see "Order"). An acknowledgment of order form often contains more than a mere acknowledgment (i.e., verification of details on material ordered, shipping instructions, etc.). May be cross-referenced under "To Certify."

Action (subject)—An act, thing done, deed, or enterprise. In forms control "Action" is used only when the particular operation or action cannot be identified with a specific, single subject. If the subject about which the action takes place can be identified, classify the forms involved under the specific subject followed by an operation descriptive of the action.

Addition, to (operation)—The act or process of joining or uniting, as one thing to another, so as to increase the number, augment, or enlarge.

Address (subject)—The name, title, and place of residence of a person; the location by street and city of a person, organization, firm, etc.

Address Label (form)—See "Label."

Adherence, to (operation)—Quality, act, or state of adhering; to abide by; to be devoted; to hold or be attached to.

Adjustment or Correction of (operation)—The act of bringing a thing or things into proper or exact position or condition; the act of making that right which was wrong; the act of bringing to a standard, or changing to remedy an error or defect. See also "Change of."

Admission—The act or practice of admitting; granting permission or privilege to enter into a place. In forms control "Admission" is not used as such. Instead, "Passage of," which includes exit as well as entry, is used with a specific subject (i.e., "Person, Passage of" or "Personal Property, Passage of," etc.). See "Passage of" (operation).

Admission (legal, subject)—A legal term indicating the granting of an argument that has not been wholly proved.

Admission of (operation)—The act or process of accepting into a school, class, hospital, fraternal organization, or other type of institution. In forms control, "Admission of" is used only in relation to students in schools, patients in hospitals, and members of an organization, etc., and should not be confused with "Passage of," which can relate to anyone or anything in an office, building, or premises of any sort. "Admission of" refers only to persons, normally students, patients, members, etc., and usually embraces considerably more in its significance than the mere passing of someone or something through an entrance or exit, usually implying an acceptance or granting of admission or membership. "Passage of" can include reference to things or objects as well as persons, but has to do only with the entrance or exit from a particular place or location.

Advertising (subject)—A public notice, especially in some public print, as a newspaper, periodical, book, poster, or handbill; anything that advertises; the overall publicizing of a product or object as part of a merchandising operation.

Advertising material—Material the purpose of which is to advertise or promote something. File under a special category "Advertising."

Advice (form)—A sworn statement in writing; especially, a declaration in writing, made upon oath before an authorized magistrate or officer. In forms control, affidavits should be classified under "To Certify" and the specific subjects under that function.

Agency (subject)—The place of business of an agent; the business organization of an agent. In forms control "Agency" is not generally used as a subject; use "Agent" instead.

Agent (subject)—One who acts for or in the place of another by authority from him or her.

Aging of (operation)—The act or process of arranging according to age, like aging of accounts receivable.

Agree, to (function)—To offer and accept in writing; to concur in; to come to terms or common understanding; usually applying to actions or events to take place in the future as opposed to "To Certify," which applies to past actions.

Agreement (form)—A form the function of which is to agree; a formal writing between two or more persons to do, or not to do, something; a contract. In forms control, agreements should be classified under the function "To Agree" and the specific subjects under that function.

Allocation of (operation)—See "Distribution of" or "Placement of."

Allow to (function)—To approve of; to sanction; to grant, give, admit, accord, afford, or yield; to own or acknowledge. Use the function "To Authorize."

Analysis (Subject)—The consideration or examination of each component or individual part of a thing, object, or organization, either separately or in their relation to the whole. In forms control, analysis is used as a subject when the analysis itself is the subject matter of the form rather than the thing or object being analyzed. When the thing or object is identifiable, file the form under the subject, modified by "Analysis of," as an operation.

Analysis of (operation)—The act of determining one or more qualities, or separating one or more ingredients of a substance as to kind, amount, weight, hardness, strength, etc. In forms control the distinction between the operations "Analysis of," "Examination of," and "Inspection of" should be carefully noted. "Analysis of" refers only to inanimate things, figures, statistics, substances, and the determination of the identity and characteristics of their ingredients. "Examination of" refers to the determination of the physical or mental qualifications or fitness of an individual, and is used only in relation to persons. "Inspection of" refers to scrutiny of inanimate objects or substances to determine their consistency with set standards of quality. See also "Examination of," "Inspection of," "Rating of," and also the definitions of "Sample" and "Specimen."

The operation "Analysis of" is not treated as an operation when used in relation to persons but is included in the operation "Rating of" under the subject "Employee" or other applicable subjects.

Annual Statement (form)—The annual statement or report made by a company of the details of its business at the close of the calendar year, stating the company's receipts and disbursements, assets and liabilities. The annual report in a condensed form may be issued to the stockholders of the company. File under "Company, Status of."

Annul, to (function)—To reduce to nothing; to annihilate; to make void or of no effect; to nullify. Use the function "To Cancel."

Appeal (form)—A form the function of which is to appeal; to seek aid, consideration or decision, usually from someone in authority. In forms control, such forms should be classified under the function "To Apply" and the specific subjects under that function.

Applicant (subject)—One who applies for something; a petitioner. In forms control an applicant will most commonly be applying for employment but may also be applying for a loan, membership, or any one of several other things.

Application (form)—A form the function of which is to apply for something; a petition. In forms control, applications should be classified under the function "To Apply" and the specific subjects under that function.

Forms that are supplemental to insurance applications and become part of the application when it is made out should be filed as applications with the subject and the condition "Insurance of" with the function "To Request." If the form furnishes information about the applicant, file under "Applicant, Information About, to Report." Such information will not be made part of the policy and should not be filed as applications even though the information may be used as the basis of a rate or premium.

If the insurance has been issued and the information is for the possible extension or change of the policy, file under "Insurance, Information About," and the proper function. When a form changes the existing coverage use "Insurance, Adjustment, Correction of" and the proper function. Forms that report data about buildings, property, premiums, etc., are sometimes entitled "Applications" but unless they actually are applications they should be filed under the pertinent subjects (property, etc.) "Status of" and the proper function.

Applications for liability insurance need not carry the signature of the applicant but are signed by the agent.

Application for (operation)—The act of applying for something.

Application of (operation)—See "Use of."

Apply, to (function)—To make application for something that may or may not be granted; to ask consideration—usually a request made without formal authority to demand action, to be decided under conditions beyond control of the applicant as opposed to "To Request," where action may definitely be expected as a result.

Appointment (subject)—An arrangement or engagement for a meeting; the designation by authority of a person to a place or position.

Appointment of (operation)—To assign, designate, or set apart by authority.

Appraisal of (operation)—The act of establishing a value on "Land and Buildings," "Premises," and "Housing." When the form refers to Machinery and Equipment and other contents of the above, use the specific subject that applies and the conditions "Value of."

Appraise, to (function)—To estimate; conjecture; to set a value on. Use "To Estimate."

Appropriation (subject)—An amount of money set aside or allocated for a specific purpose, usually a project. In forms control "Appropriation" should be used only when the appropriations themselves are the subject of the form and not when the project itself is the subject. In the latter case use "Project" as the subject and "Cost of" as a condition.

Appropriation of (operation)—To set apart for, or to assign to a particular purpose.

Approval of (operation)—The act of approving; to grant approval.

Ask, to (function)—To interrogate or inquire of as concerning; to put a question to or about; to question. Use "To Request."

Assets (subject)—All the property of a person, firm, or estate that may be used to pay up his or its debts; property in general or any piece of property.

Since assets are made up of things, the word "assets" is normally not used in forms control as a subject. Use instead the particular thing that represents the asset (i.e., machinery and equipment, land or buildings, etc.).

Use the subject "Assets" if it is not possible to identify the particular assets referred to.

Assigned Risk (subject)—A risk that underwriters do not choose to insure but that, because of state law or otherwise, must be insured. The insurance, therefore, is handled through a pool of underwriters and assigned to companies in turn. Classify the same as "risk."

Assignment of (operation)—The act or process of making over or transferring one's right, title, or interest in property or anything of value to someone else.

Assured (subject)—See "Insured."

Attendance of (condition)—The fact of being present or in attendance. In forms control, attendance is seldom recorded as such but is implied in the reverse "Absence of." All absence records indicate the attendance of the person or employee on all days when he or she was not absent. All forms recording attendance or absence should be filed under "Employee, Absence of."

Attest, to (function)—To bear witness; to certify; to affirm to be true or genuine; to authenticate officially. Use "To Certify."

Audit (subject)—A report made as the result of auditing the records of accounts of a business organization. In forms control "Audit" can be used only when the report itself is the subject of consideration, not when the operation "Audit of" is involved.

Audit of (operation)—The act or process of formally and officially examining and authenticating the records of account of a business organization.

Authorization (form)—A form the function of which is to authorize; a formal writing to provide authority or right to act, to empower, or to legalize. In forms control, authorizations should be classified under ''To Authorize'' and the specific subjects under that function.

Authorize, to (function)—To permit, allow, or make possible in an action; to clothe with authority; to grant license or liberty; usually where subsequent action is mandatory.

Automobile—See ''Machinery/Equipment.''

Availability of (condition)—The state of being available; accessible, attainable, ready.

Award (subject)—A granting or giving after due deliberation and consideration of relative merit; that which is awarded. Includes all types of recognition of achievement. See also ''Benefits.''

Back-Order of (operation)—The act of holding an order in reserve or in a state of restraint, usually after part of the order has already been delivered.

Bad Debt (subject)—An account receivable determined to be uncollectable. ''Bad Debt'' is usually also an item of expense in the accounts of the company. If the bad debt is being considered as an account receivable, file the form under that subject. If it is considered as an expense in the operations of the company, file under the subject ''Costs.''

Bail Bond (subject)—A bond that guarantees the appearance of a person in court to answer to a legal summons. Treat the same as ''Bond.''

Bank (subject)—An organization formed for the purpose of carrying on banking operations. Banks may be of the commercial or savings type with somewhat different functions. Federal Reserve banks perform even different functions. The subject ''Bank'' should be used in the same manner as ''Company.'' See that definition.

Bank Account (subject)—An individual's or business organization's account with a bank or financial institution. In forms control, ''Bank Account'' refers to the account only, and not to the cash or its equivalent on deposit in the account. See also ''Account.''

Bank Check (subject)—A written order directing a bank or banker to pay money as therein stated; a bill of exchange drawn upon a banker payable upon demand. When used as a subject in forms control, ''Bank Check'' refers to the checks themselves and not to their equivalent cash. Bank Checks should be filed under the subject ''Cash,'' the operation ''Payment of,'' and the function ''To Order.'' They should not be filed under the subject ''Bank Check.''

Batch Header (form)—Term for a document or form used as the lead document in a collection of checks, drafts, or other similar documents. It is usually used in machine operations, such as sorting, and may contain magnetic ink identification relating to the following or subsequent documents. Classify under the subject ''Records'' or a more specific subject and the function ''To Identify.'' Ordinarily a condition or operation is not necessary.

Batch Separator (form)—Similar to a batch header except that it separates the records into subgroups instead of heading up the entire lot. Classify the same as batch header.

Beneficiary (subject)—One who receives anything as a gift; one who receives a benefit or advantage; the person designated to receive the income or proceeds of a trust, estate, insurance policy, etc.

Benefit Plan (subject)—A plan, organization, or association by which life insurance, sick allowances, the payment of funeral expenses, provision for old age, recreational or social privileges, or other similar benefits are secured by means of regular dues or special assessments, to be paid by the members (employees of a specific company, usually) of the plan. In forms control, all insurance and savings plans and "employees' Associations" in general are grouped under this category, including those of purely social or recreational character. Forms pertaining to the plan, organization, or association itself, or membership or affiliation in it, or activities, are classified under this subject. Forms pertaining to the benefits or privileges themselves should be classified by specific subject.

Benefits (subject)—Remuneration due or paid to someone as the result of the sustenance of a loss, usually arising out of the hazard against which the person was insured. Care must be taken not to confuse the loss sustained with the benefits that may be claimed or paid. In many instances the same form may be used to report the loss and claim the benefit. All forms for reporting loss due to the occurrence of a hazard should be filed under the subject "Loss" and not under "Benefits." See also "Awards."

If the form is for the purpose of claiming benefits as the result of a loss use "Benefits, To Claim." If the benefits relate to employment benefit plans use the subject "Employee Benefits."

Bid (subject)—A quoted price. In forms control, "Bid" is not used as a subject. Use "Quotation" or "Price" as defined under these subjects instead.

Bill (form)—A form the purpose of which is to set forth an account of goods sold, services rendered, or work done, with the price or charge; a statement of a creditors's claim in gross or by items. In forms control, bills are classified under "To Notify" and the specific subjects under that function. See also "Invoice."

Bill of Lading (form)—A type of delivery receipt on which the carrier acknowledges receipt of the material from the consignor. Additional copies serve functions other than "To Acknowledge," which is the function of the original or first part of the form. Other functions may include "To Order" (i.e., one copy serves as a shipping order); "To Record" (i.e., a memorandum or record of the bill of lading itself to go to accounting, traffic, or shipping departments). The shipping order copy is retained by the carrier while the original signed by the agent of the carrier, goes back to the consignor. Bills of lading are standard, being adopted as such by common carriers or the Interstate Commerce Commission and usually carry a statement of conditions and liabilities on the reverse side. Some bills of lading are made up in combination with invoices or acknowledgments of the order, in which case the form should be cross-referenced from the file "To Acknowledge" to the files "To Notify," etc.

Bill of Material (form)—A detailed listing of all parts and part numbers required for the processing of a product through materials and supplies and work-in-process. In forms control, all "Bill of Material" forms should be filed under the specific subject to which they pertain, the condition "Specifications of," and the function "To Notify."

Binder (subject)—A preliminary agreement to provide immediate insurance until a policy can be written. It should contain the elements of the insurance policy itself. In forms control, the binder should be treated the same as the policy.

Birth of (operation)—The act or fact of coming into life or existence—being born.

Blue Print—See "Print."

Bond (form)—An instrument made by a government or corporation as an evidence of debt, usually for the purpose of borrowing money; any interest-bearing instrument issued by a corporation. In forms control, forms pertaining to "Bonds," used in the sense of a security or invest-ment, should be classified under the subject "Securities." See also "Securities."

Also, a writing under seal by which a person binds himself to pay a certain sum of money on or before a certain day in the future. Usually a condition is added that if the obligor shall do (or abstain from doing) a certain act on or before the time specified, the obligation shall be void, but otherwise shall remain in full force. In forms control, forms pertaining to the subject "Bond" when used in the sense of a person's bond should be classified under the subject "Bond." When the form relates to the person being bonded, file under the subject "Person," the operation "Insurance of," and the function "To Agree."

Book (subject)—A written or printed narrative, record, representation, or series of these, designed to perpetuate information or literary art, and bound together for some degree of permanency.

Bordereau (form)—A form used in insurance containing summary informa-tion concerning insurance policies and the details of insurance represented thereby. Classify under "Insurance," "Information About" and "To Re-port" or "To Record."

Budget (form)—A form of financial statement, the purpose of which is to set forth the position or condition of a business organization, or measures proposed by it. A budget is not necessarily limited in scope to matters of a purely financial or accounting character. In forms control, budgets as such should be classified under "To Estimate" and the specific subjects under that function. See also "Costs," "Payment of," and "Cash."

Budget (subject)—An estimate of probable income and/or expenditure for a given period.

Budget of (operation)—The act or process of setting forth the position or condition of a business organization, or measures proposed by it; the act of estimating probable income and expenditure for a given period, with proposals for maintaining a proper balance between the totals. In forms control, the operation "Budget of" is used in a broad sense to include all items that may fall under budgetary control (i.e., personnel, payroll, and office expense, etc.). Use the subject affected and the operation "Budget of" following that subject.

Building—See "Land and Buildings." A structure designed to stand more or less permanently, and covering a space of land, for use as a dwelling, storehouse, factory, or some other useful purpose. In forms control, forms pertaining to buildings as such should be classified under the subject "Land and Buildings."

Bulletin (form)—A form the function of which is to set forth authoritative and formal statements of operation, policy, or conduct, usually pertaining to a specific subject and its treatment, in the business organization. In forms control, bulletins can be classified under any one of four subjects: "Procedure," "Policy," "Rules and Regulations," or "News," depending on the type of material the bulletin form is designed to carry. The definitions and distinctions of these four subjects should be reviewed before final disposition of a bulletin form is made. Bulletins should be classified under the function "To Order" or "To Notify" and one of the four subjects listed above.

Burden (subject)—See "Overhead."

Calculate, to (function)—To reckon; to estimate, compute; to form as estimate or make a calculation. Use the function "To Estimate."

Calibration of (operation)—The act or process of determining, checking, or rectifying the graduations of any instrument giving quantitative measurements.

Call Sales (subject)—A call made on a prospect. See also "Contact."

Call, Telephone—See "Communication."

Cancel, to (function)—To cause or bring about the annulment, revocation, or recall of things; to abolish or repeal things or former actions.

Cancellation (form)—A form the function of which is to cancel, annul, revoke, recall, or deprive of validity. In forms control, cancellations should be classified under "To Cancel" and the specific subjects under that function, unless the cancellation forms themselves are the subject under consideration, in which case the form dealing with the cancellations may be filed under the subject "Cancellation."

Cancellation of (operation)—The act or process of bringing about the annulment, revocation, or recall of something.

Candidate (subject)—One who offers himself or herself or is put forward as an aspirant or contestant for an office, privilege, or honor.

Car—See "Railroad Car."

Cargo (subject)—The lading or freight of a car, truck, ship, or other vessel; the goods, merchandise, or whatever is conveyed in a vessel or boat. The term "Cargo," in law, is usually applied to goods only, and not to live animals or persons. In forms control, forms pertaining to cargo should be classified under the specific subject being conveyed (i.e., merchandise, materials, supplies, machinery, equipment, etc.), followed by the operation "Transportation of." If what makes up the cargo cannot be identified as a specific subject, which will normally be the case, classify under the subject "Shipment."

Carrier (subject)—A person or company in the transportation business. In insurance this is an insurance company that "Carries" the insurance.

Cash (subject)—Coin or specie, bank notes, drafts, or commercial paper easily convertible into money. In forms control, the subject "Cash" includes coin and specie and all other items equivalent to coin and specie. Thus, for example, the subject "Cash" includes all items normally handled through the "Cash Account" on the books of the company.

Forms dealing with cash or determining how much cash is to be needed or handled should not be confused with that for which the cash is spent. For example, forms dealing with requests for "Project Appropriations" are "Cash," not "Project."

Wages and salaries are considered as "Earnings" prior to the time of actual payment, but are considered as "Cash" when cash or its equivalent actually enters the picture as the medium of payment.

Cash Item (subject)—Term used in banking to indicate checks and other negotiable instruments or documents of value, usually in terms of collection or being sent elsewhere for collection. In addition to checks, cash items may include drafts, trade acceptances, bills of lading, warehouse receipts, insurance certificates, etc.

Use the subject "Cash Items" only when the documents are not specifically identifiable or when more than one type of document is included.

Cash receipt (form)—A form the purpose of which is to acknowledge that someone has paid money to someone else. Both the functions of receiving and paying are involved since the money could not be paid unless it was also received. Since the form is usually given to the person who made the payment as his or her evidence of the payment, such forms are to be filed under the subject "Cash," the operation "Receipt of," and the function "To Acknowledge."

Certificate (form)—A form the function of which is to certify, as a written declaration legally authenticated, or a certified statement; a written testimony to the truth of any fact; or anything that produces the same result as such a document. In forms control, certificates should be classified under the function "To Certify" and the specific subjects under that function.

Certificate (subject)—A written declaration legally authenticated; a certified statement; a written testimony to the truth of any fact, or anything that produces the same result as such a document. When used as a subject in forms control, "Certificate" refers to the certificate only, not to that which is certified. See also "Record."

Certification of (operation)—To prove to be true; to confirm; to substantiate or test the accuracy or exactness of. See also "To Certify."

Certify, to (function)—To attest, verify, endorse, or guarantee authoritatively, usually applying to existing or past conditions as opposed to "To Agree," which applies to future conditions.

Change of (operation)—To alter, to make different, to cause to pass from one state to another. In forms control the distinction between the operations "Change of" and "Adjustment—Correction of" should be carefully noted. "Change of" involves action only in the sense of alteration, whereas "Adjustment—Correction of" involves action because the existing state, for some reason, is wrong and must be corrected or adjusted.

Charge to (operation)—See "Debit to."

Charges (subject)—See "Costs."

Charge-off of (operation)—The act of writing off an account or any item or part of the account for any reason. Usually this operation takes place in accounting practice in relation to accounts receivable after continued failure to collect, but it is not necessarily limited to that subject. The Term "Charge-off" should not be confused with the operation "Termination Of." An account can be subjected to a charge-off without being terminated.

Check (form)—A form that may have any one of several purposes or functions depending upon its makeup and usage. If used to direct or order a bank or banker to pay money as therein stated upon demand, it is classified under the function "To Order," the subject "Cash," and the operation "Payment Of." If used to prove ownership or title, or to identify something as a coat, hat, etc., it is classified under the function "To Claim," the subject "Personal Property." If used to set forth an account or itemized statement of merchandise with the charges or prices indicated and totaled, as in restaurants, taverns, etc., it is classified under the function "To Notify" and the specific subjects under that function. See also "Bank Check," "Personal Property Check," and "Waiter's (Food and Beverage) Check," as the case may be.

Check (subject)—See and use the definition now under the term "Bank Check." Let "Bank Check" cross-reference to "Check." See also "Cash Item."

Check List (form)—A form, usually containing a list of items to be checked for completion. File under the applicable subject and operation or condition with the function "To Follow-Up."

Check-off (subject)—Term used by unions and management to indicate sums withheld from employees' earnings and turned over to the union as dues or other payments. Do not use as a subject. Use "Earnings," "Withholding of."

Citizenship of (condition)—The state or quality of being a citizen. In forms control, the condition "Citizenship of" is usually used in relation to the subject "Employee."

Claim (form)—A form the purpose of which is to claim, or to demand a right or supposed right; or to call on another for something due or supposed to be due; or to assert a right or fact. In forms control, claims should be classified under the function "To Claim" and the specific subjects under that function.

Claim (subject)—A demand or a calling on another for something due or supposed to be due, or a right or supposed right, or an assertion of a right or fact. In forms control, the subject "Claim" applies only in those cases when the claim as such is the subject matter of the form involved rather than to the subject to which the claim pertains. In the latter case file the form under the subject to which the claim applies and the function "To Claim." If the major purpose of the form is to claim benefits from an insurance policy, use "Benefits, to Claim."

In insurance, all forms used for the purpose of reporting the details of a loss as the result of the occurrence of a hazard should be filed under the subject "Loss" even though there may be, and usually is, a secondary function of claiming benefits as the result of the loss.

Forms relating the details of the loss are usually entitled "Proof of Loss." These forms should be classified under 'Loss." If a form deals only with the claim as such, or is predominately concerned with the amount of money being claimed as the result of the loss, it should be filed under "Benefits, to Claim." Only when a form deals with the loss with no substantial reference to the claim should they be filed under "Loss."

Claim, to (function)—To ask for or seek to obtain something in the possession of another; to demand something due or supposed to be due, usually when there is actual or potential question as to the right of possession or justification for the claim.

Class (subject)—A group of persons brought together for a common purpose such as a school class engaged in learning; things or objects of similar characteristics grouped together for common identification.

Classification (subject)—This term is used in some instances to indicate the special trade or occupation followed or practiced by anyone. In forms control, this subject is not used as such but rather is included in the subject "Job."

It may also apply to either aspects of persons, things or objects, in which case file under the applicable subject.

Classification of (operation)—To arrange in a class or classes; to assign to a given category.

Clearance of (operation)—The act of clearing; testifying that certain conditions have been met and that subsequent action is thereby in order.

Closing of (operation)—The termination or bringing to an end of a relationship, such as a business relationship or a physical part of the business, such as an office or branch operation.

Code (subject)—An organized method of communication, usually in a secretive or esoteric form not understandable by others than those for whom the message is intended; a system of symbols for use in manual procedures charting or in computerized information handling.

Collateral (subject)—The designation of some tangible or physical security, such as stocks or bonds, property or real estate, against the payment of an obligation, such as a note, to ensure that the terms of payment will be met.

In forms control, the subject ''Collateral'' is used only when the security is specified as being given against the payment of the obligation. When the security is itself the subject of the form, use the subject ''Security'' or the stocks or bonds or property that makes up the security.

Collection of (operation)—The act of demanding and obtaining payment of, as an account, or other indebtedness; the act of collecting, gathering, or accumulating together. In banks, the act of sending through bank channels for payment.

Commission (subject)—Reward, usually in the form of cash or its equivalent, for work or services rendered, usually predicated on the amount of sales resulting from the effort expended. In forms control the subject ''Commissions'' is included in the subject ''Earnings.''

Commission, to (function)—To give a commission to; to appoint and authorize. Use the function ''To Authorize.''

Committee (subject)—A person or group of persons elected or appointed to investigate, report, or act in special cases. In forms control, ''Committee'' is used as a subject only when forms deal with the committee itself and not to the findings or reports they may submit.

Commodity (subject)—An item of commerce; goods or products handled, sold, or transferred in the conduct of business. Use the term ''Product'' instead of ''Commodity.'' See ''Product.''

Communication (subject)—That which is communicated or imparted, as intelligence or news; a verbal or written message. Telephone or telegraph messages should be filed under the function ''To Notify,'' ''To Report,'' ''To Record,'' etc., the subject ''Communication,'' and the operation ''Receipt of,'' ''Transmittal of,'' etc.

Community (subject)—A number of people living within a circumscribed area or related by geographic, historical, or cultural limits, usually having the same or similar interests or intentions.

Company (subject)—An organization formed for the purpose of carrying on a business. In forms control the subject ''Company'' should be used only when the organization as a whole is the subject of the form, such as a financial statement of the company. See also ''Organization.''

Complaints—Trouble (subject)—An expression of grief, regret, censure, grievance, or resentment; a formal allegation or charge against a party; a statement of trouble, uneasiness, annoyance, disturbance, misfortune, or embarrassment. In forms control, expressions of grief, uneasiness, or complaint from employees in regard to their personal status are treated as a "Grievance." All reports of grief, annoyance, disturbance, etc. from any source other than employees are treated as "Complaints—Trouble." See also "Grievance."

Completion of (operation)—The act of completing or making complete. Example: "Completion of," "To Request."

Computation of (operation)—The act or process of computing; the finding of a result through reckoning or calculation.

Compute, to (function)—To determine by calculation, to reckon or count. Use the function "To Estimate."

Conditions (form)—A form the function of which is to formally set forth something established, or agreed upon, as a requisite to the doing or taking effect of something else, as stipulations or provisions. A good example is "Conditions of Employment," or the conditions of a purchase order, printed separately, but afterward attached to, and made a part of, the purchase order. In forms control, such forms are classified under "To Agree" and the specific subjects under that function. The example noted would be classified under the function "To Agree," the subjects, "Employment," or "Purchase."

Condition of—See "Status of."

Confirm, to (function)—To strengthen, establish, ratify, sanction, or corroborate something. Use the function "To Certify."

Confirmation (form)—A form the function of which is to confirm, strengthen, establish, ratify, sanction, corroborate, or verify something, usually a statement, position, or action. In forms control, confirmations should be classified under the function "To Certify" and the specific subjects under that function.

Consent, to (function)—To agree; to give assent or approval. Use the function "To Agree."

Contact (subject)—A personal visit, meeting, telephone call, or other contact between two or more persons, or with a prospect or customer in the course of business or for other purposes. The subject "Contact" is broad in nature and can be used collectively if desired. However, if the number of forms in the category becomes large a further breakdown can be made. Sales calls forms can be filed under that subject (see definition) or under "Entertainment" if that applies.

Container (subject)—A vessel, bottle, drum, or other receptacle used to hold materials. In forms control, it is treated as a separate subject only when there are sufficient forms to classify as such. Otherwise file under the subject "Material and Supplies."

Contents of (condition)—That which is contained inside of something else.

Contract, to (function)—To enter into with mutual obligations; to establish or undertake by contract; to make a contract. Use the function "To Agree."

Contract (subject)—A written agreement under which something will or will not be done for consideration. In forms control, "Contract" is used as a subject only when the agreement papers themselves are the subject of another form.

Contribution (subject)—Something of value, usually money, given voluntarily for a special purpose, such as donations to charity or employee, or company contributions to pension funds, etc. In forms control, "Contribution" is used as a subject only when the form deals with the donation, and not to the requesting, etc., of contributions, in which case the subject would be "Cash."

Control (subject)—A method of checking or regulating something; to keep within the limits of prescribed boundaries; in banking or other business it may take the form of an account in a general ledger used to carry the total of several subaccounts. Anything affecting the subsidiary accounts will be reflected in the control account, thereby giving the control.

Control of (operation)—The act of controlling something.

Correction of (operation)—See "Adjustment or Correction Of." The act or process of correcting, or making that right which was wrong. In forms control, the term "Correction" is not treated as a specific operation, but is included in the operation "Adjustment, Correction Of."

Correctness of (condition)—The state of being correct or without error.

Correspondence (subject)—See "Records." The actual records (i.e., letters, postcards, etc.) that pass between correspondents; the tangible instrument of communication upon which the message is transmitted. In forms control, correspondence as such should be classified under the subject "Records." See also "Records."

Correspondence should be treated as a subject only after the letterhead, memo, etc., has been filled in, and the body material thereof constitutes correspondence. Letterheads, etc., before use should be filed under a special category "Letterheads," "Memoranda," "Envelopes," "Postal Cards," etc.

Correspondence should be used as a subject only when the body or subject matter of that correspondence, or a group or correspondence as a whole, is the subject. Forms relating to correspondence in this sense may be filed under "Correspondence."

Cost of (condition)—Cost or costs as they apply to a given specific item. In forms control, only those forms that relate solely to costs of such a specific item should be filed under the subject modified by the condition "Cost of." An example is travel expenses. When such costs are under consideration, they should be filed under the subject "Travel" and the condition "Cost of." When costs cannot be identified with a specific, individual subject, they should be filed under the general subject "Costs."

Costs (subject)—The amount or equivalent paid, given, charged, or engaged to be paid or given, for anything bought or taken in barter, or for service rendered; the expenditure or outlay as of money, time, labor, etc., usually measured in dollar value; or, that which has involved the expenditure of money, labor, time, etc.

Forms pertaining to costs should be filed under the subject "Costs" only when they are accounting forms that recapitulate or list costs in accounts—journal, ledger, etc. See also "Cost of" (condition).

Course (subject)—A program of instruction or learning, as in a school or learning effort.

Coverage of (condition)—To comprehend, include, or embrace. In banking, the amount of resources to meet liabilities.

Credit, to (operation)—The act or process of recording payment by entering in an account; to give credit for, or to place to the credit of. The subject to which this operation applies will vary, usually being merchandise, supplies, etc. Although the act of crediting is actually done in an account (receivable, payable, general, etc.) the operation actually applies to the specific subject, not to the account. Thus a form may be filed under the subject "Account," the operation "Credit to," and the function "To Notify." When the credit is indicated as an operation but the subject is not definable, the subject may then be considered as "Account Receivable." See also "Debit–Credit to" (operation).

Credit (subject)—Trust given or received; expectation of future payment for property transferred, or of fulfillment of promise given; the relation between one person and another who trusts in him or her to pay or render something in the future; the commercial reputation entitling one to be trusted, as to buy goods on credit.

Use "Credit" as a subject only when the person or organization to which the credit applies cannot be identified. When it can be identified use that subject with the condition "Credit of."

Credit Card (subject)—An identification card that entitles the bearer to credit within stated limits of time or amount. As in the case of all forms, the subject "Record" should be used, assuming that the form being filed relates to the credit card itself and not to some other subject, until the number of forms in the "Record" category indicates the need for a further breakdown.

Credit Memorandum (form)—A form used to notify some person, usually a customer, that an account has been credited in some manner. It may also be used to credit other accounts within the same accounting system. In forms control, the "Credit Memorandum" should be filed under the particular subject to which it applies, the operation "Credit to," and the function "To Notify." The operation may, in some instances, be other than "Credit to" (i.e., "Return of," etc). If the "Credit Memorandum" cannot be identified as dealing with some specific subject, file under the subject "Accounts Receivable." In some cases this might also change and become "Accounts Payable" or "General."

Credit of (condition)—The status of any particular person or organization in relation to credit. See also "Credit."

Cross-up—A term used in commercial banking to indicate a certain type of error on the paperwork of the bank. Classify forms having to do with this subject under "Error."

Curriculum (subject)—A specified, fixed course of study.

Customer (subject)—One who regularly or repeatedly makes a purchase of, or has business dealings with, a tradesperson or business house; a buyer or purchaser; a patron.

In forms control, forms keeping a record of sales by customer rather than by sales irrespective of customer should be filed under the subject "Customer" rather than "Sales."

Customer Service (subject)—The performance of labor for the benefit of another, or at another's command, usually with nominal or no charge in view of the fact that the labor is performed on things or objects sold to the customer as merchandise. Customer service may, under varying circumstances, take on the aspects of repair if the thing or object sold has been damaged through no fault of the customer or is faulty for some reason or other, or maintenance if it is only a matter of keeping the object sold in good working condition, or adjustment if only a matter of assuring installation to obtain the maximum degree of efficiency. The type of service rendered by the business organization usually depends entirely upon the product sold and prevailing practice of the industry.

Customer service does not include repair work done at a fixed schedule of prices with no relation to the carrying out of a performance guarantee or warranty. Forms applying to such repair should be filed under the subject "Work."

Damage to (condition)—The state of being damaged, usually as the result of an accident. In forms control, the condition "Damage to" applies only to inanimate objects or things, such as equipment or property, never to individuals or persons. See also "Injury—Illness."

Damages (subject)—The estimated or actual reparation in money for injury sustained.

Dealer—Use "Agent."

Death of (condition)—State of being deceased; the cessation of physical life.

Debit, to (operation)—The act or process of recording a charge or debit by entering in an account; to charge with or to enter on the debtor (debit) side of the account.

Debit—Credit, to (operation)—The act or process of charging or debiting an account and for crediting an account. In forms control, this operation is to be used only when a form can be used for either debiting or crediting an account; or when a form recaps debits and credits to an account or group of accounts without reference to the resultant balance of the account or group of accounts.

Debit memorandum (form)—A form used to notify some person, usually a customer, that an account has been debited in some manner. May also be used to debit other accounts within the same accounting system. In forms control, the "Debit Memorandum" should be filed under the subject to which it applies (i.e., Merchandise, Supplies, etc.), the operation involved (i.e., Rejection of, Return of, etc.), and the function "To Notify." If the memo cannot be identified as dealing with a particular subject, file under the proper account as a subject (i.e., Accounts Payable, Accounts Receivable, Accounts General, etc.), the operation "Debit to," and the function "To Notify."

Declaration (form)—A form the purpose of which is to declare, proclaim, or make an explicit assertion; the instrument of such formal expression. In forms control, declarations should be classified under "To Certify" and the specific subjects under that function.

Deduction of (operation)—The act of taking away; separating; removing; subtracting; or setting apart.

Deferment of (condition)—The state of being deferred; a delay or postponement. In forms control, the condition "Deferment Of," is usually used with the subject "Employee" and has to do with "postponement of induction into the armed forces under a Selective Service Act.

Delay of (operation)—To put off, postpone, defer, to prolong the time of or before, to procrastinate.

Delinquency of (condition)—The state of being in arrears, the failure to meet an obligation within the specified time.

Delivery of (operation)—The act of putting merchandise, goods, or commodities into the possession of another.

A distinction should be drawn between the operations "Delivery of," "Transportation of," and "Shipping of." "Transportation of" applies to the physical act or means of transporting things. "Shipping of" applies to the preparation of the things for transportation and "Delivery of" applies to the overall act of getting or putting things into the possession of another. Thus, a requisition may request the delivery of supplies and this may subsequently entail a shipping order for preparing the supplies and a trucking order for its actual transportation whereby the delivery is completed.

The operation "Delivery of" should, therefore, be applied only when the overall operation is involved and not when the limited operations of shipping or transportation are involved. See "Requisition" (form).

Delivery Receipt (form)—A form used to acknowledge the receipt of material delivered by one means or another. Usually made up in more than one part, the additional parts serving functions other than "To Acknowledge." Copies usually include one for the consignee as a record of material received and for which he or she has receipted. Another copy may serve as a freight bill for the carrier. See also "Bill of Lading."

Demand to (function)—To ask or call for with authority; to claim as due. Use the function "To Claim."

Demonstration of (operation)—The act or process of demonstrating, usually for the purpose of showing the characteristic or quality of a product.

Demurrage (subject)—Charge made against transportation equipment when waiting for loading or unloading. Forms pertaining to demurrage should be filed under this subject and the proper functions.

Department (subject)—A subdivision of an organization performing a single part of the total work of the whole organization. When a form deals with the reporting of various factors or the general condition of a department, file under the subject "Department." See also "Organization."

When a report is of a single factor or a few closely related factors, file under the more specific subject. Example: "Production," "Time," etc. (Also see "Production.")

Departure of (operation)—A departing or going away; hence, a setting out, as on a journey. Usually relating to persons and never to inanimate objects.

Dependent (subject)—One who is dependent upon another for something. Examples in forms control are dependent persons in income tax withholding and in certain insurance forms.

Deposit (subject)—That which is placed anywhere, or in anyone's hands, for safekeeping; something entrusted to the care of another; anything given as a pledge or security. In forms control, use the term "Deposit" as a subject only when the specific thing being deposited is not identifiable and, therefore, cannot be treated as a particular subject to be followed by the operation "Deposit of" (i.e., "Personal Property, Deposit of").

Deposit of (operation)—The act of lodging something, for safekeeping or as a pledge; to commit to custody, or to instruct as to put on deposit in a bank.

Depreciation (subject)—A predetermined reduction in the value of a capital investment of a business organization. In accounting practice, depreciation is usually considered as a subject in itself, but in forms control, it is not so treated because it always applies to some object or thing that is in itself identifiable as a subject. The thing or object therefore becomes the subject, and depreciation is treated as an operation applying to the subject." See also "Depreciation of."

Depreciation of (operation)—The act or process of reducing the capital investment of a business organization according to a predetermined schedule, which ordinarily considers the original cost, the estimated salvage value, and the estimated life or depreciation period. In forms control, the forms classified under this category should not be confused with forms pertaining solely to the capital investment. For instance, "Equipment Ledger" forms normally make provision for a record of the depreciation taken on the specific item of equipment named but are classified under the subject "Machinery—Equipment," and the function "To Record." On the other hand, a form devised to schedule depreciation on certain items of capital investment such as machinery—equipment will be classified under the subject "Machinery and Equipment," the operation "Depreciation of," and the function "To Schedule."

Description of (operation or condition)—The act of describing a person, thing, or object or a written description of it.

Design of (operation)—The act or process of drawing, outlining, or sketching as a conception or plan; the act of artistic invention or the artistic idea as executed.

Designation of—See "Appointment of."

Destination of (condition)—The place set for the end of a journey, or to which something is sent. In forms control, the condition "Destination of" is that place or location, stated or inferred, to which the subject is being sent, and becomes a specification or limitation of the subject.

Destruction of (operation)—The act of destroying, ruining, or spoiling.

Development of (operation)—The act of developing or disclosing that which is unknown. A gradual unfolding process by which anything is developed. In forms control, this would apply chiefly to the improvement of an old product or the introduction of new products, and should be filed under the subject "Product."

Dictation (subject)—The act of telling, uttering, or mechanical recording so that another may write down; that which is dictated.

Die (subject)—A device for cutting or forming material.

Diploma (subject)—A document awarded by a school to a student who has satisfactorily completed a prescribed course of learning; a certificate of achievement.

Disbursement of (operation)—The act of disbursing or expending or paying out. In forms control, the term "Disbursement of" is not treated as a specific operation, but is included in the operation "Payment of."

Discount of (operation)—To deduct from an account, debt, charge, or the like; to make or take an allowance, usually at a predetermined rate.

Disposition of (operation)—The act of disposing, the state or manner of disposal. In forms control, a careful distinction should be made between the operations "Disposition of" and "Distribution of." The operation "Disposition of" has to do with or implies final disposal, whereas "Distribution of" refers to a separation for allocation for further use or action.

Distribution of (operation)—Act of distributing; state of being distributed.

Distributor (subject)—One engaged in the general distribution or marketing of some article or class of goods. One who distributes the manufacturer's products.

Dividend (subject)—A sum of money or quantity of commodities to be divided and distributed; the share that falls to each individual. In insurance, the share of surplus earned by or allocated to any policy.

Division—A part of a company larger than a department but less than the company as a whole. When the subject covers the general operations of a division in an industrial company use the subject "Plant." In insurance companies or financial institutions use "Department" or "Company," whichever seems the more appropriate.

Document (subject)—A piece of paper on which has been recorded information or data to be preserved. The term is often used in a special sense, implying something special or important, as a legal document. Documents are included under the subject "Records."

Donation—See "Gift."

Draft (subject)—An order from one person or party to another directing the payment of money. A draft can be drawn on a person whereas checks are drawn on a bank as an order to pay cash. In forms control drafts and checks are normally classified together since each orders or directs the payment of cash.

Drawing (subject)—That which is drawn; a representation drawn by pen or pencil; sometimes, a slight or preliminary representation, as a sketch. In forms control, the subject "Drawing" does not include reproductions made from drawings; such reproductions, regardless of how made, are treated as "Prints." See also "Prints."

Drilling (subject)—The act or process of performing work necessary to sinking or drilling a well. Encountered mostly in the oil and gas industry. File under the subject "Work."

Dues (subject)—That which is due or owed, especially pertaining to membership in an organization or society, as membership dues. In forms control, forms pertaining to dues should be filed under the subject "Cash."

Duty (subject)—An impost or customs recoverable by law, as upon goods imported, exported, or consumed. Use the subject "Tax."

Earnings (subject)—Wages or reward gained by work or services. That to which the employee is entitled after having performed work or service. In forms control, the distinction between the subjects "Earnings" and "Cash" should be carefully noted. "Earnings" is that to which the employee is entitled after having performed work or services, and is not in itself cash although usually measured in dollars and cents. On the other hand, when the actual payment to the employee for his services is considered, cash, or its equivalent, is normally used to meet the liability.

There can, however, be exceptions to the matter of actual payment of the employee in cash or its equivalent. For instance, a part-time employee might work for room and board, and obviously, under those circumstances, no cash, as such, would ever pass between the employer and the employee. However, under even those circumstances, one can assume that the cash value of the room and board was given to the employee, and that the employee, in turn, reimbursed the employer for room and board. The important thing to remember is that "Cash" is coin or specie, or its equivalent in commercial paper, and that "Earnings," while measured in cash value, is not actually cash. See also "Cash."

Earnings (subject)—The excess of income in relation to cost in any transaction, or series of transactions; the excess of income in relation to costs as in a business, or any of its departments, during a given period of time; or, any benefit or advantage, usually measured in dollar value, accruing from the management, use of sale of property, or from the carrying on of any process of production, or from the conduct of business; profit. In forms control, the term "Earnings," in the sense of profits, is not treated as a specific subject, but is included in the subject "Profit and Loss." See also "Profit and Loss."

Earnings Statement, Earning Record (form)—A form used to set forth the amount or amounts of earnings made by employees as salaries or wages. Since these forms refer to the earnings as such and not to the cash used to reimburse the employees, they are under the subject "Earnings" and the functions "To Record," "Report," "Notify," etc.

Education (subject)—The act or process of educating; discipline of mind or character through general study of instructions. In forms control, care must be taken not to confuse the subject "Education" with the subject "Training."

Training is regarded as the process directed toward qualifying an employee for a specific job, whereas education is used in a general sense with respect to peculiar situations (i.e., American firms operating in foreign lands in many instances must provide an educational system for their American employees' children, etc.).

Efficiency of (condition)—The quality or degree of being efficient; effective operation as measured by certain predetermined standards.

Electrotype (subject)—A facsimile for use in printing, consisting of a thin shell of metal deposited by electrolytic action in a wax, lead, or plastic mold of the original and backed with lead alloy.

Eligibility for (condition)—Quality or state of being eligible for something.

Employee (subject)—One employed by another; a worker in the service of an employer; a person employed by another person or by a business organization. A person becomes an employee only after he or she has been employed. Prior to that time, he or she is an applicant. See "Employment" for distinction to be drawn between "Employee" and "Employment." Also see "Labor."

Employee Benefits (subject)—Benefits that may accrue to an employee as the result of being an employee of the company and having met certain qualifications of eligibility for such benefits in addition to regular earnings. Educational assistance is an example. If the benefits are the result of having been insured against loss or damage, use the term "Benefits" without the qualification of "Employee."

Employees' Accounts Receivable (See "Accounts Receivable")—A written or printed statement of business dealings with an employee of such a nature that payment should be had. In forms control, the term "Employees' Accounts Receivable" is not used as a specific subject but is included in the subject "Accounts Receivable" under the department "Payroll." See also "Account" and "Accounts Receivable."

Employment (subject)—The act or state of being employed; the conditions under which employees work for or render service to an employer. The condition of being employed by another for hire. In forms control, a distinction must be drawn between "Employee" and "Employment." Forms should be filed under "Employee" only when the subject matter of the form refers personally to the employee; example, "Employee Identification Cards, Records of Employees, etc. When the subject matter refers to the condition of employment, the forms should be filed under the subject "Employment." Example: Change of Status, Termination of Employment, etc.

Forms having to do with facts about the employee that are constant regardless of his or her employment (i.e., age, marital status, etc.) should always be filed under "Employee." Forms dealing with facts pertaining to the employment should be filed under "Employment." Many forms deal with both and should be cross-referenced.

Employment deals with several specific subjects such as rate, etc., and should include such forms unless there are enough forms in any such category to warrant setting up a separate subject. In that case, cross-reference those subjects with "Employment."

Applications for employment should be filed under "Employment" even though they contain essential information about the applicant.

Employment Notice (form)—A form used to notify an applicant that he or she has been approved for employment. The applicant becomes thereby an employee, sometimes after having signed an employment agreement. An employment notice should be filed under the subject "Applicant," the operation "Employment of," and the function "To Notify."

Employment of (operation)—The act of employing or hiring; to make use of the services of another. In forms control, the operation "Employment of" is used only in relation to persons, usually "Applicants."

Endorse, to (function)—To write on the back of; to sanction. Use the function "To Certify."

Endorsement (subject)—A signature added to a document as further verification. In insurance it is an amendment in writing added to and made a part of the insurance contract, and should be filed under subject "Insurance," operation "Change of," and function "To Agree."

Enrollment of (operation)—The act of enrolling, such as the listing of approved students in a course of learning.

Engraving—See "Plate."

Entertainment (subject)—The act of receiving and providing for a guest; the provision of meals, shelter, amusement, etc. for one's business or social guests.

Entrance (operation) (See "Passage of")—The act of entering into a place, or granting permission to enter into a place. In forms control, the term "Entrance" is not used as a specific operation, but is included in the operation "Passage of," including exit as well as entry, used with a specific subject (i.e., "Person," "Passage of," or "Personal Property, Passage of").

Envelope (form)—Envelopes, strictly speaking, are not forms insofar as functions, subjects, and operations are concerned. It is true that the function "To Route" could be ascribed to them but they are so completely in a category of their own that it is more practicable to set them up in the arbitrary category "Envelopes."

Error (subject)—A mistake or inaccuracy. Errors occur as the subject of forms principally in such organizations as banks and insurance companies where there is a large clerical force, or in the area of quality control in industrial companies. Use as the subject only when the forms deal specifically with the errors themselves. The operation is normally, but not necessarily "Adjustment, Correction Of."

Establish, to (function)—See "To Identify."

Estate (subject)—A person's possessions or fortune, either during life or thereafter. Estates are often left in the care and management of banks, and forms relating to the estate as such should be classified under that subject. If the securities or property making up the estate are the subject of the form, use that subject but if the estate generally is the subject use "Estate." See also "Trust."

Estimate (form)—A form the purpose of which is to set forth a valuation or rating of something, especially from incomplete data, as a rough or approximate calculation, or a judgment or opinion, usually implying careful consideration or research. In forms control, estimates are classified under "To Estimate" and the specific subjects under that function.

Estimate (subject)—The calculation of the approximate cost or price of something; a calculation of value, time, quantity, etc., in relation to some given object or thing. In forms control, "Estimate" should be used as a subject only when the estimates themselves are the subject matter, not when some other thing is being estimated. See also "To Estimate" and "Quotation."

Estimate, to (function)—To fix or calculate approximately; to form an opinion of something in the absence or unavailability of all actual facts, usually pertaining to values, quantities, or time; usually subjects or matters treated in the singular as opposed to "To Schedule," which usually treats of repetitious or recurring events.

Evaluation of (operation)—To grade according to a prescribed set of standards; to appraise.

Event (subject)—A scheduled or planned incident that falls outside the routine of usual happenings (e.g., programs, banquets, conventions, parties, dances, concerts, etc.).

Examination of (operation)—The act of examining, searching, or investigating; usually an act or process prescribed or assigned for testing qualifications. In forms control, the distinction between the operations "Examination of," "Inspection of," and "Analysis of" should be carefully noted. "Examination of" is the only one of the three relating to persons, and has to do with determining the physical or mental qualifications or fitness of the individual. "Inspection of" refers to scrutiny of inanimate objects to determine their consistency with set standards of quality. "Analysis of" refers to the determination or separation of one or more ingredients of a substance as to kind, amount, weight, strength, etc. See also "Inspection of" and "Analysis of," and "Investigation of."

Exemption of (condition)—The state of being exempt, or free, from any charge, burden, etc., to which others are subject.

Expenditure (operation)—The act of expending; a laying out as of money; a disbursement. In forms control, the term "Expenditure" is not treated as a specific operation, but is included in the operation "Payment of." See also "Payment of."

Expense (subject)—That which is expended, laid out, or consumed, as a charge or cost. In forms control, the term "Expense" is not treated as a specific subject, but is included in the subject "Cost." See also "Cost."

Expense Report—See "Travel Expense Report."

Experience (subject)—That body of factual data that represents the past happenings and contingent circumstances over a given period of time affecting any given object or thing. In insurance, experience is measured in relation to known hazards in the determination of future rates or action. Experience is used as a subject in forms control only when the form deals with a recounting of experience on any given object for the purpose of recapitulation prior to its use in subsequent action, rate fixing, etc.

Expiration of (condition)—A coming to a close; end, as expiration of a contract or insurance policy.

Exportation of (operation)—The act or process of sending, transporting, or carrying something, usually a product, abroad, or to a foreign country.

Extension of (condition)—The act of reaching or stretching out; state of being lengthened or widened; enlargement. In forms control, the condition "Extension of" pertains to employment beyond retirement age; the increase in length either in space or in time, increase in range as of kinds of influence, extension of credit, lengthening of a road, etc.

Facility (subject)—A thing that promotes the ease of any action, operation, or course of conduct; the physical means whereby the operation of a service is made possible. The distinction between "Service" and "Facility" is that one provides the physical means of operation whereas the other is the resultant service made possible by the facility. Examples: laundry facilities and laundry service; telephone facilities and telephone service. See also "Service."

File (subject)—An orderly collection of paper, as a file containing the complete case history of a specific subject, case, or incident.

Filing (operation)—The act of placing records or other items in a file for storage and future reference. Also, the act of placing on official record such as the filing of a suit or other legal instrument. In the latter sense filing is not used as an operation. Use instead "Listing of."

Filling of (operation)—The act or process of pouring a liquid or other substance into a suitable container or vessel with the idea of filling it.

Fingerprint (subject)—An impression made by a finger or thumb, especially a print made by the inside of the first joint showing its characteristic lineation, or marking. This lineation varies with the individual and is unchanged throughout life; hence fingerprints are now widely used as a means of identification. In forms control, the term "Fingerprint" is not treated as a specific subject, but forms pertaining to fingerprints may be classified under the operation "Identification Of" following a specific subject, normally "Employee."

Follow-up (function)—To pursue an initial effort; to keep attention fixed upon or to recall attention to.

Food (subject)—That which is eaten or taken into the body for nourishment.

Forecast (form)—A form the function of which is to set forth a prophecy or estimate of a future happening or condition, or an indication of what may be expected. In forms control, forecasts are classified under the function "To Estimate" and the specific subjects under that function.

Foreign Exchange (subject)—Technically the trading in or exchange of foreign currencies at currently established exchange rates. In forms control it may apply to the foreign money itself that has been purchased, sold, or otherwise handled by the bank.

Forms (subject)—A prearranged blank upon which data or information is entered. See also "Publication."
   "Forms" is ordinarily not used as a subject when filled-in records are referred to. Use the subject "Records."

Formula (subject)—A prescription or list of ingredients of a mixture, giving the exact proportions of each together with proper directions for compounding, especially when end mixture or product has industrial or commercial use; as opposed to "Recipe," which usually denotes a dish in cooking.

Freight (subject)—Compensation paid for the transport of goods.

Funds (see "Cash")—Money and negotiable paper immediately or readily convertible into cash. In forms control, the term "Funds" is not treated as a specific subject, but is included in the subject "Cash."

Garnishment (subject)—A warning to a person, in whose hand the effects of another are attached, not to pay money or deliver goods to the defendant, but to appear in court and answer to the suit of the plaintiff to the extent of his or her liability to the defendant; also, the proceeding so begun by service of this warning. In forms control, "Garnishment" usually occurs in relation to employees. This usage should not be confused with the operation "Garnishment of" applying to the subject "Cash." The distinction is simply that a garnishment happens to be one of the subjects about which the personnel department is usually concerned, whereas in the payroll department, a garnishment irrevocably affects the operations of that department in relation to a subject "Cash" with which it is concerned. Hence, "Garnishment" as a subject in relation to employees and "Garnishment of" as an operation in relation to "Cash."

Garnishment of (operation)—The act of warning or giving notice to a person, in whose hands the effects of another are attached, not to pay the money or deliver the goods to the defendant, but to appear in court and answer to the suit of the plaintiff to the extent of his liability to the defendant. In forms control, the operation "Garnishment of" is used in relation to the subject "Cash," although its use is not necessarily limited to that subject.

Since the subject "Earnings" is also used and the operation "Garnishment of" is usually spoken of in relation to "wages or earnings" it might seem that the operation "Garnishment of" should modify the subject "Earnings," in the sense of that to which the employee is entitled, or has earned, remains unchanged by garnishment proceedings. Only the "take home" cash of the employee is affected; hence, the use of "Garnishment of" in relation to the subject "Cash" instead of the subject "Earnings."

Gauge (subject)—An instrument for measuring or automatically recording or testing an amount or quantity, or the use of an amount or quantity, of anything (e.g., a gas meter or gauge, a pressure gauge, etc.).

Gift (subject)—Something given or donated.

Grant, to (function)—To agree or assent to; to allow to be fulfilled; to give by consent. Use the function "To Acknowledge."

Graph Paper (form)—See "Work Sheets."

Grievance (subject)—A cause of uneasiness and complaint, or that which gives ground for remonstrance or resistance, as arising from an injustice, imagined or real. In forms control, the term "Grievance" is used as a subject only in relation to employees, and then only when such complaints refer to the employee's personal status in the business organization. All other complaints of grief, annoyance, disturbance, etc., are included under the subject "Complaints—Trouble." For instance, an employee's report of a faulty light fixture should be treated as "Complaints—Trouble," whereas an employee's taking exception to his or her rate of pay or general working conditions should be treated as a "Grievance."

Guarantee, to (function)—To be a guarantee, warranty, or surety for; to be responsible for the fulfillment of. Use the function "To Certify."

Handling of (operation)—In forms control, the manner of handling a situation.

Hazard (subject)—Risk, danger, or peril; in insurance all forms dealing with a condition, operation, activity, material, or combination of these which creates or increases probability of loss is classified under subject "Hazard."

Health and Accident (department)—In forms control, "Health and Accident" refers to that phase of operations, and that portion of a business organization, having to do with the recording, investigation, reporting, and compensation of bodily injury or illness sustained in normal business operations by employees of the organization. Included also are those operations related to the treatment granted, offered, or paid for in cases of injury or illness, and those operations pertinent to the determination of the physical fitness of employees to perform the tasks to which they are, or may be, assigned.

Hearing (subject)—A listening to arguments or evidence in a matter of dispute.

Hiring of (operation)—See "Employment of."

Housing (subject)—That structure utilized as a shelter for business associates or employees. The subject "Housing" should not be confused with the operation "Housing of" in forms control. "Housing" refers to the specific structure or house as such that is or can be utilized as shelter for business associates or employees, whereas "Housing of" refers to the processes utilized in locating suitable housing accommodations for business associates or employees, or to the process of establishing a person under shelter, as in a room, or housing a guest in a hotel.

Furthermore, the distinction between the subjects "Housing" and "Land and Buildings" should be noted. "Housing" refers to that structure, building, or house that is or may be used as shelter but beyond the control of the business organization as owners, tenants, lessees, etc. As soon as such a structure becomes property of the business organization, or through contractual agreement comes within the jurisdictional control of the business organization, it immediately falls in the category of the subject "Land and Buildings," and is usually treated in a much different manner from a control and record point of view than it would if remaining under the category "Housing."

Housing of (operation)—The act of putting or receiving under shelter. As used in forms control, the operation "Housing of" refers to the processes utilized in locating suitable housing accommodations for business associates or employees, or to the process of establishing a person under shelter, as in a room, or housing a guest in a hotel.

Idea (subject)—A concept, design, or preliminary plan for a thing or a course of action intended to lead to a preconceived result. In forms control, the use of the subject "Idea" usually pertains to someone's idea of a product or service that can be marketed or lead to a course of action that will lead to a product to be marketed. Such ideas are normally protectable by copyright or patent.

"Idea" should be used as a subject only when applying to a protectable concept and not for a suggestion given under a company-sponsored suggestion plan. See also "Suggestion."

Identification of (operation)—The act of identifying, regardless of the means.

Identify, to (function)—To establish the identity of; to recognize or establish something or someone to be the same.

Incident (subject)—Something that occurs; an event.

Income (subject)—That recurrent benefit derived from labor, business, or property; commercial revenue or receipts of any kind. In forms control, the subject "Income" is not used in the sense of profits, nor in the sense of wages, but is used in the sense of revenue, proceeds, or receipts. Income is primarily material value in the form of cash, or the evidence or equivalent of material value, brought about through the sale of merchandise, services, or the use of property or cash.

Incorrectness of (condition)—The state of being wrong or in error. Use the operation "Adjustment or Correction of."

Indemnity (subject)—Protection or exemption from loss or damage, past or to come. In forms control, "Indemnity" is usually not considered as a subject; rather, the subjects "Damage" or "Loss" are used with the condition "Protection from."

Indoctrination of (operation)—See "Orientation of."

Inform, to (function)—To give instructions or directions to; to communicate knowledge of; to make known. Use the function "To Notify."

Information About (condition)—Knowledge or intelligence, particularly of a special situation or of special circumstances. In forms control, the condition "Information About" is always used to modify a specific subject, regardless of its nature, and becomes in effect a description or statement of fact about the subject. Hence, the use of "Information About" as a condition. Care must be taken not to use this condition too generally or as a substitute for a more specific condition. A call to check on the references of a prospective employee is a request for information about the "Applicant" and should be so filed, but a report on the inventory of material should be filed under the condition "Status of" even though the "Status of" represents information about material.

Injury—Illness (subject)—Harm, hurt, sickness, disease, ailment, malady, wound, or disorder of health. In forms control, the subject "Injury—Illness" includes only those items of harm or sickness sustained by persons, never by inanimate objects or things, and usually as the result of an accident, or exposure to occupational hazards.

In insurance companies, "Injury—Illness" is synonymous with "Loss" but is used in the personal situation to specify the loss more closely.

Inquire, to (function)—To ask about or ask; to seek to know by asking or questioning. Use the function "To Request."

Inquiry (subject)—A seeking for information by asking questions; a form or record used for the purpose of transmitting an inquiry.

Inspection of (operation)—The act or process of inspecting, as a strict or prying examination or close or careful scrutiny or investigation, usually to determine adherence to set standards of quality. In forms control, the distinction between the operations "Inspection of," "Analysis of," and "Examination of" should be carefully noted. "Inspection Of" refers to scrutiny of inanimate materials, matter, or objects, or the product of labor—production, for the purpose of determining their consistency with set standards. "Analysis of" refers to the determination or separation of one or more ingredients of a substance as to kind, amount, weight, strength, etc. "Examination of" refers to persons only, and has to do with determining the physical or mental qualifications or fitness of the individual. See also "Analysis of" and "Examination of."

Installation of (operation)—The act or process of installing, as a fixture or pieces of equipment in an office or factory.

Instruct, to (function)—To impart knowledge to; to teach, or furnish with direction; to educate, train, or indoctrinate; usually without authority to enforce subsequent action, as opposed to "To Order," which carries authority.

Instructions (form)—A form the purpose of which is to instruct, or to impart knowledge or intelligence in order to instruct. In forms control, instructions are classified under the function "To Instruct" and the specific subjects under that function.

Instruction of (operation)—The act or process of imparting knowledge to, as through teaching or lessons.

Instructor (subject)—One who instructs, or imparts knowledge; a teacher.

Insurance (subject)—The fact of having insured against loss or damage by a contingent event; the insurance held by any one person or company as a whole or a group.
  Three main factors affect or form the basis of considering the subject of insurance in forms control, as follows:

1. The persons, person, or organization protected by the insurance (i.e., person, company, etc., or the objects or things against which the hazards may occur or to which the insurance applies, property, automobile, plate glass, etc.).
2. The hazard or hazards against which the protection is received (e.g., fire, theft, property damage, death, collision. personal injury, etc.).
3. The physical or geographical limits of the coverage afforded by the insurance (e.g., building, garage, ship, or unlimited, etc.).

In forms control, care must be taken not to confuse the subject ''Insurance'' itself with the subject matter of insurance issued. Item No. 3 above identifies the subject of insurance after it has been issued, whereas the subject ''Insurance'' applies to the broader fact of the mere existence or nonexistence of coverage. Care must be taken also not to confuse the premium paid for insurance with the insurance itself. See also ''Premium.''

Applications for insurance present a problem in classification owing to the tendency to use ''Insurance'' as a subject and ''To Apply'' as the function. If this is done all applications will come together regardless of the type of insurance involved. A more practical way is to use the objects or things that are being insured, the operation ''Insurance of'' and the function ''To Apply.''

Application forms normally carry much detailed information about or description of the objects or things to be insured as well as the hazards against which they are insured. This should not confuse the classification.

The key is found in the possibility of a policy being written as the result of the form in question. If a policy can be issued on the basis of the form under consideration, it should be considered as an application. If a policy cannot result directly from the form, it must be considered as something other than an application (e.g., an inspection form, etc.). If the application has a binder clause it must be considered as a policy and not as an application, although the two must then be cross-referenced in the index. Binder clauses may be buried in the body of the form and not easily visible. Many applications carry the reverse of the binder, stating specifically that the company is not bound.

Insurance of (operation)—The act of insuring against loss by contingent event.

Insured (subject)—The person, persons, or organization protected against loss of damage by contingent event through the issuance of insurance.

Interest (subject)—A charge made for the use of money or its equivalent.

Interview of (operation)—The act or process of mutual sight or view, as meeting another face to face, usually formally, for the purpose of consultation, examination, inspection, or view of something.

Invention (subject)—A device, contrivance, process, design, or the like originated after study and experiment.

Inventory, to (function)—To make an inventory of; to make a list or schedule of. Use the function ''To Report.''

Inventory (form)—A form the function of which is to set forth an itemized list of goods or valuables, usually with their known or estimated worth. In forms control, inventory forms are classified under the specific subjects on which the inventory applies, the condition ''Status of,'' and the function ''To Report.''

Inventory (subject)—Use inventory as a subject only when the item being inventoried cannot be specifically identified or classified, or when the coverage is broad and includes a variety of items.

Inventory—Perpetual (form)—A form the purpose of which is to record the receipts, issues, and balances on hand of a given item or product. It is kept current and may or may not show the price or value of the product; often included is the bin location, etc., for filling orders. The difference in classifying inventory forms is that one type is "To Report" while "Perpetual Inventory" is "To Record."

Investigation of (operation)—To follow up by inquiry or observation; to ascertain the facts in relation to a given situation, occurrence, or person. Care must be taken not to confuse the operations "Investigation of," "Inspection of," "Examination of," and "Analysis of." See also the definitions of those operations.

Use "Investigation Of" only when the representative of the company or organization is making the investigation. When information is requested from an applicant or some third party, use "Person," "Information About," "To Request."

Investment—A source of income or profit, or that in which money is invested. In forms control, the term "Investment" is not treated as a specific subject, but is included in the subjects "Securities," "Land and Buildings," etc. See also "Securities" and "Land and Buildings."

Invoice to (function)—To make a written list or account of, as goods sold and to be sent to a consignee; to insert in a price list; to enter in an invoice. Use the function "To Notify."

Invoice (form)—A form the purpose of which is to provide a written account or itemized statement of merchandise shipped or sent to a purchaser, consignee, etc., with the quantities, values, and prices or charges shown. An invoice applies to a given order or shipment whereas a statement usually recaps all invoices sent over a given period of time and represents the status of the account receivable as of a given date. The invoice relates to the specific subject (e.g., "Merchandise," etc.), whereas a statement relates to an account. (See "Account.") File invoices under the applicable subject, "Product or Merchandise," the operation "Sale of," and the function "To Notify."

Invoices can be used as a subject in itself only when the invoice form is that with which another form deals (e.g., Invoice Register, etc.).

Issuance of (operation)—The act of issuing or giving out.

Itinerary—See "Travel."

Job (subject)—A piece of work, especially of an odd or occasional kind or one undertaken at a fixed price; the special trade or occupation followed or practiced by anyone; a situation or occasion in which one's trade or occupation may be performed or exercised.

The difference between "Job" and "Work" lies in the performance; "Work" is the actual performance or exertion of effort whereas "Job" applies to the ability to do the work or the situation in which the work may be performed.

The difference between "Job" and "Project" is usually in the relative size of the undertaking and in the fact that a project is usually related to a special appropriation granted for the purpose.

Journal (form)—A record of original entry. Journal forms may be handwritten or made by machine when the entries are posted. The journal is a chronological record of transactions as they take place or are posted. Journal entries are posted subsequently to the ledger, either to the general ledger or to the specific ledger containing that kind of accounts, such as payables or receivables.

Forms for journal entries should be classified under "Account," either general or more specific.

Journal Voucher (form)—A form used in accounting for summarizing individual voucher entries in order to reduce the number of journal entries. The journal vouchers are kept in a binder that becomes a book of original entry. File under the subject "Accounts General" and the function "To Record."

Justification of (condition)—Use "Certification of."

Key (subject)—An instrument by means of which the bolt of a lock is shot or drawn, usually a removable metal instrument with wards shaped to fit the mechanism of a particular lock and operated by turning or pushing.

Label (form)—When labels cannot be identified with a specific subject, they are filed under the arbitrary subject of "Labels" without reference to operation or condition. An alternate classification may be "Shipment," "To Route."

Labels, Address (form)—Forms used for showing the person, organization, and address to which something is to go. File under the subject that applies (e.g., material, merchandise, etc.), the condition "Destination of," and the function "To Notify."

Labor (subject)—Physical or mental toil or exertion; laborers as a body or class or those performing work as a group.

When the form pertains to the toil or exertion "Labor" is not used as a subject; use instead the subject "Work."

When the form treats of laborers as a group the subject "Labor" is used. Example: A form that deals with the total number of persons on a payroll or that measures labor turnover should be filed under the subject "Labor."

Land and Buildings (subject)—Any portion of the earth's surface or an edifice designed to stand more or less permanently for use as dwelling, storehouse, factory, shelter, or for some other useful purpose.

Land and buildings when owned are fixed assets of the company and in banking are assets on which loans can be made. Land and buildings may be rented also.

The distinction between "Land and Buildings" and "Premises" usually relates to actual or potential tenancy and use. See also "Premises."

Law (subject)—A rule or action established by a recognized authority; to enforce justice and prescribe duty or obligation; a legislative enactment.

Lawsuit (subject)—A suit in law; a case before a court. Do not use as a subject. Instead use "Suit."

Lead (subject)—A prospective customer or account; a name given or otherwise obtained for the purpose of calling on to qualify as a potential customer.

Lease (form)—A form the purpose of which is to set forth the agreement of two or more persons in regard to property, or the rights or privileges in relation to a certain property. In forms control, leases should be classified under "To Agree" and the specific subjects under that function.

Lease (subject)—A contract by which one conveys property, or rights or privileges in relation to property, for a specified period of time, usually for a certain rent or compensation. In forms control, the term "Lease" is used as a subject only when the contract or lease instrument itself is the subject matter of the particular form. If the subject matter of the lease itself is under consideration, the subject should be used, modified by the operation "Lease of."

Lease of (operation)—The act of granting or conveying property, or rights or privileges in relation to property, to another by a lease or contract.

Leave of Absence (form)—A form used to request or grant, or both, permission to be absent from work. File under the subject "Employee," the condition "Absence of," and the function "To Request."

Ledger (subject)—The final book of record in business transactions in which all debits and credits from the journal, etc., are placed under appropriate heads.

Legal Documents—Legal documents constitute a special category of forms and present problems not encountered with other forms. Some of the factors that set such forms apart are:
1. They are, in fact, legal and are used with a recognized context of legality. They cannot, therefore, be changed as to content or wording without legal clearance and approval, usually difficult if not impossible to obtain and, in fact, there is no need to change them.
2. Although many, if not most, of them are printed in such a way that they are difficult for the average person to read and most could well be redesigned as to typographic format to make them easier to read, there is no compelling reason for doing so since most of those who use them are lawyers and judicial persons who are so well acquainted with their content and format that a change would probably be

frowned upon. The change would necessitate new composition, which would be too expensive to justify itself. Laws now regulate the readability of certain legal forms.
3. Such forms are used in quite small annual quantities and are available from stationery stores or legal suppliers in those small quantities at relatively low prices.

The legal forms commonly encountered include judgments, summonses, liens, garnishments, quit claims, mortgages, notes, assignments, and others of similar nature.

Legal forms can be handled in one of two ways in the functional index. First, they may be classified in one category as "Legal Documents, General" with all such forms included in that one category. Second, they may be classified by subject, operation, and condition, as are all other forms. In banks and insurance companies there may well be enough legal forms to so classify them. Some of the more common legal forms and the subjects to which they apply are:

Under Property—Sale agreements, transfer of equity, leases (when the form deals with the actual leasing of property), chattel mortgages, bills of sale.

Under Lien—Release of lien, assignment of lien, extension of lien.

Under Power of Attorney—Appointment of power of attorney.

When the legal document itself is the subject of another form, that form should be filed under the subject of the legal document itself (bond, mortgage, etc.) and the suitable operation and function. If there are few such forms they may be filed under the general category of "Records."

Letterheads (form)—Letterheads, strictly speaking, are not forms, insofar as functions and subjects are concerned, until after the letter has been written. They should, therefore, be filed under the arbitrary classification "Letterheads and Memoranda," without reference to functions, subjects, operations, and conditions.

This does not apply to requests for information, instructions, orders, etc., on specific subjects when most of the form is printed or mimeographed on a letterhead and is to be filled in somewhat as a memorandum or letter. Whenever the form is identifiable with a specific subject it should be filed under that subject, the condition "Information About," and the proper function, "To Request," "To Report," etc.

Letter of Credit (subject)—A document issued by a bank on another bank or banks, foreign or domestic, whereby the purchaser has the backing, prestige, and guarantee of payment of drafts drawn against the letter of credit for the specified amounts under the specific conditions.

In forms control use the subject "Letter of Credit" only when the actual letter itself is being referred to; otherwise use the applicable terms. The letter itself should be classified as "Cash, Payment of, to Certify." Personal letters of credit are usually accompanied by other documents identifying the bearer and his signature. Classify such forms under the applicable subjects (e.g., person, name, etc.).

Liability (subject)—Broadly speaking, any legally enforceable obligation. The term is most commonly used in a pecuniary sense. In insurance it is the limit of liability under a policy. In reinsurance the liability is split between two or more companies. Forms should not be filed under the subject "Liability" unless they specifically deal with the liability itself (Limit of, etc.) or the distribution of liability between companies insuring and reinsuring.

License (form)—A form the purpose of which is to authorize certain acts, or the operation of a certain business, which otherwise would be illegal. In forms control, licenses are classified under "To Authorize" and the specific subjects under that function.

License (subject)—A formal permission from the proper authorities to perform certain acts or to carry on a certain business that, without such permission, would be illegal. In forms control, the term "License" is used as a subject only when the license itself is the subject matter of the particular form.

Licensee—Use "Agent."

Lien (subject)—A right to control or to enforce a charge against the property of another until some claim of the former is paid or satisfied.

Limitation of (condition)—A confinement or limiting; or the establishment of upper and/or lower limits, as a limitation on a customer's credit.

List (form)—A form the function of which is to list or catalog, as names, objects, or items. In forms control, lists should be classified under "To Report" and the specific subjects under that function, or under "To Record" and the specific subjects under that function. Only careful analysis of the particular form will indicate which function is applicable. In some instances, there may be forms that deal with the actual lists themselves in which case "List" may become the subject (e.g., "Mailing Lists," "To Record").

List (subject)—See "List" (form).

Listing of (operation)—The act of entering a security or property on the list of one officially or publicly recognized as dealing in such items, as listing stock with a broker, or listing real estate with a realtor. In forms control, the term "List" is not treated as a separate function, but is included in the function "To Report." See also "To Report."

Loading of (operation)—The act or process of placing material in proper position for processing or transportation (e.g., loading in a truck or railroad car, or loading into a hopper or a machine).

Loan (subject)—That which one lends or borrows, especially money lent at interest.

Loans represent the fact of having granted money to another, usually for a specified use and covered by certain collateral (see definition) put into the hands of the lender as a guarantee of repayment. Loans are usually covered by a note setting forth the terms of the loan and repayment.

In forms control the distinction may be made between the loan (the act of loaning or having loaned) and the note (the evidence on paper of the loan and its terms). If only a few forms are involved they may be all classified under the subject "Loan" since a loan may be made without a note. If many forms are involved, put them under the separate subjects "Loan" and "Note."

Loan of (operation)—The act of lending; the granting of permission to use, as the loan of a book, money, equipment, or services.

Location of (condition)—The state of being in a specific and certain place, locality, or place of residence. As used in forms control, the condition "Location of" modifies inanimate things, objects, or persons. When used as a condition, "Location of" becomes a specification of limitation of the subject to which it applies.

Lock Box (subject)—See "Safety Deposit Box."

Loss (subject)—Act or fact of suffering deprivation; unintentional parting with something. In insurance a settlement, usually measured in monetary value, made by an insurance company as the result of the occurrence of a hazard against which the insurance was made.

The terms "Loss" and "Claim" are very confusing and must be carefully distinguished in dealing with forms. The key is found in the viewpoint; the insured suffers a loss and puts in a claim. The insurance company gets a claim and, if it is settled in favor of the insured they suffer a loss. To the insurance company it becomes a loss only when the decision is reached, the amount settled and paid.

Since the forms control is in the area of the insurance company and not the insured, all forms for reporting the details of a loss on the part of the insured should be classified under the subject "Claim," "To Report" even though to the insured he or she is reporting a loss. In some cases it may be more desirable to classify them under the subject "Benefits" and the function "To Claim."

When the claim has been paid and the forms relate to the payment of the money on the part of the insurance company, the forms should be classified under the subject "Loss."

Some forms are not claims as such but are certifications as to the extent or details of the loss. In that case, classify under the term "Loss, to Certify."

Loss of (condition)—The state in which a thing or object exists when lost or unintentionally out of one's possession. In forms control, the term "Lost" is not treated as a specific condition, but is included in the condition "Lost and Found." See also "Lost and Found."

Lost and Found (condition)—The state in which a thing or object exists when lost, or unintentionally out of one's possession, or is met with accidentally, is discovered, or appears by one's seeking or detection. As used in forms control, the condition "Lost and Found" is usually applicable to things or objects in the category of "Personal Property," although not necessarily limited or restricted to this usage alone. See also "Personal Property."

Machinery and Equipment (subject)—Constructions or contrivances of a mechanical nature, articles of convenience or decoration, used to equip or furnish a place of business usually representing a capital investment and necessary to the operation of a business. Items considered as "Machinery and Equipment" are usually nonexpendable, not for resale, and not produced by the user but procured elsewhere. This category includes such things as desks, chairs, work benches, typewriters, adding machines, lathes, drill presses, storage shelves, shop mules, trucks, cranes, barges, railroad cars, vessels, vehicles, etc. See also "Materials and Supplies."

Magazine—See "Publication."

Mail (subject)—That which is sent through or comes in the mail; letters, etc., sent or received through the post office. In forms control, the subject "Mail" is broad in scope, including all items, regardless of nature, handled through mail service channels. Prior to dispatch and after delivery, those items making up the classification "Mail" may be treated under different identities (reports, records, publications, etc.), but while in transit through established mail channels, these same items lose their separate identity and are collectively treated as "Mail."

Mailing List (subject)—A listing of names and addresses of persons, businesses, or organizations that are to receive literature at intervals.

Maintenance of—See "Repair–Maintenance of."

Manifest (form)—A form authoritatively listing or invoicing a ship's cargo and certifying that it was laden for shipment, specifying the marks, numbers, contents, shipper, consignee, etc., of each package of goods. In forms control, manifests should be classified under "To Certify" and the specific subjects under that function. In the event the goods making up the cargo are unknown or unidentifiable, which is not unusual, use the subject "Shipment" under the function "To Certify." See also "Shipment."

Manual—See "Publication."

Manufacture of (operation)—The fabrication or construction of products or things, usually in quantity and according to a predetermined set of specifications.

Manuscript (subject)—A typed or written document, such as the original copy of a story or book as the author has written it.

Market (subject)—The state of, or conditions affecting, trade as determined by prices, supply, demand, and location and number of potential customers.

Marriage of (operation)—The act or process of uniting in the holy estate of matrimony. Also the act or process of uniting two prefabricated assemblies into one unit. (Commonly used in the aircraft and shipbuilding industries.)

Material receipt (form)—A form used to acknowledge the receipt of material or supplies. See also "Delivery Receipt."

Materials and Supplies (subject)—That which is needed or furnished currently for the physical operation of a business; the substance or substances, or the stock or goods or parts of which the product is made, or that which is used in the making of the product; the items necessary in the day-by-day conduct of the business, generally thought of as supply items.

Materials and supplies are expendable in the conduct of the business and are of a noncapital nature. They are not for resale and are not usually produced by the user but are procured from other sources.

Included in materials and supplies are both the raw materials of the business and the office supplies, stationery, janitorial and maintenance supplies, etc.

The distinction between "Materials and Supplies" and "Work-in-Process" should be clearly understood. Items are materials and supplies only to the point where they are taken from stock and entered into the manufacturing or conversion process; then they become "Work-in-Process."

A company may have two plants, one of which sells its product to the other. In that case the product of the first plant becomes the raw material of the other plant. Forms pertaining to the item in the respective plants should be classified accordingly.

Maturity of (condition)—The date upon which a note, time draft, bill of exchange, or other negotiable instrument becomes due and payable.

Meal (subject)—The portion of food taken at one time to satisfy the appetite; also, the act or time of eating a meal.

Media (subject the plural of medium)—The collective means by which communication is attempted or achieved, such as magazines, newspapers, radio, television, and film.

Medical examination (subject)—An examination by a doctor, usually given to an employee or applicant for employment. File under the subject "Applicant" or "Employee," as the case may be, the operation "Examination of" and the function "To Authorize," "To Report," etc.

Medicine (subject)—A remedy for disease or illness or for the prevention of disease or illness.

Meeting (subject)—A group of persons composing a society, community, party, or organization, usually considered to be on an officially approved basis. A group of individuals gathered together for the purpose of discussing a subject or taking action.

Membership (subject)—The state or status of being a member; the collective body of members, as a society or group.

Memorandum (form)—See "Letterhead" and treat similarly.

Merchandise (subject)—The objects of commerce; whatever is usually bought or sold in trade, or market, or by merchants, as wares, goods, commodities—provided the objects have been purchased for resale without intervening manufacturing or assembling activities, in which case they are classified under "Products." Personal services, when offered on the open market on a fee basis, instead of a wage or salary basis, can be considered as merchandise.

After the goods are sold they cease to be merchandise or product and become, in the eyes of the purchaser, materials, supplies, machinery, equipment, personal property, etc. If it is returned to the seller for any reason, however, it again becomes merchandise or product.

Forms relating to such items after they have been sold and passed from the possession of the seller usually are classified under the subject "Customer Service." When the merchandise is sold, the transaction is completed. The invoice relates to the merchandise because it is concerned with the individual order or shipment. At the end of the month or accounting period, the statement sent to the customer applies to the account receivable and not to the merchandise. From the seller's view, merchandise has lost its identity when it has passed from the possession of the seller. See also "Product" and "Commodity."

Merchandise Receipt (form)—See "Material Receipt" or "Delivery Receipt."

Message—See "Communication."

Messenger Service (subject)—The service of bearing messages or doing errands; bearing oral or written communications, notices, invitations from one person to another, usually by a company engaged in their transmission. In forms control the subject "Messenger Service" is used only when the service itself, and as such, is the subject matter of the particular form.

Minutes of (condition)—The official record of proceedings at a meeting of an organized body.

Model (subject)—A representation, generally in miniature, to show the construction or serve as a copy of something.

Mold (subject)—The matrix or cavity in which anything is shaped; also, the body containing the cavity. A frame or body on or about which something is made.

Money (subject)—Any particular form or denomination of coin or paper that is lawfully current as money. In forms control the term "Money" is not treated as a specific subject, but is included in the subject "Cash." See also "Cash."

Money Order (subject)—Treat the same as "Check" or "Draft."

Mortgage (subject)—The designation of property as security for the payment of a debt, transferring the ownership with the proviso that the transfer is void when the debt is paid. The mortgage is usually considered the piece of paper by which the designation of transfer of ownership is made, and in classifying forms the subject should be used only when the piece of paper itself is referred to. If the money loaned is referred to, the subject "Loan" should be used except when it is paid to discharge the debt; then the subject "Cash" should be used. The mortgage itself should be classified under the applicable subject, "Property," etc.

Mortgage of (operation)—The act of mortgaging something.

Movement of (Operation)—The act of moving, carrying, or conveying any inanimate thing or object from one location to another. (Used in lieu of "Transportation Of" only when the movement is within the confines of the premises.) Do not use "Movement of" when transfer of ownership or rights is involved; use "Transfer of" in all cases where other than physical things are involved.

Name (subject)—The title by which any person or thing is known or designated.

News (subject)—Fresh information of something that has recently taken place. In forms control, news releases should be filed under the subject "News," the operation "Release Of," and the function "To Notify."

Note (subject)—An evidence on paper of a loan having been made. The note sets forth the terms of the loan and the repayment. In forms control, "Note" is used as a subject only when the actual piece of paper itself is referred to. They may be classified under "Loan" (see definition) if there are few forms in the category.

Notice (form)—A form the function of which is to communicate intelligence, information, or warning, especially a formal nature, as an announcement, or a written or printed sign, or the like, communicating information or warning. In forms control, notices are classified under the function "To Notify" and the specific subjects under that function.

Notices as such are not forms, inasmuch as they ordinarily do not have blank spaces for subsequent entry of data for clerical purposes. If they do have blank spaces, they should be identifiable under specific subjects and functions. If they do not have spaces, they should be filed under a blanket category of "Notices" similar to "Envelopes," "Letterheads," etc.

Notice (subject)—The communication of intelligence, information, or warning, especially of a formal nature. Notice should be used as a subject only when the subject matter of the notice is not identifiable as such. When it is identifiable it should be filed under the applicable subject and the function "To Notify."

Notify, to (function)—To give notice of or make known facts that were not known before, usually where another person will be bound to some degree by the information as opposed to "To Report," where no binding action is carried.

Number (subject)—The use of a numerical code or symbol as a means of identification. Use as a subject only when the number itself is being referred to as a subject and not when the thing to which the number refers can be identified, in which case use the applicable subject and the condition "Identification of."

Obsolescence of (condition)—The state of being obsolete; out-of-date; out-moded.

Office supplies (subject)—See "Materials and Supplies."

Opening of (operation)—The act or process of establishing or setting up, as of an account.

Operation of (operation)—The act of operating, or putting into or maintaining in action, as the operation of a machine or a piece of equipment. Also the operation of a department or company (e.g., operating report). See also "Use of."

Order (form)—A form, issued by competent and recognized authority, the purpose of which is to provide direction to purchase, sell, or supply goods or services, or to perform work. A sales order form is not an actual order but a notification to the company that a sale has been consummated. In forms control, a salesperson's order form is filed under the subject "Product," the operation "Sale of," and the function "To Notify."

Order (subject)—A commission to purchase, sell, or supply goods, or services, or to perform work, always issued by competent and recognized authority. In forms control, "Order" is used as a subject only when the order itself is the subject matter of a particular form.

A rule or regulation made by competent authority. In forms control, the term "Order" in the sense of a rule or regulation is not treated as a specific subject but is included in the subject "Rules and Regulations." See also the definition of that subject.

Order, to (function)—To rule or regulate by competent authority; to commission the purchase or sale of things or the performance of services or work, usually where subsequent action is optional, or to "To Instruct," where no binding action is involved.

Organization (subject)—A number of individuals systematically united for some work, as a business organization. The terms "Company," "Corporation," and "Organization" are easily confused, and a decision will have to be made as to which one will be used. If only a few forms are involved, the term "Organization" is probably desirable, whereas if many forms are involved they may be broken down into the separate categories. "Company" and "Corporation" are more applicable when the legal entity is involved, while "Organization" is more applicable where people, departments, etc., are involved.

Organization of (condition)—The state or manner of being organized; the state or manner of arrangement in interdependent parts, each having a special function, act, office, or relation with respect to the whole.

Orientation of (operation)—The act or process of making familiar with one's surroundings or conditions, like the orientation of a new employee. To place all things in their proper relative position.

Overage of (condition)—The state of being in excess or excessive; an overplus unaccounted for. See also "Overage−Shortage of."

Overage −Shortage of (condition)—The state of being in excess, or excessive and/or the state of being in deficiency or deficit. In forms control, this condition is used only when a form can be used for either shortages or overages, or both.

Overhead (subject)—Those general charges, collectively, in any business that cannot be charged to any particular part of the work or product, as rent, taxes, depreciation, insurance, lighting, heating, accounting, and other office expenses.

Overtime (subject)—Time beyond, or in excess of, a limit, especially extra working time. In forms control, the term "Overtime" is not used as a specific subject, but is included in the subject "Time." See also "Time."

Ownership of (condition)—The state, relation, or fact of being an owner; lawful claim or title.

Package (subject)—A bundle made up for transportation, as a packet, bale, parcel, or package of goods. See also "Personal Property" and "Shipments."

Packaging of (operation)—The act or process of wrapping, crating, or packing. A careful distinction should be drawn between "Shipping of" and "Packaging of." The goods or commodities may be packaged for storage with no reference to subsequent shipping, in which case use "Packaging of." On the other hand, if the goods or commodities are wrapped, crated, or packed for the specific purpose of putting into the hands of a transportation agent, use "Shipping of." See also "Shipping of."

Parent (subject)—A father or mother or a foster parent acting in a surrogate capacity for natural patents.

Part (subject)—One of the portions, equal or unequal, into which a manufactured product is, or can be, divided, or regarded as divided; something less than the end product in its finished state. As used in forms control, the term "Part" is not treated as a specific subject, but is included in the subject "Materials and Supplies" and "Work-in-Process." See also the definition of those subjects.

Participation in (operation)—To take part in or to assume a part of. In banking participation loans are made when the amount of the loan is beyond the legal means or the desire of the bank to handle.

Pass (form)—A form the function of which is to grant permission or license to pass, or to go and come; a written permit allowing a person or property to pass. Such permission or license to pass actually falls in the category of an authorization, and, in forms control, passes are classified under the function "To Authorize" and the specific subjects under that function. Many passes possess a secondary function of the category "To Agree." However, in forms control, this function is considered subordinate to the primary function "To Authorize" and, consequently, a condition to the authorization.

Passage of (operation)—The act of passing, or permitting admission or exit, or allowing to enter or leave a particular place or location. In forms control, the operation "Passage of" is used with a specific subject, regardless of its nature.

Passport (subject)—A formal document issued by a state officer to a citizen of the country, certifying citizenship and authorizing leaving that country, requesting protection abroad and permitting reentry as a citizen.

In forms control "Passport" should be used as a subject only when the passport itself is the subject of another form. Otherwise file "Passport" under the subject "Person," the operation "Passage Of," and function "To Authorize."

Patent (subject)—A right or privilege, given legally, to someone for the exclusive right to the manufacture or sale of a given product or thing.

Patient (subject)—A person under medical or surgical treatment.

Pattern (subject)—Anything designed as a guide or model for making things, as a pattern for making parts in manufacturing operation, or a dressmaker's pattern. A pattern is that after which something is made.

Payment of (operation)—The act of paying or giving compensation; the discharging of a debt or an obligation; a laying out, as of money.

Payroll (subject)—The total amount of earnings due all or a group of employees for work performed or services rendered. Payroll applies to more than one employee and only when they are not individually identified, whereas "Earnings" applies to one employee only or a group of employees individually identified. See also "Labor."

Pension (subject)—Allowance received or payment made for some meritorious service, or for length of service or employment, usually upon retirement from that service or employment.

Performance of (operation)—The act or process of doing something, such as the performance of work. The manner of operation when measured by or compared with some given norm. See also "Operation of."

Period (subject)—In forms control, a prescribed interval of time, such as a class period in school; the number of hours a student spends in the classroom.

Permit, to (function)—To consent to; to allow to be done; to grant express license or liberty to do an act; to authorize. Use the function "To Authorize."

Person (subject)—An individual human being.

Personal Property (subject)—Property belonging to a person, consisting in general of things temporary or movable; chattels personal. As used in forms control, "Personal Property" is used as a subject only when it is broad in scope and used in a collective sense. When the items are identifiable as such they may and usually are classified under their specific subject headings unless, for convenience in filing, it is more desirable to group them under the general heading.

Example: A billfold is personal property but it may contain cash, keys, passes, records, photographs, etc., in which case the billfold would be a specific item with all the other items grouped within it, or the entire lot including the billfold itself could be classified under the subject "Personal Property."

Personal Property Check (form)—A form, ticket, certificate, or token by which ownership or title may be proved, or a thing may be identified, as a check for a coat, hat, etc. In forms control, "Personal Property Checks" should be classified under the function "To Claim" and the subject "Personal Property." Personal property checks also serve to identify personal property items, but this function is considered subordinate to the function of claiming.

Pickup Order (form)—A form used to instruct someone to pick up something and deliver it to another place, usually applying to things located somewhere else to be brought to the place where the pickup order originated. Material to be transported away from the point of origin is usually covered by a shipping order. Pickup orders should be filed under the applicable subject (materials, merchandise, etc.), the operation "Transportation of," and the function "To Order."

Picture—Use "Print."

Placard—See "Warning Placard."

Placement of (operation)—The act of placing in a particular spot or place, or in a certain relative position; to put or set in a particular rank, office, or position; to secure a position, office, or the like. In forms control, the operation "Placement of" is usually used only in relation to persons, usually in the category of employees. The distinction between the operation "Placement of" and the condition "Location of" should be carefully noted. "Placement of" refers to persons only, usually employees, and the act or process of fitting them into the business organization according to their wishes and the physical and mental qualifications. "Location of" refers to the state of animate or inanimate objects or things in relation to a particular place, locality, or place of residence. In insurance, it refers to placing a risk with an insurance company by an agent or reinsurance.

Plant (subject)—A factory, workshop, or apparatus complete for the manufacture of a particular product; the machinery, apparatus, fixtures, etc., and sometimes also the real estate employed in carrying on a trade or a mechanical or other industrial business.

File plant reports under "Plant" only when the report is general in nature and reports a variety of factors. When the report is of a single factor or a few closely related factors, file under the more specific subject "Production," "Time," etc. See also "Premises."

Plate (subject)—In printing, the original linecut or halftone engraving, planographic offset plate, or intaglio from which the printing images are produced. See also "Electrotype." Plates are to printing what tools, dies, etc., are to fabrication processes. Plates are also known in the trade as "cuts."

Policy (form)—A document setting forth an agreement and the terms of insurance between the insurer and an insured. In forms control, policies are filed under the subject that applies (person, property, automobile, etc.), the operation "Insurance Of," and the function "To Agree." Use the subject "Policy" only when another form deals with the policies themselves.

Policy (subject)—A settled course adopted and followed by an organization, usually emanating from management or its representatives; in insurance companies or in relation to insurance, those documents that set forth the agreement between the insurer and the insured. In forms control, "policy" can be used as a subject only when the documents themselves are under consideration as the subject matter. Example: policy register would be a form on which policies themselves are recorded and the subject would be "Policy," but a policy itself would have as the subject the things against which the hazard might occur. Binders are considered and treated as policies.

In businesses other than insurance companies, forms pertaining to policies should be classified under "Records" until it is determined that enough such forms exist to set up a specific "Policy" group.

Policy Holder—See "Insured."

Postage (subject)—The charge made for sending material through the mails; also, in forms control, the postage stamps used in payment of the postage charges.

Power of Attorney (subject)—Legal authority or right given to one person to act for another who is bound by the action. In forms control, use the subject only when the power itself is the subject and not the exercise of the power. The latter case should prevail, for instance, in the case of a proxy in which the subject is "Vote," although the proxy form grants the power of attorney to cast the vote.

Premises (subject)—Land, building or buildings, ship or vessel, or other property capable of tenancy and use of any combination of these within the jurisdiction of a person or a business organization as owner, tenant, or operator thereof.

The distinction between "Premises" and "Land and Buildings" is one of specific versus general treatment. When the form treats specifically of the land or the building as such with no reference to tenancy or use, the subject "Land and Buildings" should be used. If the treatment applies to the land or buildings as a place of occupancy, use the subject "Premises." Example: "Premises, Inspection of, To Report" as against "Land and Buildings, Cost of, to Record."

Premises usually deals with not only the land buildings but also part or all of the contents relating to occupancy and use.

Premises can also apply to rented property as against company-owned property.

Premium (subject)—An amount of money paid or to be paid at regular intervals for insurance. The consideration given for a contract of insurance. In forms control, a distinction must be drawn between "Premium" and the cash used to pay the premium. When the actual money or cash becomes involved in the transaction, the subject must be "Cash." "Premium" refers to the amount or value of the amount due without reference to the cash actually then being involved. Example: The determination of the amount due as a premium refers to the subject "Premium," but when the premium is paid, it is cash that changes hands and not the premium.

The insurance premium is actually an invoice (Service, Sale of, to Notify), but its use is so typically established in the insurance industry that forms relating to the premium should be filed under that subject.

Premium notices (Premium, Payment of, to Notify) are an example. When a form recaps premiums on many policies or on classes of insurance, they can still be filed under "Premium" although they may be cross-referenced with "Accounts Payable" or "Accounts General."

If the premium is payable as a note given in advance, the note becoming payable on the premium due date, the forms specifying the note schedule are still under the subject "Premium" but the actual notes themselves represent cash and should be filed under that subject.

Prevention of (operation)—The act of avoiding the occurrence of a known hazard.

Price (subject)—The quantity of one thing, usually money, exchanged or demanded in barter or sale for another thing. Price is what is asked or demanded, especially for goods or commodities. See also "Quotation."

Price of (condition)—The amount of money or its equivalent asked for anything offered for sale or barter. In forms control "Price of" usually applies to an answer to a customer or prospect's request for quotation. Use the subject "Product," condition "Price of," and function "To Notify."

Prints (subject)—An impression, copy, or reproduction taken from anything. As used in forms control, the subject "Print" refers to photographic prints, blueprints, ozalids, photostats, etc.—in short, reproductions. The subject "Prints" does not include the original or that from which reproduction is made, which is treated as the subject "Drawing." See also "Drawing."

Problem (subject)—A question proposed for solution usually requiring some research or analysis. In forms control "Problem" is usually used in connection with laboratory research and should not be confused with "Project," which applies more to construction, etc., and which does not involve a research problem.

Procedure (subject)—A specified and authorized manner of handling a particular subject in the business organization, including treatment of that subject in its relationship to the departments or subdivisions of the organization structure and the various operations, conditions, and activities affecting that subject. Procedure usually takes the form of formal and authoritative releases emanating from management or its representatives setting forth manner of handling a particular subject or group of related subjects.

Procurement of (operation)—The act or process of acquiring something by any means (purchase, production, hire, etc.) In forms control, the operation "Procurement of" is used to modify a specific subject, regardless of nature. See also "Purchase."

Product (subject)—The end result of a manufacturing or production process, usually offered for sale as an object of commerce; also, anything produced by generation or growth such as the products of agriculture.

The difference between "Product" and "Work-in-Process" lies in the point at which the latter ceases to be work-in-process and becomes a product. This is usually at the point of final inspection, after which it becomes salable as a product.

The difference between "Product" and "Merchandise" lies in the point of production. A product is produced by the organization that sells it, whereas merchandise is purchased for resale. A retail store sells merchandise whereas a factory sells its product. Some manufacturing concerns not only manufacture and sell their product but also may deal in resale merchandise (i.e., the product of another organization along with their own product).

See also "Merchandise," "Invoice," "Statement," and "Commodity."

Production (subject)—A measurement of output; the result of a manufacturing, producing, or growing process measured in terms of output.

The distinction between "Production" and "Work-in-Process" lies in the physical aspect of the work-in-process (see also the definition of "Work-in-Process"). Production may be measured in terms of several things: units, pieces, weight, or quantity, but it is always a physical measurement of output.

Production can be applied to intangible as well as tangible things. A clerk may report production on the number of checking operations performed, a telephone operator may report the number of calls handled, and a factory worker or department may report on the number of units produced.

Production is usually associated with a product of work-in-process, as semifinished parts or material, but this association or the identification of the product or item being produced should not confuse the classification of the production form. If the form refers to the thing or object being produced and not to a measurement of production, file under ''Work-in-Process.''

The distinction between ''Production'' and ''Work'' lies in the physical aspect of work. Work is the physical or mechanical effort that goes into production, whereas production is a measurement of output as a result of the work.

The distinction among ''Work,'' ''Job,'' and ''Production'' may be stated as follows: (1) Work is the expenditure of energy in a (2) job, which is a set of conditions in which one's trade or occupation is practiced to bring about (3) production, which is the measurement of output.

If a form reports several things about a department or plant, such as materials used, amount produced, quantities on hand, time operated, costs, etc., with no particular emphasis on any of them, classify under ''Department'' or ''Plant,'' condition ''Operation of,'' and function ''To Report.'' However, if there is appreciable emphasis on any factor, classify under the factor and cross-reference to the others.

Do not use ''Production'' when the measurement is of the movement of work-in-process from one place or process within the total production process. Use ''Work-in-Process, Movement of.''

Profit and Loss (subject)—The excess or deficiency of income in relation to costs in a given transaction or series of transactions, or in a business or any of its departments, during a given period of time.

Profit includes any benefit or advantage, and loss includes any diminution of value, usually measured in dollar value, accruing from the management, use, or sale of property, or from the carrying on of any process of production, the rendering of services, or from the conduct of business.

In forms control, all forms possessing the elements necessary to constitute a profit or loss figure of any sort are included under the subject ''Profit and Loss.'' All profit and loss statements of the ordinary or general accounting type are considered as reports and are to be so filed. Other profit and loss forms may be records, particularly when they represent data taken from other reports and recapped on the profit and loss form as original entries.

Program (subject)—A brief outline of the order to be pursued, or the subjects embraced; plan of future procedure.

Project (subject)—A planned or designed undertaking (e.g., a construction or work program). A project may be in process, planned for the future, or already completed or accomplished. In forms control, the subject ''Project'' should be used only when referring to the undertaking as an entity, not to the work or effort going into it or to the status of production on the undertaking at any one time. A project applies only to items of a capital nature and not to items of current expense or recoverable expenses against production.

A project usually has a starting and stopping date and becomes completed at some date as opposed to "Work," which is effort currently expended, or "Production," which is a continuous or recurrent process with no planned termination date, even though products are continuously being completed in the process. See also "Work," "Production," "Job," and note under "Cash."

Promise, to (function)—To engage to do, give, make or to refrain from doing, giving, making, or the like; to afford reason to expect; to assure emphatically. Use the function "To Agree."

Proof (form)—A form the purpose of which is to verify the accuracy of a situation or condition. In banking the proof sheet may apply to a "batch" of work or documents or it may apply to the overall condition of a department or work section at the end of a given period of time. In the latter case the forms should be filed under "Department," the condition "Condition of" or "Status of," and the function "To Certify." If it applies to a batch of work use the subject "Work." Proof sheets may also be referred to in terms of "Control."

Properties of (condition)—Used generally in connection with chemical laboratories when "Analysis of" becomes too broad a term. Physical characteristics, such as weight, color, and strength, are properties. "Analysis of" is then used to cover constituent parts. Properties are usually applicable to solids, analysis to liquids.

Property (subject)—All things or rights of value; possessions or that which is one's own. Use the subject "Property" only when the treatment is broad and cannot be tied down to any one particular kind of property (e.g., securities, tools, land and buildings, merchandise, etc.).

The distinction between "Property" and "Premises," insofar as forms control is concerned, lies in the implication of ownership. If the form deals with or implies the actual ownership of the things, use the subject "Property," but if the form deals with the things without reference to ownership, use the subject "Premises" or such other subject as may apply more specifically.

Prospects (subject)—Potential customers, known or thought to be interested in procuring the products, merchandise, or services of the business organization; potential employees of an organization should be filed under "Applicant" rather than under "Prospect."

Protection of (condition)—The act of protecting; state or fact of being protected.

Proxy (subject)—Authority held by one person to act for another usually in the matter of casting a vote. The document that grants the authority itself is usually spoken of as a "proxy," and this document can be classified under that term although the general term "record" can be used in all ordinary cases since there will probably be few such forms.

The proxy grants power of attorney to act in all matters covered by the proxy but it is usually limited to the casting of a single vote or the votes in a single meeting. It is most commonly used in votes to be cast at director's meetings of corporations. Care should be taken to distinguish between the proxy as such and the power granted by it.

Publication (subject)—That which is published, especially any magazine, manual, pamphlet, etc., offered for public or private distribution but not bound in the ordinary manner of books. See also "Forms."

Publicity—See "Advertising."

Public Utilities—See "Utilities."

Purchase of—Use "Procurement of."

Purchase (subject)—The act of acquiring title to, or property in, anything for a price; buying for money or its equivalent. In forms control, the term "Purchase" is treated as a subject because of the broad scope of the purchasing activity and the nonidentity of that which is purchased. As a rule, the same purchasing form can be utilized in the procurement of a box of safety pins, a piece of heavy equipment or machinery, or canned food for the employees' cafeteria, or most any item one might name. Hence, the use of the word "Purchase" as a subject in lieu of that specific subject, whatever it might be, with which the form deals.

"Purchase" should be used as a subject only when it is not possible to identify the objects or items being purchased. When identification is possible the form should be filed under the proper function: the subject (materials, supplies, etc.,), and the operation "Procurement of." See "Procurement of."

Qualifications of (condition)—The state of being qualified; or possessing the necessary requisites or essentials. In forms control, the distinction between the condition "Qualifications of" and the operation "Examination of" should be carefully noted. "Qualification of" has to do with state of being or not being qualified, whereas "Examination of" has to do with the act or process of determining whether or not a person might be qualified.

Question, to (function)—To inquire of by asking questions; to examine by queries. Use the function "To Request."

Questionnaire (form)—A form containing a set of questions for submission to a number of persons, the purpose being to obtain information on a certain subject. In forms control, questionnaires should be classified under the applicable subject (e.g., applicant, equipment, etc.), the condition "Information About," and the function "To Request."

Quotation (subject)—The price, terms, or conditions named or published as currently applying to any commodity. Quotations may be requested from a supplier or may be given to customers or prospects. If the quotation is being given out, use the subject "Quotation" with "To Notify"; if it is being requested use "Quotation" with "To Request."

When bids or prices are being tabulated and the thing to which the price applies cannot be identified, or when the bids or prices cover numerous items, use the subject "Price."

R. R. Car (subject)—A conveyance designed to be pulled by a locomotive over railroad tracks. In forms control, this equipment is usually considered under the subject "Machinery and Equipment." However, if the number of forms involved is excessive, the subject "R. R. Car" may be used.

Rate (subject)—A charge or price fixed by a ratio, scale, or standard (e.g., railroad rates, price per hundred, insurance rates, rates of pay, etc.). The rate of pay may be considered as one of the conditions of employment in the case of personnel matters, or it may be set up as a separate subject in itself if there are sufficient forms to warrant doing so. If established under "Employment," they should be cross referenced to the subject "Rate." It may also be classified as the condition "Rate of" under the subject "Earnings."

In insurance the rate is the amount per designated unit of insurance upon which the premium for a given policy is established. Before the premium is established the subject should be rate; after the premium is established the subject "Premium" should be used.

Rate of (condition)—The proportion, scale, or ratio determined as the norm for finding a rate determination according to a predetermined set of standards for the purpose of placing in a scale or finding a rate.

Rating of (operation)—Classification according to grade; the act of considering, regarding, or evaluating. As used in forms of control, the operation "Rating of" usually refers to a job, an employee, or a group of employees treated as a unit of the organization (e.g., division, department, district, etc.) It should not be confused with the operation "Examination of." "Rating of" has to do with the evaluation of a job, an employee, or a group of employees in a particular job, position, or status, while "Examination Of" has to do with determining the physical or mental qualifications or fitness of them for the particular job, position, or office.

Real Estate (subject)—Lands; tenements; freehold interests in landed property; property in houses and lands. In forms control, "Real Estate" is not used as a subject; see "Lands and Buildings."

Recall of (operation)—The act or process of calling back; usually in relation to calling an employee back to work.

Recall to (function)—To revoke; to annul; to take back; to withdraw. Use the function "To Cancel."

Receipt (form)—A form the purpose of which is to acknowledge the taking or receiving of goods or money delivered or paid. Both the operations of paying or delivering and taking or receiving are involved but, inasmuch as the receipt is given to the person making the payment or delivery and constitutes primarily an acknowledgment of the payment or delivery, such forms should be filed under the applicable subject, the operation "Receipt of," and the function "To Acknowledge."

Receipt of (operation)—The act of receiving, to take possession of.

Receipt, to (function)—To put a receipt on; to give a receipt; act of receiving; a writing acknowledging the taking or receiving of goods or money delivered or paid. Use the function "To Acknowledge."

Receiving Report (form)—A form for reporting the receipt of materials, supplies, etc.; also often known as a "receiving slip." File under the applicable subject, the operation "Receipt of," and the function "To Report."

Recipe (subject)—A formula or prescription for making some combination, mixture, or preparation, especially, a dish in cooking.

Reconciliation of (operation)—The act of reconciling, reduction to congruence; removal or explanation of inconsistency, to bring into harmony; as to reconcile one's cash account with the banks's statement.

Record, to (function)—To copy or reduce to writing as evidence to perpetuate a knowledge of events or facts; usually where the making of a record of some permanency is the primary function of the document, as opposed to forms in which the record is secondary to another primary function.

Records (subject)—That which is written or transcribed to perpetuate a knowledge of acts or events; a reduction to writing as evidence; a compilation of facts set down for permanent or semipermanent retention for purposes of reference when need arises. In forms control, the distinction between "Records" and "Reports" should be carefully noted. It is normally found in the primary use of the document. A person can make a record either for himself or for another person. A person can make a report only to another person and cannot make a report to himself. The subject "Records" should be used only when the subject matter of the record cannot be specifically identifiable. If identifiable, use the subject of the record itself and the function "To Record" (e.g., equipment, insurance policy, note, etc.). If more than one specific and identifiable record is involved, they should be treated collectively under the subject "Records."

When the subject "Records" is applicable to all forms or documents coming under the classification, they can be filed together and, if the group becomes too large, they can be broken down into specific types of records (e.g., invoices, bills of lading, etc.). If only a few forms are involved they can be left under the general subject "Records." Routing slips are a common example of form to be classified under "Record," the function being "To Route."

Recovery of (operation)—The act of restoring, receiving, repossessing, or reclaiming anything.

Recreation (subject)—Refreshment by any means, or refreshment of the strength and spirits after toil; a diversion. In forms control, the subject "Recreation" does not involve time away from work and is usually a period of short duration, whereas "Vacation" inherently involves time away from work and is usually a period of leisure or rest of some duration.

Referral to (operation)—To direct attention to another thing or place; to assign or reassign a person to another location or place.

Refusal of (operation)—The act of refusing something. Use the operation "Rejection of."

Refund of (operation)—See "Return of."

Registration of (operation)—To enter into a prescribed listing; to enroll a student in a school course.

Regulate to (function)—To adjust or control by rule, method, or established mode; to direct by rule or restriction; to subject to governing principles of laws. Use the function "To Order."

Regulation (subject)—A rule or order prescribed for management or government. In forms control, the term "Regulation" is not used as a specific subject, but is included in the subject "Rules and Regulations." See also "Rules and Regulations."

Reinstatement of (operation)—The act or process of returning or putting back into a previous state or condition.

Reinsurance (subject)—The process by which an insurance company protects itself against excessive loss by reinsuring a part of its risks with other companies and paying such sharing companies a portion of the premium it receives.

Reinsurance is the same as insurance but once removed from the original transaction. File forms for reinsurance the same as for insurance except that the form for the original transaction specifies the subject of the insurance, whereas the reinsurance usually refers only to a policy with no specification of the subject; therefore, reinsurance forms may have to be filed under the subject "Insurance," "Placement of," and the function.

Rejection of (operation)—The act or process of rejecting, usually following a process of inspection to determine adherence to set standards because that which is rejected fails to measure up to set standards and is set aside or rejected as unsatisfactory.

Release of (operation)—To let loose, to set free from restraint or confinement, to liberate from obligations.

Remittance Advice (form)—A form the purpose of which is to transmit money—cash, checks, drafts, etc.—to someone else. File under the proper subject (e.g. Accounts Payable) and the function "To Notify."

Remittance of (operation)—Transference of or sending of something, often a document, to someone else.

Remittance Receipt (form)—See "Cash Receipt."

Rent (subject)—The return made by the tenant or occupant of land or property to the owner for the use thereof. The return made by the hirer or user of personal property to the owner for the use thereof. Since rent normally involves cash or its equivalent, forms pertaining to rent are classified under the subject "Cash" and the operation "Payment of," or "Receipt of," as the case may be. Rent should be used as a separate subject only when no handling of cash is implied or involved as an operation. If cash is being received, paid, or handled in any way, the subject "Cash" should be used.

Rental of (operation)—The act of permitting the use of property, land and buildings, products, machinery and equipment, etc., for a stipulated sum usually payable at specified intervals. Do not confuse with "Lease of."

Repair—Maintenance of (operation)—The act or process of repairing, or restoring, to a good or sound state after decay, waste, injury, etc., or maintaining in a good or sound state to preclude decay, waste, injury, etc. In forms control, the operation "Repair—Maintenance of" is used only in relation to inanimate things or objects.

A distinction should be drawn between repair done, as a maintenance factor on equipment or tools within the organization, and repair work done as a commercial service for a price. The former should be classified under the subject "Equipment," "Tools," etc., the operation "Repair Maintenance of," and the function that applies, whereas, the latter should be classified under the subject "Work," and the applicable operations and functions.

Repeal to (function)—To recall; to revoke; to rescind or abrogate by authority; to annul; to cancel; to reverse. Use the function "To Cancel."

Replacement of—Use "Issuance of."

Replenishment of (operation)—The act of replenishing, or state of being replenished; filling again after having been diminished or emptied; stocking anew; refilling.

Report to (function)—To give an account of events, happenings, performance, things or conditions; to communicate knowledge of, to make known, tell, or enlighten; to gather data or information from records to present a current picture of conditions; to gather primary data or information from which records are to be compiled, usually where the other person is not particularly bound to specific action by the information, as opposed to "To Notify," where it is known that action will be affected or circumscribed by the information.

Report (form)—A form the purpose of which is to give an account of events, happenings, performance, things, or conditions, or to present, tell, enlighten, or communicate knowledge that was not known before, usually where the other person is not particularly bound to specific action by the information. In forms control, reports are classified under the function "To Report" and the specific subjects under that function.

Report (subject)—An account or relation, either of a routine performance or of some matter specially investigated; an official statement of facts, oral or written, for transmission to another point or person, made up from original source data or from already compiled records, or from other reports. It should be understood that the person receiving the report is not bound to specific action by it. Many reports are for advice or information only.

In forms control, the distinction between a "Record" and a "Report" should be carefully noted, and that distinction is normally found in primary use of the document. A person can make a record either for himself or for another person. The subject "Report" is used in forms control only when the report itself constitutes the primary purpose of a particular form.

Care must be taken not to use the subject "Report" when actually a report is being made of another distinct and identifiable subject. Use "Report" as a subject only when the reports themselves are the subject matter, not when a report is being made of another subject.

Repossession of (operation)—The act of taking possession of something after it has been previously transferred as to ownership; usually due to the failure to meet payments of an obligation for which the property had been given as collateral.

Reprimand of (operation)—The act of administering a reproof, censure, or reprimand, especially when given with authority. In forms control, the operation "Reprimand of" is used only in relation to the subject "Employee."

Reproduction of (operation)—The act of making a copy of something.

Request (form)—See "Requisition."

Request, to (function)—To ask for something; to requisition the procurement or delivery of things, materials, or personnel required for operation, usually by those in a position to expect action as a result, as opposed to "To Apply," where the request carries no assurance of action.

Requirements of (condition)—The quantity of anything needed for a given purpose.

Requisition (form)—A form the function of which is to ask for something, or for some action desired, by one in a position to expect action. Requests are commonly known as "Requisitions" and should be filed under the subject to which they apply (materials, etc.), the operation "Delivery of," and the function "To Request." When the requisition is of a general nature to be used for the requisitioning of many items or things, it should be filed under the subject "Materials and Supplies."

Requisition to (function)—To make a requisition or authoritative demand for. Use the function "To Request."

Reservation (subject)—An evidence of having reserved something, such as space on a train, a room in a hotel, etc., especially for oneself or for another person. In forms control, the subject "Reservation" is used only when the reservation, as such, is the subject matter of a particular form, and is not to be confused with the operation "Reservation of" used with a specific subject, as "room, reservation of."

Reservation of (operation)—The act or process of preserving or keeping, as to reserve a room in a hotel.

Reserve (subject)—Funds kept on hand to meet demands; something reserved for a particular purpose. Reserves may be represented by cash or other resources of the business.

Resolution (subject)—A formal expression of the opinion or the will of an assembly, adopted by vote.

Responsibility for (condition)—The state of being responsible for the acts of another or for the safekeeping of something; accountability or liability for being called on to give satisfaction for something to someone.

Retention of (operation)—The act or process of retaining, safeguarding, or holding, usually the records of a company.

Retirement of (operation)—The act of withdrawing from an activity or a position of employment, usually in a prescribed manner or plan.

Returnable Container (subject)—A receptacle returnable by the customer to the supplier for credit. See "Container."

Return of (operation)—The act of returning or coming back, to or from a place or location; the giving back or returning of something by one person to another.

Revenue (subject)—Return, proceeds, yield, or profits. In forms control, the term "Revenue" is not treated as a separate and specific subject, but is included in the subjects "Income," and "Profit and Loss," depending upon its meaning and usage. See also the definitions of the subjects "Income." and "Profit and Loss."

Review of (operation)—Use the operation "Inspection of." See the definition of that subject.

Rework of (operation)—The act or process of correcting to specification the parts, sub-assemblies, or the finished products of a manufacturing operation. In forms control, the distinction among the operations "Repair—Maintenance of," "Adjustment or Correction of," and "Rework of" should be carefully noted. "Repair—Maintenance of" has to do with restoration of inanimate objects, notably machinery and equipment, buildings, etc.; "Adjustment or Correction of" has to do with making right that which was wrong—usually in a clerical sense; "Rework of" has to do with correcting to specifications that which is produced by a manufacturing operation. It usually modifies the subject "Work-in-Process."

Rights (subject)—That to which one has just claim; any power or privilege vested in a person by the law, custom, contract, or agreement.

Risk (subject)—Conditions surrounding the possibility of the occurrence of a hazard. In insurance risk is related to hazard; forms relating directly to risks should be filed under "Hazard." See also "Experience."

Risk is also the probability of the occurrence of a loss. Hazard is the thing that might occur; risk is the probability of its happening. The distinction between the two is so finely drawn that risk forms may be filed under "Hazard." If the file contains too many forms the two may be separated.

Room (subject)—One part of a building, an enclosure within a building.

Rooming of (operation)—The act of putting or receiving under shelter, as rooming a guest in a hotel. In forms control, "Rooming of" is not treated as a specific operation, but is included in the operation "Housing of." See also "Housing of."

Route to (function)—To send forward or transmit by a certain route or to a specified place or person.

Routing of (operation)—The act or process of sending by, or the determination of a certain route to, a specified place or person.

Royalties (subject)—A compensation paid to the owner of a patent or a copyright for the use of it or the right to act under it. In forms control, forms dealing with "Royalties" are filed under the subject "Cash."

Rubbish (subject)—Waste or rejected matter; trash; debris.

Rule to (function)—To control the will and actions of; to exercise authority or dominion over; to control or direct by influence. Use the function "To Order."

Rules and Regulations (subject)—A prescribed guide, or series of guides, for conduct; a rule or order prescribed for management or government of subjects within the jurisdiction of such management or government. In forms control, a careful distinction must be drawn between "Rules and Regulations" and the subject to which they apply. A form setting forth the rules and regulations themselves should be filed under the subject "Rules and Regulations." Example: A set of rules governing the award of prizes should be filed under the subject "Rules and Regulations" and the function "To Notify." On the other hand, a form on which a record is kept of the issuance of rule books falls under the subject "Publication," the operation "Issuance of," and the function "To record."

Safe Deposit Box (subject)—A receptacle, such as a vault or safe, used for the purpose of storing valuables for safekeeping, usually under rental arrangements under the care of a bank, safe deposit company, or warehouse acting as bailee.

Safety of (condition)—The state or condition of being safe; freedom from danger, risk, or injury.

Salary (subject)—See "Wages" and "Earnings."

Sale—The transfer of ownership of property from one person or company to another for a consideration.

In forms control do not use "Sale" as a subject; use the subject to which it applies, the operation "Sale of," and the proper function that applies. Also see "Sales."

Sales (subject)—The cumulation of more than one sales transaction for any given period of time, or a particular class or kind of commodity, or with a particular customer. Use "Sales" as a subject only when the form refers to sales as a group and is treated collectively. When the form refers to a single sale use the subject to which the sale applies, the operation "Sale of," and the proper function. See also "Sale."

Sales Call—See "Call, Sales."

Sale of (operation)—The act of selling or transferring the ownership of property from one person or company to another for a consideration.

Sales Proposal (form)—A form used to transmit prices and conditions under which merchandise is offered for sale. File under the subject "Merchandise," the condition "Information About," and the function "To report."

Salvage (subject)—A part or portion of material or product scrapped or rejected in a manufacturing process that has been determined to be suitable for rework or reuse (e.g., an assembly that has been scrapped or rejected by reason of a defective part or parts may be broken down and other component parts salvaged and used in another assembly).

In insurance "Salvage" is the value of property after it has been partially damaged by fire or other hazards.

Sample (subject)—A part of anything presented for inspection, or shown as evidence of the quality of the whole; a specimen. Use "Sample" as a subject only when

1. the sample is an entity in itself, such as a sample of a product put up for advertising purposes or for submission to someone for trying out or testing apart from the parent organization. Samples for testing may be of raw material, work-in-process, or finished products.
2. the thing or substance being analyzed is not identifiable as such.
3. a sample of an alien product or the product of another company comes in for an analysis.

Schedule (form)—A form the purpose of which is to set forth the times of projected operations or events, placing them chronologically in the element of time. In forms control, schedules are classified under "To Schedule" and the specific subjects under that function.

Schedule, to (function)—To set forth the times of projected operations; to outline regularly occurring events or to write a plan of future events placing them in the time element; to place chronologically, as opposed to "To Estimate," which involves elements other than time and is only an approximation in the absence or unavailability of all actual facts.

School (subject)—An organized place of learning; a place where planned instruction is given, usually to an organized class of students; the building or structure in which instruction is given on a planned basis to enrolled students.

Scrap (subject)—A small piece, a detached, incomplete portion; a fragment; waste material of any kind. In forms control "Scrap" as a subject refers to that generated usually through processing materials in a manufacturing operation or that which has been determined to be unfit for use in the same manufacturing process. Scrap may also be the completed product, part, or subassembly scrapped because of not meeting standards.

Securities (subject)—An evidence of debt or of property, as a bond, stock certificate, or other instrument; a document giving the holder the right to demand and receive property not in his or her possession; an investment. As used in forms control, the subject "Securities" does not contemplate a company's investment in its own stock. All forms pertaining to the control or handling of company stock are included in the subject "Stock." See also "Stock."

Selective Service (subject)—The statutes providing for the selection of citizens for service in the armed forces of a nation. As used in forms control, the subject "Selective Service" refers to all operations performed by business organizations in effecting compliance with federal statutes governing Selective Service, or for their own benefit in relation to Selective Service, and records and reports pertaining thereto. The subject "Selective Service" is used only in relationship to employees of the business organization.

Semifinished Parts (subject)—Materials processed up to a point in the manufacture of a product but not completely finished; usually held in stock for further processing or for assembly. Parts purchased from an outside source should be treated as materials and supplies, but parts manufactured by the company that will finally assemble them should be treated as semifinished parts.

"Semifinished Parts" is not ordinarily used as a subject; use instead the subject "Work-in-Process."

Seniority of (condition)—The quality or state of being senior, or priority of service, usually measured in relation to the provisions of seniority clauses of labor contracts or in relation to stated company seniority policies and practices. As used in forms control, the condition "Seniority of" refers only to the subject "Employee."

Service (subject)—The performance of labor for the benefit of another, or at another's command; the act of fulfilling some general demand, as telephone service. Also, the performance of duty over a period of time, as in personnel (e.g., 15 years' service). Service performed in relation to merchandise after it has been sold is included under the subject "Customer Service." See also the definition of that subject.

Settlement of (operation)—The act of settling; the payment of an account or of a claim for benefits under an insurance policy. In forms control "Settlement of" is not used as an operation. Use "Payment of" instead.

Setup of (operation)—To give a specific or desired position to; to put into a certain place or relation in order to secure a special end; to put in order for use or prepare for working; to arrange or make ready, as setting up a machine for a manufacturing operation.

Shipment (subject)—Goods or commodities being committed to any conveyance for transportation or in the process of being transported from one point or place to another. The subject "Shipment" is used in forms control only when the goods or commodities cannot be identified under a specific subject (e.g., "Materials and Supplies" or "Product," etc.), followed by the operation "Shipping of."

Shipper (form)—Use the subject "Product" and the operation "Shipping of."

Shipping of (operation)—The act of committing to any conveyance for transportation. In forms control, the distinction between the operations "Shipping of" and "Transportation of" should be carefully noted. "Shipping of" refers to the preparation (e.g., wrapping, crating, weighing, loading, etc.) of that which is being transported, in fact, all operations performed up to the point of actual movement toward its destination. "Transportation of" refers to the actual movement of the person or object from one place to another. A further distinction is noted in the fact that "Shipping of" can never refer to a person, whereas "Transportation of" is commonly used in relation to persons' as well as inanimate objects.

Shipping Tag (form)—A form the purpose of which is to convey instructions on the destination to which objects are to be transported. File under the operation "Destination of" and the function "To Notify." The subject may vary and usually is not identifiable. When the subject is specifically identifiable the form should be filed under that subject; when it is not identifiable, file under "Materials and Supplies."

Shortage of (condition)—The state of being in deficiency or deficit. See also "Overage–Shortage of."

Shrinkage of (condition)—The loss in weight, value, volume, or count brought about by processing, use, changing temperatures, or humidity, evaporation, etc. (e.g., a loss in the gallonage of a tank car filled with gasoline resulting from a sudden drop in temperature, or exposure to open air).

Shutdown of (condition)—The shutting down of a piece of machinery or equipment or the discontinuance of work in a department or plant, usually for a temporary period of time.

Signature (subject)—The name of any person, written with his or her own hand.

Size of (condition)—The spatial or numerical dimension of a thing; measurement of a thing by means of dimensional or bulking factors.

Social Security (subject)—The federal statutes providing for deductions from earnings of certain classes or categories of labor to afford a reserve for benefit payments under certain conditions at a later date. As used in forms control, the subject ''Social Security'' refers to all operations performed by business organizations in effecting compliance with federal statutes governing Social Security, and records and reports pertaining thereto.

Specifications (subject)—A notation or setting forth of limits, the designation of restrictions or the peculiar properties of a thing; limits of tolerances in measurements.

As used in forms control, ''Specifications'' usually refer to size, weight, color, hardness, strength, elasticity, and other properties of a thing together with allowable tolerances, if any, for each of their properties and is never used in relation to persons.

Specifications can be used as a subject only when the specifications themselves are the subject of another form; otherwise use the applicable subject, the condition ''Specifications of,'' and the function that applies.

Specifications of (condition)—The notation of limits; the designation of restrictions or the peculiar properties of a thing that have been set forth as authoritative.

Specimen (subject)—Not used as a subject; use instead the subject ''Sample.''

Standard (subject)—A definite rule, principle, or measure set up and established, especially by authority as a means of determining quantity, weight, extent, time, value, or quality; a means of ascertaining the level reached by a thing, its degree in a scale, or the like.

Standard Practice (subject)—A specified and authorized manner of handling a particular subject in the business organization, including treatments or subdivisions of the organization structure and the various operations, conditions, and activities affecting that subject. ''Standard Practice'' usually takes the form of formal and authoritative releases emanating from management or its representatives setting forth manners of handling a particular subject or group of related subjects. In forms control, the term ''Standard Practice'' is not treated as a specific subject, but it is included in the subject ''Procedure.'' See also ''Procedure.''

Statement (form)—A form used to notify someone, usually a customer, of the status of an account, usually an account receivable, as of the end of a given period, usually a month, quarter, or year. This periodic aspect differentiates between a statement and an invoice, which applies to a given order or shipment of merchandise, etc., rather than to the cumulative account over a period of time. File under the subject ''Account Receivable,'' the condition ''Status of,'' and the function ''To Notify.''

Status of (condition)—The state in which anything or anybody is at any given time, the state existing. See also ''Inspection of.''

Stock (subject)—The capital of a company or corporation in the form of transferable shares, each of a certain amount. As used in forms control, the subject "Stock" refers only to the company's stock, not to stock of other companies procured as an investment. See also "Securities."

Stocking of (operation)—The act or process of placing or carrying in stock, as the stocking of products or supplies or materials.

Stop Payment Order (form)—To order payment stopped on some negotiable paper, usually a bank check. File under the subject "Cash," the operation "Payment of," and the function "To Cancel."

Storage of (operation)—The act of storing, state of being stored; the placing of goods in a warehouse or other depository for safe keeping.

Student (subject)—A person engaged in study or devoted to learning; one who attends a school or who seeks knowledge from teachers or books. In forms control, the subject "Student" is used only in relationship to employees of the company and hence is listed as a subject under the department "Personnel."

Subrogation (subject)—The assignment to an insuror by the terms of the policy or by law of the rights of the insured to recover, after payment of a loss, the amount of the loss from one legally liable for it. Forms referring to subrogation may be filed under "Cash, Recovery of, to Agree."

Substitute (operation)—The act or process of placing one thing or person in the place of another. In forms control, the term "Substitute" is not treated as a specific operation, but is included in the operation "Change of." See also "Change of."

Suggestion (subject)—A suggesting; a presentation of an idea; a bringing before the mind for consideration, action, solution, or the like. As used in forms control, the subject "Suggestion" refers to suggestions pertaining to work, working conditions, and matters associated with these general subjects.

Suit (subject)—A court action for the recovery of a right or claim. The forms or documents relating to suits are generally judgments, admissions, quit claims, etc., and may be filed under the category of "Legal Documents" or, depending on how many forms there are, under the subject "Suit" or the specific subjects involved in the forms. Another term that may be encountered is "Action," but this is usually synonomous with "Suit" and should not be used.

Summons (subject)—A document, usually legal, calling upon someone to appear at a given place at a given time to answer some charge, such as a lawsuit.

Supplier (subject)—One who supplies; a vendor.

Supplies—See "Materials and Supplies."

Survey of (operation)—Use "Review of."

Suspension of (operation)—To stop or cease an action; to prevent participation in a given activity, such as suspension of a student from a school course.

Switching of (operations)—The act or process of changing, moving, placing, etc. R. R. cars for loading or unloading. In forms control, this operation is used only in relation to the subject "R. R. Car."

Tariff (subject)—A schedule of rates, charges, and the like. Do not use as a subject; use "Rate" instead.

Tax (subject)—A charge or assessment, imposed or levied by authority; a charge laid upon persons or property for public use.

Teacher (subject)—One who teaches or instructs another; a schoolteacher.

Telegram (subject)—See "Communication."

Telephone Message (subject)—See "Communication." Telephone slips for recording calls should be filed under the subject "Communication," the operation "Receipt of," and the function "To Notify."

Teletype (subject)—See "Communication."

Tell to (function)—To relate in detail; narrate, make known; disclose; divulge; inform; report or communicate to. Use the function "To Report."

Termination of (operation)—The act or process of terminating, ending, or concluding.

Test (form)—A form containing a predetermined set of questions the purpose of which is to determine the qualifications of an individual in relation to a given purpose. Such forms should be filed under the subject "Person," "Employee," etc., the operation "Examination of," and the function "To Report."

Testify, to (function)—To make a solemn declaration, verbal or written, to establish some fact; to bear witness to; to support the truth of by testimony. Use the function "To Certify."

Testing of (operation)
1. The act of determining one or more qualities or separating one or more ingredients of a substance as to kind, amount, weight, hardness, strength, etc. In forms control, the term "Test" used in the sense outlined above is not treated as a specific operation, but is included in the operation "Analysis of." See also "Analysis of."
2. The act of examining, searching, or investigating, usually prescribed or assigned for testing qualification, mental or physical, of an individual. In forms control, the term "Test" used in the sense outlined above is not treated as a specific operation, but is included in the operation "Examination of." See also the definition of the operation "Examination of."
3. The act or process of inspecting, as a strict or prying examination or close or careful scrutiny or investigation, usually to determine

adherence to set standards of quality. In forms control, the term "Test" is not used as a specific operation in the sense outlined above, but is included in the operation "Inspection of." See also "Inspection of."

4. The act of following up by inquiry or observation; to ascertain the facts in relation to a given situation, occurrence, or person. "Test" is not used as a subject in the sense outlined here; rather the operation "Investigation of" should be used.

5. The act of determining performance under a given set of conditions or circumstances that will be encountered in actual use.

Ticket (subject)—A certificate as evidence of a right, as of admission to a place of assembly or passage in a public conveyance.

Time (subject)—Time given to or taken away from work; the amount of time one has worked. See also "Absence Of" and "Attendance of."

Title (subject)—That which constitutes a just cause of exclusive possession; the instrument that is evidence of a right; a claim or right to property.

Tool (subject)—Any implement or object used in performing an operation or carrying on work of any kind, especially where the implement or object is used or worked by hand, and is movable, as distinguished from power-driven machinery. In forms control, the distinction between the subject "Tools" and "Machinery and Equipment" should be carefully noted. "Tools" differ from "Machinery and Equipment" in that tools have a relatively short life and are accordingly regarded as semipermanent instead of permanent investments. They are generally small and designed for hand use, or for machine attachments, such as the cutting tools used on lathes, planners, reamers, taps, and dies. Tools are applied directly to material in process, and consequently they wear out with greater rapidity than do machines, and because of their usual small size are easily lost or stolen. See also "Machinery and Equipment."

Tracer (form)—A form the purpose of which is to follow up some thing or action to determine the present status thereof. File under the applicable subject, the condition "Status of," and the function "To Follow Up."

Trade Acceptance (form)—An acknowledgment of a debt for goods sold, given by the purchaser to the seller of the goods and promising to pay the indebtedness at a certain time and at a certain bank. Trade acceptances represent an acknowledgment of debt, but the primary function is to order the bank to pay money; therefore they should be filed under the subject "Cash," the operation "Payment of," and the function "To Order." A cross reference may be made in the file to other functions: "To Acknowledge" and To "Agree."

Trade acceptances are negotiable instruments representing cash and may be made between two or three parties in addition to the bank. Trade acceptance forms have been standardized and approved by the National Association of Credit Men and the Federal Reserve System.

Trade Mark (subject)—A word, letter, device, or symbol used in connection with a product or merchandise and pointing distinctly to the origin of ownership of the article to which it is applied.

Training (subject)—The act or process utilized in academic preparation of an employee for a specific job. Use "Training" as a subject only when the form treats of training schedules, programs, purposes, etc.

Training of (operation)—The act or process of educating or providing with instructions. Use "Training of" in relation to the actual training of an employee for a specific job (e.g., "Employee," "Training of," "To Report," etc.).

Transfer of (operation)—The act or process of making over the possession or control of, or to make transfer of, to pass, to convey, as a right, from one person to another (e.g., title to land is transferred by deed).

Transmit, to (function)—To send or transfer from one person or place to another. Use the function "To Route."

Transmittal of (operation)—The act or process of sending or forwarding, usually by mail. In forms control, the operation "Transmittal of" is used only in connections reflecting paper work (e.g., bank checks, credit memos, correspondence, etc.).

Transportation (subject)—The movement or conveying of goods, commodities, or persons from one station or place to another. Transportation should be used as a subject only when the actual transportation itself is the subject matter of the forms (e.g., freight bill, record, etc.).

Transportation of (operation)—The act of transporting, carrying, or conveying goods, commodities, or persons from one station or place to another. "Shipping of" refers to the preparation (e.g., wrapping, crating, weighing, loading, etc.) of that which is being transported; in fact, all operations performed up to the point of actual movement toward its destination are included in the operation. A further distinction is that "Transportation of" commonly relates to persons as well as objects, whereas "Shipping of" never refers to a person. See also "Delivery of."

A distinction between "Transportation of" and "Travel" should be noted. While both may pertain to persons, "Transportation of" can include reference to inanimate things (e.g., merchandise, materials, supplies, equipment, etc.), whereas "Travel" refers to persons only. Furthermore, "Transportation Of" implies an impersonal treatment of the movement of persons, usually in the plural, whereas "Travel" implies a personal treatment of the movement of a person, usually in the singular.

Travel (subject)—The act or process of making a journey, as to pass to a distant place or places; to journey; to journey from place to place for a business house. In forms control, "Travel" applies to persons only, never to things or objects such as merchandise or supplies. The distinction between "Travel," and the operation "Transportation of" should be carefully noted. While both may apply to persons, "Travel" applies to persons only while "Transportation of" may apply either to persons or things. Also "Travel" implies action taken by the person or persons themselves while "Transportation of" implies action taken by someone else to transport the persons from one place to another. Itineraries of salespeople or others should be classed under "Travel, To Schedule."

Traveler's Check—Use "Check."

Travel Expense Report (form)—A form for the purpose of reporting the expenses of travel by persons. File under the subject "Travel," the condition "Cost of," and the function "To Report."

Treatment of (operation)—The act or process of rendering or administering medical or surgical care; the act of subjecting materials or other things to a prescribed set of conditions, operations, or influences to bring about certain predetermined results. In personnel and medical work, the operation, "Treatment of" usually applies to a person or an employee.

Trouble (subject)—That which causes disturbance, annoyance, misfortune, or embarrassment. In forms control, the term "Trouble" is not used as a specific subject, but is included in the subject "Complaints—Trouble." See also the definition of the subject "Complaints—Trouble."

Trust (subject)—A right or interest in certain property without actual legal ownership to it. An amount of money left under the care of another, usually a bank, the income of which goes to certain specified persons or organizations.

In forms control the subject "Trust" is easily confused with the securities or property that makes up the body of the trust. Use the subject "Trust" only when the entire body of the money or property itself is the subject of the form. When the form deals with the specific money or property that makes up the trust use the subject "Property" or "Securities."

Tuition (subject)—A sum of money paid for the privilege of taking courses at an institution of learning. Use the subject "Cash."

Use of (operation)—To employ or make use of; to act with or by means of; to consume entirely by using. "Use of" implies actual consumption, all or in part, as opposed to "Operation of," where something such as a machine is used but not consumed.

Utilities (subject)—Elements used in operation or use of a business or property, usually water, gas, and electricity. Sometimes considered as supplies and usually furnished by a public utility company for general use of a community or territory.

Vacancy of (condition)—The state of being vacant.

Vacation (subject)—An intermission of a stated employment, as a period of leisure or rest; a holiday. In forms control, the distinction between the subjects "Vacation" and "Recreation" should be carefully noted. A "Vacation" inherently involves time away from work—a period of leisure or rest of some duration, whereas "Recreation" does not involve time away from work and is usually a period of refreshment or diversion of short duration.

Validate, to (function)—To render valid; to give legal force to; to confirm. Use the function "To Acknowledge."

Value of (condition)—The comparative estimate that an individual places on any of his or her possessions, independently of any intent to sell.

Variance of (condition)—The fact of having departed from a predetermined standard or position.

Vehicle (subject)—A conveyance in which persons or commodities may be transported. In forms control, the subject "Vehicles" refers only to the vehicle itself and not to its contents or purpose.

Vendor (subject)—One who vends, a seller. In forms control, the term "Vendor" is not treated as a specific subject, but is included in the subject "Supplier." See also "Supplier."

Verification (form)—A form the purpose of which is to verify, confirm, or authenticate. In forms control, verifications are classified under the function "To Certify" and the specific subjects under that function.

Verification of (operation)—Use the operation "Certification of."

Verification of Order (form)—See "Acknowledgment of Order."

Verify, to (function)—To prove to be true; to establish the truth of; to confirm, as by comparison with facts; to substantiate, as by reasoning. Use the function "To Certify."

Violation of (operation)—The act of infringement, transgression, or nonobservance, as of laws, covenants, promises, rules, etc.

Visa (subject)—An endorsement made on a passport by proper authorities, denoting that it has been examined and that the bearer may proceed. In forms control, use "Visa" only when the visa is the subject of another form.

Visitor (subject)—See "Person."

Vote (subject)—An officially conferred right to express an opinion by ballot on some subject, such as the election of corporate officers or public officials. Stockholders' votes are commonly granted by proxy (see that definition) to another person by giving power of attorney for the casting of the vote.

Voucher (form)—A form used in accounting to evidence the correctness of an account or accounts by listing the details regarding a transaction or series of transactions involving that account or accounts. In ordinary accounting practice it is a form designed specifically to be used as a means of recording the details of transactions affecting accounts of the company (e.g., accounts payable voucher, etc.).

Wages (subject)—Reward, usually in the forms of cash or its equivalent, for work or services rendered usually predicated on a certain amount of time spent by the recipient in rendering the work or services. In forms control, "Wages" and "Salaries" are considered under the subject "Earnings." See also the definition of that subject.

Waiters (food and beverage) Check, or Chit (subject)—An account or itemized statement of merchandise with the charges or prices indicated and totaled; normally used in restaurants, taverns, etc., to itemize food and beverages consumed, together with other charges, and assessed against the patron. When used as a subject in forms control, "Waiter's Checks" refers to the checks only. Otherwise, waiter's check is classified under the function "To Notify," and the specific subjects under that function.

Waiver (form)—A form the purpose of which is to waive something, or to intentionally relinquish or abandon some known right, claim, or privilege. In forms control, waivers are classified under "Cancelation of, to Agree" and the specific subjects under that function.

Warn, to (function)—To put on guard; to give notice, information, or intimation of beforehand. Use the function "To Notify."

Warning Placard (form)—Forms the purpose of which is to give notice of a condition requiring special care or attention. File under "Hazard."

Waste—See "Scrap."

Weather (subject)—The state of air or atmosphere with respect to heat or cold, wetness or dryness, calm or storm, clearness or cloudiness, or any other meteorological phenomena.

Weight of (condition)—The measure of the force with which bodies tend toward the earth's center, or the force thus measured, as in ounces, pounds, hundredweight, etc.

Withdrawal of (operation)—The act or process of taking back or away, removing, or withdrawing.

Withholding of (operation)—The act of holding back all or a part of something.

Work (subject)—Physical or mechanical effort, exertion of strength or faculties for the accomplishment of something. Work can be either mental or physical.

    The distinction between "Work" and "Production" is in the direction of effort; "Work" is the effort that goes into the production or performance of a job, whereas "Production" is a measurement of the output of that effort.

    Work may be ordered and performed; production may be measured as a result. Both "Work" and "Production" may be scheduled, although the difference should be carefully noted.

In service organizations such as banks, insurance companies, schools, hospitals, etc., work is more clerical or administrative than physical as is ordinarily thought of in a manufacturing organization. Forms instruction personnel, such as file clerks, business machine operators, key punchers, etc., should be classified under "Work" with the proper operation and function.

Work-in-Process (subject)—The conversion of materials into a product; the activity or operations that take place in production or in working on raw materials or semifinished products to produce or manufacture the end product.

The distinctions among "Work-in-Process" and "Materials" and "Product" lie in the progression of the materials through the entire manufacturing process. "Materials" become "Work-in-Process" as soon as they are taken from stock and put into the conversion process. "Work-in-Process" becomes "Product" only after the final inspection is made and the product becomes salable.

The distinction between "Work-in-Process" and "Production" lies in the physical aspect of the work-in-process.

"Production" is a measurement of output that, although it can be measured in terms of "Work-in-Process" or "Product," actually is neither but only the measurement of work or effort expended. If the form relates to the actual product or materials being worked upon, it should be classified as "Work-in-Process"; if it relates to the quantity produced, it should be filed under "Production."

Semifinished parts returned to stock for storage until needed for further processing should be classified as "Work-in-Process" even though they may not be actually in process at the moment.

"Work-in-Process" requires an operation as well as a function; something must be done to it or a condition must apply to it (e.g., "Inspection of," "Change of," "Status of," "Adjustment of," "Weight of," etc.). Production," on the other hand, may be reported without an operation since production in itself implies an operation.

Two categories of forms that cause difficulty are "Work-in-Process—Inspection of—To Report" and "Equipment—Inspection of—To Report." In certain industries, such as chemical, many forms make a periodic, often hourly, report on the status of the operation. These reports may be difficult to classify as between "Equipment" and "Work-in-Process." The reading may be of a gauge or depth in a tank or other mechanical measures, but the reading actually pertains to the "Work-in-Process."

If, on the other hand, the reading actually pertains to the equipment rather than to the work-in-process, the subject should be "Equipment."

A criterion may be the frequency of the report. If the reading is made on an hourly basis the chances are that it applies to the "Work-in-Process" because equipment inspections normally are not made that often. On the other hand, if the reading is on less than a daily basis, it probably relates to the "Equipment" since work-in-process readings are made more often.

Seldom does a reading apply to both the equipment and the work-in-process. The reading may also be on a gauge or valve measuring steam, gas, air, etc., used in the conversion process. Sometimes these utilities are manufactured by the company itself or purchased from a utility company. In either case use the subject "Utilities."

Another category is "Work-in-Process—Movement of." This should be used when the form has to do with the movement of the actual work-in-process from one location to another on the same premises within the confines of the total production process. There may be a measurement of the amount moved and this should be classified under "Movement of" and not under "Production."

Work Measurement (subject)—The act of measuring work or the performance of work. Forms used in work measurement programs should be classified under the subject "Work" and the applicable operation, such as "Performance of" or "Efficiency of."

Work Order (form)—A form the purpose of which is to order the expenditure of effort—physical, mental, or mechanical—for the accomplishment of an end.

Many such forms are called "Production Order," "Factory Order," etc., but all apply to the exertion that is set in motion for the accomplishment of something and should, therefore, be classified as "Work."

Work Sheets (form)—A group of forms comprising columnar sheets, graph paper, ruled forms, etc., all of which contain printing or ruling in the form of lines and rules only, with no words or copy to identify the form with a given function or subject.

Such forms are not forms in the strict sense of the word until they have been filled in with data that identifies them with some subject or function; therefore they should be filed under the arbitrary classification "Work Sheets" without references to subject operations or functions.

CODED DICTIONARY OF TERMINOLOGY FOR THE TASK INVENTORY WORK MEASUREMENT PROGRAM

This dictionary contains the large majority of terms that will be encountered in taking a task inventory for work simplification and cost reduction. It has been developed through actual application in industrial, commercial, and governmental types of organizations and has been proven successful.

Terms may be encountered, of course, in any given organization that do not appear herein, but they can be added as needed. New developments in such areas as word processing and new computer applications will account for such new terms in the area of business machines, and electronic applications may bring in new terms in data processing activities. However, in the very large majority of instances the terms contained herein will be found sufficient.

In the area of coding the forms, trouble may arise in the various ways in which forms are numbered sequentially for control. Many such numbers contain prefixes and suffixes, which cannot be conveniently coded for task inventory without the use of special codes. A convenient way to do this is to make a listing of the form numbers involved, assign a supplementary code in five digits arbitrarily to each form, and use the arbitrary codes for key punching. The forms can then be easily related back to the proper form numbers for identification.

Otherwise the terms, definitions, and codes should suffice for all ordinary applications. The codes have been applied to the task "Transcribing" in Section IVD.

Dictionary of Clerical Task Titles for Clerical Work Measurement

Code			
Prefix	Suffix	Description of Tasks	Count as Output
1	1	Accounting Classification A special task title for assigning an account number or a code to a previously prepared form or record. It involves reading the data and deciding on the proper classification by reference to an established chart of account or code list, if necessary. Includes entering the appropriate account number or code on the form.	Papers Coded
	2	Accounting Data, Compile Includes preparation of accounting and statistical reports, generally when data are compiled from a number of sources and intermittent brief calculating tasks are involved. Distinguish from Enter Data, Calculate.	None
	3	Accounting, Journalize Constructing journal entries preparatory to transfer of data from one accounting record to another. Distinguish from Posting.	None
		Accounting, Reconciliation, see Balancing	
2		Add, See Calculate	
		Address A—*Method Used* (1st digit of suffix)	Addresses Addresses
	1 – –	Use Addressing Machine, Power driven; auto feed	
	2 – –	Use Addressing Machine, Power driven; hand feed	
	3 – –	Use Addressing Machine, Manual	
	4 – –	Use Typewriter, Electric	
	5 – –	Use Typewriter, Manual	
	6 – –	Use Pen, Longhand	
	0 – –	Unspecified	
		B— *Type of Item Address* (2nd digit of suffix)	Addresses
	– 1 –	Envelope, size 14 or smaller	
	– 2 –	Envelope, larger than size 14	
	– 3 –	Card, 5 × 8 and smaller	
	– 4 –	Card, larger than 5 × 8	
	– 5 –	Sheet, smaller than 8½ × 11	

Dictionary of Clerical Task Titles for Clerical Work Measurement *(continued)*

Code		Description of Tasks	Count as Output
Prefix	Suffix		
	− 6 −	Sheet, 8½ × 11 (form letter, etc.)	
	− 7 −	Sheet, larger than 8½ × 11	
	− 8 −	Label, single	
	− 9 −	Label, perforated strip	
	− 0 −	Unspecified	
		C— *Source of Data* (3rd digit of suffix)	Addresses
	− − 1	Embossed metal plate	
	− − 2	Stencil	
	− − 3	Card, Longhand	
	− − 4	Card, Typed	
	− − 5	List, Longhand	
	− − 6	List, Typed	
	− − 0	Unspecified	
3		Addressing, Cut Stencils	Stencils
	1	On typewriter	
	2	On stencil-making machine	
	0	Unclassified stencil handling	
4		Addressing, Plate-Handling, Addressograph	Plates
	1	Emboss metal plate	
	2	Insert metal plate in frame	
	3	Remove metal plate from frame	
	4	Print cards to identify plates	
	5	Insert identification cards in frames	
	6	Proof list new plates, sight verify to original lists or cards	
	0	Unclassified plate handling	
5		Advertising Includes layout, art work, and similar tasks that cannot be identified by any specific task title. See also Writing.	None
6		Appointments, Make Telephone work with prospects, clients, or customers to set up appointments, develop leads. Includes making hotel and travel reservations.	Calls Made
7		Appraising Establishing value of property by physical inspection or examination.	None
8		Auditing A special checking task involving the examination of books and records	None

(continued)

Dictionary of Clerical Task Titles for Clerical Work Measurement *(continued)*

Code		Description of Tasks	Count as Output
Prefix	Suffix		
		Auditing [cont.] prepared by others to verify the propriety and accuracy of entries. Distinguish from Balancing, Checking, Correcting.	
11		Balancing	Records or Accounts Balanced
		Includes calculating, checking, and comparing balances of one record with prior balances of the same or other records. If totals do not agree, individual items are checked for error in computation or posting. Corrections are made or others may be instructed to do so. Adding or calculating machines may be used. Distinguish from Auditing, Checking, Correcting.	
12		Band, Bundle Includes bundling, typing mail, and similar operations.	Bundles
13		Billing, (Invoicing, Statements)	Bills Invoice Sets
		A— *Method* (1st digit of suffix)	
	1 – – –	Using Calculating Billing Machine	
	2 – – –	Using Noncalculating Billing Machine	
	3 – – –	Using Typewriter	
	4 – – –	Using Pen, Longhand	
	0 – – –	Unspecified	
		B— *Source of Data* (2nd digit of suffix)	
	– 1 – –	Sales or shipping order, Invoice copy to be completed.	
	– 2 – –	Sales or shipping order, Complete transcription required.	
	– 3 – –	Ledger Sheet (for statements)	
	– 0 – –	Unspecified	
		C— *Characters Typewritten* (3rd digit of suffix)	
	– – 1–	Under 20	
	– – 2 –	20–99	
	– – 3 –	100–199	
	– – 4 –	200–299	
	– – 5 –	300–399	
	– – 6 –	Over 400	

Dictionary of Clerical Task Titles for Clerical Work Measurement *(continued)*

Code			Count as
Prefix	Suffix	Description of Tasks	Output
		D— *Type of Form Used*	
	– – – 1	Single Sheet	
	– – – 2	Multiple copy, insert and remove carbon	
	– – – 3	Multiple copy, carbon interleaved, snapout	
	– – – 4	Continuous	
14		Blueprint Machine, Operate Includes all work details involved in operating a machine and other equipment to produce vandyke (wet-process) or diazo (dry-process) print from translucent masters. Does not include trimming, folding, or distributing prints.	Prints
15		Bursting, Separating Separate continuous forms into sets of single sheets, Remove carbons	Sheets or Sets
	1	On Machine	
	2	Manually	
		Buying, see Order Placing, Entering Data, Reading and Signing, Interviewing	
18		Calculate	Calculations Made
	1	on Listing Machine	
	2	on Nonlisting Machines	
19		Calculate, Manually, Mentally	
		A— *Type of Operation Performed* (1st digit of suffix)	
	1 – – –	Addition	
	2 – – –	Addition and Subtraction	
	3 – – –	Division	
	4 – – –	Division and Multiplication	
	5 – – –	Multiplication and Addition	
	6 – – –	Subtraction	
	7 – – –	Multiplication	
	8 – – –	Series of three computations per answer	
	9 – – –	Series of more than three computations per answer	
	0 – – –	Unclassified	
		B— *Source of Data* (2nd digit of suffix)	
	– 1 – –	Columns of figures on single form or worksheet	*(continued)*

Dictionary of Clerical Task Titles for Clerical Work Measurement *(continued)*

Code		Description of Tasks	Count as Output
Prefix	Suffix		

	− 2 − −	Calculate [cont.]
		   Figures taken from separate
		     written records	

	− 0 − −	Unclassified	
		*C— *Digits Involved in Each* *Separate Calculation* (3rd digit of suffix)	
	− − 1 −	Under 10	
	− − 2 −	10−49	
	− − 3 −	50−99	
	− − 4 −	100−199	
	− − 5 −	200−299	
	− − 6 −	300−399	
	− − 7 −	400−499	
	− − 8 −	500 and over	
	− − 0 −	Unspecified	
		D— *Disposition of Output (Answers)* (4th digit of suffix)	
	− − − 1	Post each answer and clear machine.	
	− − − 2	Post from tape as separate task.	
	− − − 3	Check with previous answer and clear machine.	
	− − − 0	Unspecified	

		*Note:
		 Estimate digits (C) as follows:
		 Addition: Items added *x* average digits
		   per item.
		 Subtraction: Sum of digits of two
		   figures involved.
		 Multiplication: Sum of digits in
		   multiplier and multiplicand.
		 Division: Sum of digits in divisor and
		   dividend.
		 Other: Sum of digits in input data.	

21		Cash Register, Operate	None
22		Chart Data Draw charts, graphs by longhand or with hand tools on cross-section paper, poster stock, or other materials including translucent stock for reproduction.	Charts
23		Check Handling	Checks
	1	Canceling Machine, Operate	
	2	Endorsing Machine, Operate	

Dictionary of Clerical Task Titles for Clerical Work Measurement *(continued)*

Code		Description of Tasks	Count as Output
Prefix	Suffix		
	3	Endorsing, Hand Stamp	
	4	Protecting Machine, Operate	
		Preparation, see Enter Data,	
		Accounting	
	5	Posting Machine, Operate, Transcribe	
	6	Signing Machine, Operate	
	7	Signing, Manual	
	0	Unspecified	
24		Checking	Items Checked
		Task involves counting quantities of	
		things including forms, checks, and	
		other documents and comparing	
		quantities, condition, and	
		specifications with stated quantities,	
		etc., on lists, reports, or other forms.	
		Also identifying articles with written	
		specifications or descriptions.	
		Distinguish from Auditing, Balancing,	
		Correcting.	
25		Coin, Currency Handling	None
	1	Count, Machine	
	2	Count, Manual	
	3	Count, and sort, Machine	
	4	Count, and sort, Manual	
	5	Denominate	
	6	Dispense, Machine	
	7	Dispense, Manual	
	0	Unspecified	
26		Collating, Gathering	Sheets
	1	Use Machine, Sheets	
	2	Use Bins or Racks, Sheets	
	3	Use Table Top, Sheets	
27		Collecting	None
		Outside collecting involving travel.	
		Inside collecting activities are to be	
		broken down into separate tasks.	
28		Compiling	None
		Task involves gathering and arranging	
		information for catalogs, pamphlets,	
		price lists, directories, etc. See also	
		Advertising, Composing, Writing,	
		Accounting, Data, Compile.	
29		Composing, Manual	None
		Paste up copy including headlines,	

(continued)

Dictionary of Clerical Task Titles for Clerical Work Measurement *(continued)*

Code			
Prefix	Suffix	Description of Tasks	Count as Output
		Composing [cont.] text, cutouts, etc., for photocopy. See also Advertising.	
30		Composing, Machine, Operate Operate veritype, headliner, or similar.	None
31		Conferring Conversations, person to person or by telephone. Distinguish from Interviewing, Instructing.	None
32		Control Board, Maintain Set up and make changes to display board using lines, cards, and other devices to record progress or status of activities (Example: Productrol Board or maps).	None
		Copy Writing, see Writing	
33		Correcting Reading and making changes to written, typed, or printed material. Includes proofreading, editing and rearrangement of data before or after transcription. Does not include preparation of a change notice. See Enter Data.	None
34		Corresponding Reading and replying to inside or outside communications: letters, telegrams, memos, etc. Use subclassifications below.	Pages
	1	Read and Reply, Longhand draft for typing	
	2	Read and Reply, Typed draft for transcription	
	3	Read and Reply, Longhand only	
	4	Read and Reply, Typed only Distinguish from Write, Compose.	
35		Counting, Tally Machine, Operate	None
36		Cutting, Trimming	Sheets
	1	Operate Machine	
	2	Use hand tools	

Dictionary of Clerical Task Titles for Clerical Work Measurement *(continued)*

Code		Description of Tasks	Count as Output
Prefix	Suffix		
37		Depositing Money Preparatory work is covered by separate task titles. Trip to bank is titled Messenger.	
38		Dictating	Pages
	1	Use recording machine	
	2	To stenographer, Shorthand	
	3	To stenographer, Stenotype	
	4	To Typist, Typewriter	
39		Dictation, Take	Pages
	1	Using Shorthand	
	2	Using Stenotype	
		Dictation, Transcribe see Transcribing	
40		Dictating Equipment, Record Reprocessing, Shaving	Discs Cylinders Belts
41		Duplicating	Sheets
	1	Operate Machine, Power driven, auto-feed	
	2	Operate Machine, Power-driven, hand-feed	
	3	Operate Machine, manual	
	4	Same as (1) slipsheets required	
	5	Same as (2) slipsheets required	
	6	Same as (3) slipsheets required	
42		Duplicating Masters, Prepare	
	1	Hectograph, Type	Masters
	2	Mimeograph, Type	Stencils
	3	Offset Paper Master	Masters
	4	Offset Metal Plate	Masters
44		Enter Data This class of Task Titles involves the *longhand* entry of data on forms or records. It is used only where the form is *substantially completed* as a single task as distinguished from POST tasks, where data may be entered on a single record on successive days. Distinguish from Address, Post,	

(continued)

Dictionary of Clerical Task Titles for Clerical Work Measurement *(continued)*

Code		Description of Tasks	Count as Output
Prefix	Suffix		
		Enter data [cont.] Write, Transcribe. Use codes below to define this task:	
		A— *Source of Data* (1st digit of suffix)	Forms
	1 – –	Single form or record	
	2 – –	More than one form or record	
	3 – –	Letter or memorandum	
	4 – –	Activities, conditions observed and reported	
	5 – –	Requirements, needs expressed (requisition, etc.)	
	0 – –	Unspecified	
		B— Volume of Data Entered (2nd digit of suffix)	
	– 1 –	50 Characters, figures, and less	
	– 2 –	51–100 Characters, figures	
	– 3 –	101–200 Characters, figures	
	– 4 –	201–300 Characters, figures	
	– 5 –	301–400 Characters, figures	
	– 6 –	401–500 Characters, figures	
	– 7 –	501 and more characters, figures	
	– 8 –	15 or less mark sensing card digits	
	– 9 –	over 15	
	– 0 –	Unspecified	
		C— *Handling Form* (3rd digit of suffix)	
	– – 1	No carbons involved	
	– – 2	2–5 copies, Assemble and remove carbons	
	– – 3	over 5 copies, Assemble and remove carbons	
		Editing, see Correcting	
45		Erasing Machine, Operate Eliminate data from previously entered form. See also Correcting.	Forms
46		Expediting Follow-up of production by vendors to insure maintenance of schedules. May involve outside travel.	
48		File This task involves the indexing of papers under predetermined classes	Items Filed

Dictionary of Clerical Task Titles for Clerical Work Measurement *(continued)*

Code		Description of Tasks	Count as Output
Prefix	Suffix		
		and placing them in containers, files, or filing devices for future reference.	
		A— *Type of Material Filed* (1st digit of suffix)	
	1 – – –	Cards 5 × 8 and smaller	
	2 – – –	Cards larger than 5 × 8	
	3 – – –	Sheets 8½ × 11 and smaller	
	4 – – –	Sheets larger than 8½ × 11	
	5 – – –	Plates, stencils, Addressing	
	6 – – –	Plates, stencils, Masters, Duplicating	
	7 – – –	Drawings, blueprints	
	8 – – –	Booklets, pamphlets, bound or stapled material	
	0 – – –	Unclassified material.	
		B— *Condition of Material Filed* (2nd digit of suffix)	
	– 1 – –	Random sequence, filed without presorting	
	– 2 – –	Rough sorted as separate task	
	– 3 – –	Fine sorted as separate task	
	– 4 – –	Same as (1) except material is coded, logged, cross-referenced, or identified manually by subject or title as it is being filed	
	– 5 – –	Same as (4) except prior Rough Sort	
	– 6 – –	Same as (4) except prior Fine Sort	
	– 0 – –	Unspecified	
		C— *Filing Sequence* (3rd digit of suffix)	
	– – 1 –	Alphabetic, 10 characters or less	
	– – 2 –	Alphabetic, over 10 characters	
	– – 3 –	Alphabetic, Numeric, 10 characters and figures	
	– – 4 –	Alphabetic, Numeric, over 10 characters and figures	
	– – 5 –	Location, Geographic	
	– – 6 –	Location, Alphabetic	
	– – 7 –	Numeric	
	– – 8 –	Subject	
	– – 9 –	Subject and date or identifying code	
	– – 0 –	Other filing sequence	

(continued)

Dictionary of Clerical Task Titles for Clerical Work Measurement *(continued)*

Code		Description of Tasks	Count as Output
Prefix	Suffix		
		File [cont.]	
		D— *Method of Filing* (4th digit of suffix)	
	— — — 1	Insert loose in folders, file in vertical file drawer	
	— — — 2	Same as (1) except attach to folder	
	— — — 3	File cards loose between dividers, vertical file	
	— — — 4	Attach card or sheet to holding device in file	
	— — — 5	In ring binder	
	— — — 6	In post binder	
	— — — 7	File in binder or other device requiring shifting of previously filed material	
	— — — 8	Fold and file, vertical file	
	— — — 9	Fold and file, flat	
	— — — 0	Unclassified	
49		File, Remove from	Items
		Use same suffix codes as for File except use 0 for 2nd digit, thereby ignoring class B.	
50		Files, Prepare, Arrange	None
	1	Label, labels previously typed	
	2	Type and affix labels	
	3	Rearrange, shift cards, folders	
	4	Miscellaneous	
51		Fold	Sheets
	1	Folding Machine, Operate	
	2	Fold single sheet, 1 fold Manual	
	3	Fold single sheet, 2 fold Manual	
	4	Fold 2 or more sheets, 1 fold Manual	
	5	Fold Prints drawings	
	0	Unclassified	
52		Fold and Insert	Sheets
	1	Single fold, Plain envelope	
	2	Double fold, Plain envelope	
	3	Single fold, Window envelope	
	4	Double fold, Window envelope	
	0	Unclassified	
53		Forms Designing and Specification Writing	None
		Gathering, see Collating	

Dictionary of Clerical Task Titles for Clerical Work Measurement *(continued)*

Code		Description of Tasks	Count as Output
Prefix	Suffix		
55		Housekeeping, Maintenance Includes dusting furniture, laying out pads, pencils, etc., taking out and putting away work. Cleaning typewriter and changing ribbons, etc.	None
57		Insert	Sheets
	1	Previously folded sheets in plain envelopes	
	2	Previously folded sheets in window envelopes	
	3	Flat sheets in envelopes	
	4	Collate two or more types of material and insert in plain envelope	
	5	Same as (4) except insert in window envelope	
	6	Insert pamphlet, booklets, etc., in envelopes, fasten with clasp or string	
	0	Unclassified	
58		Instruct Give or receive verbal instructions when new employees are being trained or when a new or revised system is being installed. Use the following codes:	None
	1	Give instructions	
	2	Receive instructions Distinguish from Conferring.	
59		Interview Talk to business callers, applicants. May involve taking notes or filling out forms while interview is taking place.	Callers Applicants
60		Investigate Investigate claims, personal histories, and other facts and report them by use of memo or form. Distinguish from Enter Data, Write Job Analysis, see Write, Enter Data Log, Register, see Post, Enter Data	Reports
62		Machine, Set Up, Adjust See also Housekeeping, Maintenance	
63	1	Mailing, Incoming Slit envelopes	Places

(continued)

Dictionary of Clerical Task Titles for Clerical Work Measurement *(continued)*

Code		Description of Tasks	Count as Output
Prefix	Suffix		
		Mailing, Incoming [cont.]	
	2	Remove Contents of envelopes	
	3	Read and classify for distribution	
	0	Unclassified	
		See also Sort, Messenger	
64		Mailing, Outgoing	Pieces
	1	Seal envelopes	
	2	Stamp Envelopes Manual	
	3	Stamp Envelopes Machine	
	4	Inserting, Sealing Stamping Machine, Operate	
	0	Unclassified	
		See also Band, Fold, Insert, Wrap, Package Handling	
65		Messenger	None
		Carry mail inside, outside, run errands, visit bank, pick up supplies at stock room. Includes all trips outside of employees' own department except travel to and from meetings or conferences or personal time.	
66		Microfilming	Items
	1	Operate Camera	
	2	Operate Reader	
	3	Process film	
	0	Unclassified	
68		Numbering, Dating, Receipting	Items
	1	Operate Power Machine	
	2	Use hand stamps	
69		Order Placing, Telephone	Calls
		Placing purchase orders by telephone. Follow-up of orders. Taking notes of conversations.	
70		Order Taking, Telephones	Calls
		Taking or discussing orders. Making notes or memos of conversations. If the sales order itself is prepared during the conversation, use instead task title Enter Data.	
72		Package Handling	Pieces
	1	Operate Tape Dispensing Machine	
	2	Operate Sealing, Labeling Machine	
	3	Operate Tying, Bundling Machine	
	4	Operate Scales	

Dictionary of Clerical Task Titles for Clerical Work Measurement *(continued)*

Code		Description of Tasks	Count as Output
Prefix	Suffix		
	5	Wrap, Unwrap Manually	
	0	Unclassified	
73		Photoreproduction	Copies
	1	Direct Process	
	2	Negative, Positive Process	
		Distinguish from Blueprinting	
74		Post	Postings Made
		Transfer data from one form or record to another when the record is not completely filled out as a task. Distinguish from Enter Data, Transcribe.	
		A— *Method Used* (1st digit of suffix)	Postings
	1 – – –	Operate Posting or Bookkeeping Machine	
	2 – – –	Manually Post	
		B— *Volume of Data Posted* (2nd digit of suffix)	
	– 1 – –	4 digits or characters and less	
	– 2 – –	5–7 digits or characters and less	
	– 3 – –	8–20 digits or characters and less	
	– 4 – –	over 20 digits or characters	
		C— *Records Involved* (3rd digit of suffix)	
	– – 1 –	Post from one record to one sheet or card	
	– – 2 –	Post from several records to one sheet or card	
	– – 3 –	Post from one record to several sheets or cards	
	– – 4 –	Post from several records to several sheets or cards	
		D— *Record Handling* (4th digit of suffix)	
	– – – 1	Remove from file and refile each card as posted	
	– – – 2	Filing and refiling performed as separate tasks	
	– – – 0	Unspecified	
75		Post Stamp	Pieces
		Enter date, similar data using hand stamp	
		Proof Read, see Correcting	

(continued)

Dictionary of Clerical Task Titles for Clerical Work Measurement *(continued)*

Code			
Prefix	Suffix	Description of Tasks	Count as Output
76		Punch, Drill	Sheets
	1	Operate Power Machine	
	2	Use Hand Tool	
79		Read, Annotate	Communications
		Reading a report or other communication, making marginal notes for use of another person who will read copy and reply or take other action.	
80		Read, Sign	Documents
81		Read, Information	Documents
82		Reception	Callers
		Greeting callers, making out visitor's pass, announcing visitors	
85		Sales, Inside	Number of Sales
86		Sales, Outside	Number of Sales
87		Sort	Pieces
		A— *Type of Material Sorted* (1st digit of suffix)	
	1 – –	Cards 5 × 8 and smaller	
	2 – –	Cards larger than 5 × 8	
	3 – –	Sheets 8½ × 11 and smaller	
	4 – –	Sheets larger than 8½ × 11	
	5 – –	Plates, Stencils, Addressing	
	6 – –	Plates, Stencils, Masters, Duplicating punched cards (see Tabulating)	
	7 – –	Punched cards, Marginal Punching	
	8 – –	Mail, Envelopes, Jackets	
	0 – –	Unclassified	
		B— *Sorting Sequence* (2nd digit of suffix)	
	– 1 –	Alphabetic, 10 characters or less	
	– 2 –	Alphabetic, over 10 characters	
	– 3 –	Alphabetic, Numeric, 10 characters and figures or less	
	– 4 –	Alphabetic, Numeric, over 10 characters and figures	
	– 5 –	Location, Geographic	
	– 6 –	Location, and Alphabetic	
	– 7 –	Numeric	
	– 8 –	Subject	

Dictionary of Clerical Task Titles for Clerical Work Measurement *(continued)*

Code			Count as
Prefix	Suffix	Description of Tasks	Output
	− 9 −	Subject and date or identifying code	
	− 0 −	Other filing sequence	
		C— *Sorting Method* (3rd digit of suffix)	
	− − 1	Rough Sort only, Table Top	
	− − 2	Rough Sort only, Box, Bin	
	− − 3	Fine Sort, Table Top	
	− − 4	Fine Sort, Box, Bin	
	− − 5	Complete, Table Top	
	− − 6	Complete, Box, Bin	
	− − 7	Sort using Sortagraph or similar machine	
	− − 8	Needle sort marginally slotted and punched cards	
	− − 0	Method unspecified	
88		Staple, Stitch, Sew	Sheets
	1	Operate Power Machine	
	2	Use hand tool	
91		Tabulating Equipment, Operate	
	10	Keypunch	Columns
	11	Verifier	Columns
	12	Sorter	Cards
	13	Multiplier	
	14	Collator	
	15	Cardatype	
	16	Printer	
	17	Gang Punch, Reproducer	
	18	Interpreter	
	19	Summary Punch	
	20	Other	
92		Tabulating, Miscellaneous Tasks	
	1	Wiring	Boards
	2	Manual Sort	Cards
	3	Filing, maintaining Master decks	None
	4	Balancing, verifying Manually	None
	5	Pull cards from files	Cards
93		Teleautograph, Operate	Messages Sent
94		Telephone, Interoffice Communications	None
	1	Operate switchboard	
	2	Operate Public Address system	
	3	Operate Music System	
95		Teletype, Operate	Messages
	1	Send, Type all data	

(continued)

Dictionary of Clerical Task Titles for Clerical Work Measurement *(continued)*

Code		Description of Tasks	Count as Output
Prefix	Suffix		
		Teletype, Operate [cont.]	
	2	Send, Type and use tape	
	3	Receive	
	0	Unclassified	
96		Time Stamping	Pieces
	1	Operate power and stamping machine	
	2	Use hand stamp	
97		Time, Observing	None
		Making time studies by observing operations being performed. Includes entering data on observation sheet.	
98		Transcribing, Typing	
		A— *Kind of Data Typed* (1st digit of suffix)	Sheets Typed
	1 – – –	Technical, Statistical, Symbols, Words, and figures, Engineering, Medicine Terminology, etc.	
	2 – – –	Nontechnical, Common usage words, some figures	
		B— *Typing Arrangement* (2nd digit of suffix)	
	– 1 – –	Lines, Single-space	
	– 2 – –	Lines, Double-space	
	– 3 – –	Fill-in blocks or spaces on forms under 100 key strokes.	
	– 4 – –	Fill-in blocks or spaces on forms, 100–500 key strokes	
	– 5 – –	Fill-in blocks or spaces on forms of over 500 key strokes	
	– 6 – –	Columnar, using 3 tabulations stops or less	
	– 7 – –	Columnar, using 4–7 tab stops	
	– 8 – –	Columnar, using over 7 tab stops	
	– 9 – –	Irregular fill-in requiring back spacing or hand adjustments of plates	
	– 0 – –	Unclassified	
		C— *Kind of Copy Transcribed* (3rd digit of suffix)	
	– – 1 –	Longhand copy	
	– – 2 –	Longhand and typed copy, combined	
	– – 3 –	Typed copy	
	– – 4 –	Typed copy requiring rearrangement	

Dictionary of Clerical Task Titles for Clerical Work Measurement *(continued)*

Code		Description of Tasks	Count as Output
Prefix	Suffix		
	– – 5 –	Dictating machine records	
	– – 6 –	Stenotype tape	
	– – 7 –	Stenographic notes	
	– – 8 –	Unclassified	
		D— *Copies Made* (4th digit of suffix)	
	– – – 1	Original	
	– – – 2	Original and 1 carbon, includes assembling sets and removing carbons	
	– – – 3	Original and 2 carbons, includes assembling sets and removing carbons	
	– – – 4	Original and 3 carbons, includes assembling sets and removing carbons	
	– – – 5	Original and 4 carbons, includes assembling sets and removing carbons	
	– – – 6	Original and 5 carbons, includes assembling sets and removing carbons	
	– – – 7	Original and over 5 carbons, includes assembling sets and removing carbons	
	– – – 8	Snap-out set, 4 copies or less, includes removing carbons	
	– – – 9	Snap-out set over 4 copies, includes removing carbons	
	– – – 0	Varying number of copies	
100		Translating, Language	None
		Verify, see Auditing, Correcting, Tabulating Machine	
101		Write	None
		This is a general task title for all work details involved in preparing drafts, either longhand or typewritten for letters, memos, bulletins, reports, articles for publication. May include research, examination of various records and files, Distinguish from Enter Data, Post, Correspond.	
	1	Nontechnical Material	
	2	Technical Material	

Relations of Office Machines and Equipment to Tasks

Note: Some modern electronic office machines may not be shown. If encountered, add to list in proper position and code sequentially in the group.

10−002		*Accounting, Adding, Billing, Calculating, Punched Card and Statistical Machines*
11−002		*Punched Card Machines*
−102		Punch (024)
−202		Verifier (056)
−302		Sorter (082)
−312		Sorter (101)
−402		Printer, Alphabetic Accounting (402)
−412		Printer, Numeric Accounting (407)
−502		Interpreter (552)
−602		Collator (077)
−702		Reproducer (519)
−712		Reproducing Summary Punch (514)
−802		Calculator (604)
−812		Calculator (521)
−902		Transfer Posting (954)
−912		Unclassified
12−002		*Billing and Accounting Machines, except Punched Card Machines*
		Descriptive (Typewriter Keyboard Type):
−112		Noncomputing, Cylindrical Platen
−122		Computing, Cylindrical Platen
−142		Noncomputing, Flat Platen
−152		Computing, Flat Platen
		Nondescriptive (Numerical Keyboard Type):
−212		10-Key Keyboard, Cylindrical Platen
−222		Full or Multiple-Key Keyboard, Cylindrical Platen
−232		Flat Platen, Full or Multiple-Key Keyboard
13−002		*Adding and Calculating (Computing) Machine*
		Nonlisting:
−112		Unit Counters
−122		10-Key Keyboard
−132		Full or Multiple-Key Keyboard
−142		Stylus or Lever-Set-Type Keyboard
		Listing:
−212		10-Key Keyboard (Including Multiple Register Bank Proof and Check Sorting)
−222		Full or Multiple-Key Keyboard
14−002		*Marginal Notched Card Sorting and Selecting*
15−002		*Peg Board Equipment*
20−002		*Cash Registering, Check, Coin, and Currency Handling and Related Machines*
21−002		*Coin Currency Handling Machines*
−102		Currency (Paper) Counting and Sorting Machines
		Coin Handling Machines:
−212		Coin sorting
−222		Coin Counting
−232		Coin Sorting and Counting Combination Machines
−242		Coin Sorting, Counting, and Wrapping Combination Machines

Relations of Office Machines and Equipment to Tasks *(continued)*

−252	Coin Counting and Wrapping Combination Machines
−262	Automatic Cashier (Coin Dispensing) Machines
22−002	*Payroll Denominating Machines*
23−002	*Check Handling Machines, Except Office Perforators (Canceling)*
−102	Check Cutting, Sorting, and Stacking
−202	Check Endorsing
−302	Signing Machines, Include Check Signing
−402	Check Writing (Include Protecting)
24−002	*Perforators, Office, Including Check Canceling Perforators*
25−002	*Autographic Registers (Manuscript Manifolding Systems)*
26−002	*Cash Registers*
30−002	*Dictating and Recording Machines and Interoffice Communicating Devices*
31−002	*Dictating (Recording) Machines, Acoustic or Electronic Pick-up, Including Combination Dictating, Transcribing Machines*
	Needle-Type Recording Media:
−112	Wax Cylinder
−122	Plastic Disc and Belt
	Magnetic Recording Media:
−212	Wire
−222	Tape
−232	Disc
−242	Belt
−302	Reprocessing Machines
32−002	*Transcribing and Cylinder Shaving Machines*
	Transcribing (Nonrecording) Machines, Acoustic or Electronic Pick-up:
−112	Wax Cylinder
−122	Plastic Disc and Belt
−202	Cylinder Shaving Machine, for Wax Cylinder-Type Recording Media
33−002	*Shorthand (Stenographic) Writing Machine*
34−002	*Interoffice Communicating Devices*
35−002	*General Communication Devices (Teletype, Teleautograph, etc.)*
−102	Text Material
−202	Graphic and Pictorial
40−002	*Office Composing, Writing and Reproducing, and Paper Handling Equipment*
41−002	*Typewriters*
	Cylinder Platen:
−112	Standard
−122	Noiseless
−132	Wide Carriage
−142	Portable
−202	Flat-Bed Platen
−203	Word Processing

(continued)

Relations of Office Machines and Equipment to Tasks *(continued)*

42-002	*Office Composing Machines*
	Interchangeable-Type and Changeable-Type Spacing Typewriter
-202	Forms Composing
-302	Strip Composing (Headliner, etc.)
43-002	*Hectographic Process Office Duplicating Machines*
-102	Composing (Gelatin) Roll and Film
-202	Liquid (Direct or Spirit) Process
-302	Transfer Posting (Forced Fluid)
44-002	*Stencil Duplicating Machines and Auxiliary Machines*
	Stencil Duplicators:
-112	Single Rotary Cylinder
-122	Multiple Rotary Cylinder
-132	Flat-Bed Types
-142	Stamp
-202	Stencil Making Machines
-502	Ticket Writing Equipment
45-002	*Offset (Plane Surface, Planographic or Lithographic) Duplicating Process (Using Direct, Offset, or Photo-Offset Methods)*
-102	Offset Duplicating Machines
-202	Cameras, Plate-Making, and Auxiliary Machines
46-002	*Raised Image (Relief)-Type Printing Duplicating Processes*
-112	Typesetting Machines
-122	Rotary and Flat-Bed Duplicating Machines, Using Ink or Inked Ribbon
-202	Embossed Metal Plate Duplicating Machines (Form Letter Writing)
47-002	*Photographic Reproduction Processes*
	Contact- (Nonlens) Type Exposing and Developing Machines:
-112	Photocopy (Wet) Contact Process
-122	Direct (Dry) Diazo Dye-Line or Brownline Print Process
-132	Blueprint (Wet) Process
-132	Photocopy Contact Process—Transfer Method
-152	Photocopy Contact Process—Nontransfer Method (Reflex)
	Camera (Lens and Prism System) Process, Other than Photo-offset:
-212	Photocopy (Wet) Camera Process
-222	Microfilm Process (Cameras, Processing, and Reading Machines)
-302	Facsimile Reproduction
48-002	*Automatically Operated (Perforated Tape Controlled) Typesetters*
-102	Tape Punching or Perforating Machines
-202	Tape Reading (Typewriter Operating Machines)
49-002	*Paper Handling Machines and Devices*
-102	Cutting, Trimming
-202	Collating and Gathering Machines
-302	Folding
-402	Punches and Drills (Except Perforators—See 24-002)
-502	Stapling and Stitching Machines
-602	Continuous Forms Feeding, Separating, Bursting, etc. Devices
-702	Document Destroying Equipment (Shredding, etc.)
50-002	*Time Recording, Job Recording, and Time Stamping Machines*

Relations of Office Machines and Equipment to Tasks *(continued)*

51–002	*Time Recorders—Office Type (Excluding Program Clocks, Master Clock Time Systems, etc.)*
52–002	*Job Recording Machines*
53–002	*Stamping Machines*
54–002	*Numbering, Dating, Receipting Machines*
60–002	*Addressing and Mailing Machines*
61–002	*Addressing Machines*
62–002	*Address Plate Embossing Machines*
63–002	*Postage Meter and Postal Permit Mailing Machines*
–102	Postage Meter
–202	Postal Permit
64–002	*Canceling Machines Except Check Canceling*
65–002	*Stamp Affixing and Dispensing Machines*
66–002	*Envelope Opening and Sealing*
–102	Envelope Opening
–202	Envelope Sealing
67–002	*Folding and Filling Machines*
–102	Office Folding Machines (Letters, Bulletins, and Notices)
–202	Envelope Inserting-of-Contents Machines
68–002	*Package Handling Machines and Devices*
–102	Tape Moistening, Dispensing, Sealing, and Labeling Machines (Mail Room Type)
–202	String Tying and Other Wrapping or Packaging Machines (Mail Room Type)
–302	Package Marking Stencil Die-Cutting Machine
–402	Postal Scales (Parcel Post Type)
70–002	*Filing and Sorting Equipment*
71–002	*Filing Equipment*
	Vertical Types:
–111	Drawer, Letter Size
–121	Drawer, Legal Size
–131	Drawer, Card
–141	Drawer, Desk
–151	Box, Letter Size
–161	Box, Card
–171	Rotary
–181	Shelf
–191	Tray, Tub
	Visible Types:
–331	Panel Type
–531	Vertical Visible
–360	Motor Driven
	Special Purpose Filing Equipment:
–411	Blue Print, Map
–421	Insulated, Safety Cabinet, Safe
–431	Microfilm
–441	Addressing Plates, Metal

(continued)

Relations of Office Machines and Equipment to Tasks *(continued)*

71−002	*Filing Equipment* [cont.]	
−451	Addressing Plates, Stencil	
−461	Duplicating Masters	
−471	Tabulating Card	
−481	X-Ray	
	Filing Accessories:	
−511	Filing Guides, Indices	
−521	Filing Hangers	
−531	Filing Miscellaneous	
72−002	*Sorting Equipment—Racks*	
80−002	*Electronics*	
81−002	*Digital Computers*	
82−002	*Analog Computers*	
83−002	*Components*	
90−000	*Miscellaneous—Equipment and Office Supplies*	
−101	Baskets	
−201	Binders (Material Filed in Binders)	
−301	Bindings (the Binders Separately from Contents)	
−401	Bookcases, Stands, Stacks	
−501	Books	
−601	Booths	
−701	Boxes, see also Cabinets	
−801	Brushes	
91−101	Cabinets and Cases, Storage, also see Files	
−201	Cabinets and Cases, Supply	
−401	Calculating Charts, Tables	
−501	Calendars	
−601	Copy Holders	
−701	Counters, Hand Tally	
−801	Dispensers, Tape	
−901	Display Panels, Maps, Control Boards	
93−101	Price Markers	
−401	Scales, Other than Postal	
−501	Shears, Scissors	
−601	Scopes, Stencil Tracing	
−701	Stamps, Hand (Rubber)	
94−000	*Drafting Room Equipment*	

Standard Classification Blank Paper – Forms

Code
11 Loose Sheets—Under 8½ × 11—Unprinted or heading only
12 Loose Sheets—8½ × 11—Unprinted or heading only
13 Loose Sheets—Over 8½ × 11—Unprinted or heading only

Printed Forms—Loose sheets or padded (No Carbons)
21 Printed Forms—Under 5½ × 8½
22 Printed Forms—5½ × 8½ to 8½ × 11 excluded
23 Printed Forms—8½ × 11 only
24 Printed Forms—Over 8½ × 11

Printed Forms—Card stock
31 Printed Forms—6 × 9 and smaller
32 Printed Forms—Over 6 × 9
33 Printed Forms—Tabulating punched cards (IBM or Rem-Rand type)
34 Printed Forms—Marginally punched cards (McBee-type)
35 Printed Forms—Mark sensing cards
36 Printed Forms—Margin perforated common language program cards
37 Printed Forms—Perforated tape—common language

41 Printed Forms—Padded sheets with carbons inserted
42 Printed Forms—Snap-out interleaved carbon sets
43 Printed Forms—Continuous with carbons
44 Printed Forms—Continuous without carbons
45 Printed Forms—Carbon backed forms
46 Printed Forms—Carbon backed continuous forms

51 Work Sheets—Columnar ruled—4 columns or less
52 Work Sheets—Columnar ruled—5 to 8 columns
53 Work Sheets—Columnar ruled—over 8 columns
55 Bound Record

61 Tags
62 Tickets—Perforated strips

71 Envelopes—Plain—Size 14 and smaller
72 Envelopes—Plain—Over size 14
73 Envelopes—Plain—Outlook
75 Bags—Labeled
76 Jackets
81 Labels—Single
82 Labels—Continuous
91 Hectograph Masters—Plain
92 Hectograph Masters—Preprinted
93 Litho Mats—Plain
94 Litho Mats—Printed
95 Stencils—Mimeo
96 Stencils—Addressing
99 Unclassified

INDEX